THE

FORCE

IS WITH US

THE
FORCE
IS WITH US

The Higher Consciousness
that Science Refuses to Accept

Thomas Walker, D.C.

Theosophical Publishing House
Wheaton, Illinois * Chennai, India

Quest Books
Theosophical Publishing House
P. O. Box 270
Wheaton, IL 60187-0270

www.questbooks.net

Cover image: Imagewerks Japan/Getty Images
Cover design by Margarita Reyfmann

Library of Congress Cataloging-in-Publication Data

Walker, Thomas, Dr.
The force is with us: the higher consciousness that science refuses to accept / Thomas Walker.—1st Quest ed.
  p.   cm.
Includes bibliographical references and index.
ISBN 978-0-8356-0867-1
1. Parapsychology and science.   I. Title.
BF1045.S33W35 2009
130—dc22   2009010435

Printed in the United States of America

5 4 3 2 1 * 09 10 11 12 13 14

To the memory of my beloved son, Clint:

Son, if you're not sitting in God's shadow right now,
the rest of us just don't stand a chance.

Contents

I went looking for the Truth,
and this is what I found . . .

Foreword

Of all the tyrannies to which humanity has subjected itself, the despotism of words is among the most insidious. A word is a highly mutable signifier, and theorists have gone so far as to say that a given word never means the same thing twice. But we usually forget this unsettling fact and treat a word as if it were an object—sometimes as an object of reverence. And if the same word has more than one meaning, we find it easy to conflate them and mistake one meaning for another.

Such is our situation with the word *science*. The word has (at least) two meanings that are far from identical. One has to do with the scientific *method*: experimentation, observation, repeatability of results. As the twentieth-century philosopher Karl Popper pointed out, science in this sense is not concerned with proving anything. Rather, its aim is to frame hypotheses that are *falsifiable*, that can be tested and verified and possibly proved false. If they are not proved false, then they have a provisional authority. But only a provisional one: the hypothesis (even when given a certain sanction by being rebaptized as a theory) always stands open to further refutation. If a hypothesis is not falsifiable, it falls out of the purview of science.

How, for example, would you prove or disprove the existence of God? I saw a cartoon once (it was *Life in Hell* by Matt Groening, creator of *The Simpsons*) in which a little boy finds a dead squirrel on the street. The little boy looks up and says, "God, if you exist, I pray that you revive this dead squirrel!" But the squirrel doesn't come back to life. Does this mean the little boy has disproved the existence of God? Clearly not. The existence of God can't be proved false in this way or in any other, and so it is beyond the range of science.

This is all plain enough. The problem comes when we use *science* in a second sense: we forget these facts and take the findings of science as objects of dogmatic belief. This attitude is often reckoned as science, and is called by that name, but it is no such thing; it would be better to call it *scientism*. It is not a method, but rather taking the current or recent findings of that method and enshrining them as truth.

I remember seeing a peculiar volume on a bookstore table in 2006. The contents were unremarkable: Darwin's *Voyage of the Beagle*, *The Origin of Species*, *The Descent of Man*, and *Expressions of the Emotions in Man and Animals* bound together in a single volume, with an introduction by the Harvard biologist E. O. Wilson. What was curious was that the book's large format and lavish binding made it look like a Bible—as it was meant to be: a bible of the religion of science, with Darwin as its Moses and Wilson as its John the Baptist.

Such is scientism: being a religion, it needs (or thinks it needs) a bible, and the works of Darwin will serve that purpose just as well as any. But whatever the strengths and weaknesses of the Darwinist theory may be, it is not and was never meant to be a dogma of blind belief. Probably in the end it will, like Newtonian physics, be discovered to have validity within certain limits but not to explain everything about the nature of life or, for that matter, about the development of species.

The situation in physics is even more baffling. We all "know" that there is a solid, objective, three-dimensional world out there and that it resembles our own perceptions to a greater or lesser degree. Much of scientism is based on this assumption. And yet it is the most tenuous and unfounded claim of all. Advanced physics already has to resort to bizarre hypotheses such as ten-dimensional strings or a holographic universe to explain its paradoxical findings. Moreover, these hypotheses apply only to physical data, but physical data are only a small part of the picture. We know that our experience of the world is tightly constrained by the limits of our physical senses. Currently, for example, scientists estimate that 93 percent of the universe consists of "dark matter"—matter that neither we nor our apparatus can perceive directly but that by certain indirect indications we know must be there.

Are there realities beyond these, realities that we can't perceive or know of, even indirectly? Almost certainly. Devotees of the scientistic faith can accept this statement because it demands nothing of them; they are already comfortable with agnosticism, at least of a kind. But we can push the question one step further: are there realities we can perceive in ways that scientism refuses to accept? Are there such things as precognition, clairvoyance, telekinesis? Is there a "life force" that animates every creature, even if the dissection scalpel cannot find it?

Thomas Walker's fascinating and highly enjoyable work speaks to this question. His findings match what practically every objective investigator has found: that there are indeed such things and that *science* has proved their existence. But *scientism* has constantly and willfully blinded itself to these phenomena and has made every effort to blind the public to them as well.

If, for example, you read about such matters as extrasensory perception (ESP) or remote healing in the mainstream press, you will almost always be left with the impression that there is no such thing, that science has long since proved that this is all nonsense. In fact science has done exactly the opposite. Whenever it has attempted to look at such matters with genuine objectivity, it has validated the truth of these supposed superstitions, or at least discovered that there is more to them than a constrained and materialistic worldview would like to admit.

Take for example ESP, tested scientifically by methods such as card guessing. Say there are five different types of cards, and a subject is told to guess blindly which one is turned up at a given time. If she guesses right to a degree statistically greater than pure chance would allow, this result can be taken as validation of ESP. Have such experiments been done? They have. The nineteenth-century psychic investigator Henry Sidgwick urged, "If they will not believe fifty experiments, give them fifty more and then another fifty until they must believe." In his recent book, *A New Science of the Paranormal* (also published by Quest), parapsychologist Lawrence LeShan comments, "We have certainly done this with far more experiments than Sidgwick suggested," but, he adds, "the data of psychical research have still not been accepted by the scientific mainstream—not necessarily for scientific reasons."

Another noted parapsychologist, Dean Radin, delivers the same verdict on the *Reality Sandwich* Web site: "This form of investigation has been going on for over a century, and despite official denials, the jury is in: some psychic phenomena do exist. But like blindingly obvious gorillas, not everyone can see them. (Actually, like the majority of the general public, many scientists do have these experiences, but as in the parable of the Emperor's New Clothes, fledgling science students quickly learn in college that it is not politically expedient to talk about it.)"

The late sociologist Marcello Truzzi was one of the founders of the Committee for the Scientific Investigation of Claims of the Paranormal (CSICOP). Truzzi was also the founder of a journal called *Explorations*, whose name was later changed to *The Zetetic* and finally to its present title, *The Skeptical Inquirer*. It is one of the most ruthlessly scientistic magazines published today, and CSICOP (pronounced, not coincidentally, "psi cop," as Walker notes) is the closest thing scientism has to an Inquisition. Thus you might expect that Truzzi would have descended upon claims for the paranormal with the zeal of Torquemada, but actually his views were quite nuanced (which would eventually lead with his break with CSICOP). Truzzi has warned against another type of mislabeling: calling someone a skeptic when he is really a scoffer. Truzzi writes: "The term *skepticism* is properly defined as "doubt," not "denial." It is a position of agnosticism, of nonbelief rather than disbelief. The true skeptic (a doubter) asserts no claim, so has no burden of proof. However, the scoffer (denier) asserts a *negative* claim" [emphasis Truzzi's]. Organized skepticism is a fundamental norm in science, but scoffing is nothing more than dogmatism dressed up as objective inquiry. Truzzi goes on to say:

> As proponents of anomalies produce stronger evidence, critics have sometimes moved the goal posts further away. This is especially clear in the case of parapsychology. To convince scientists of what had been merely supported by widespread but weak anecdotal evidence, parapsychologists moved psychical research into the laboratory. When experimental results were presented, designs were criticized. When protocols were improved, a "fraud proof" or "critical experiment" was demanded. When those were put forward, replications were demanded. When those were produced, critics argued that new forms of error might be the cause (such as the "file drawer" error that could result from unpublished negative studies). . . . And in one instance, where the scoffer found no counter-explanations, he described the result as a "mere anomaly," not to be taken seriously and so just belonging on a puzzle page. The goal posts have now been moved to the point where some critics hold unfalsifiable positions.[1]

And, as we learned from Karl Popper, an unfalsifiable position is an unscientific position.

The story that Thomas Walker tells in this book is a story of individuals who have struggled against this type of prejudice: figures such as Anton Mesmer, J. B. Rhine, Karl von Reichenbach, and Wilhelm Reich. Some, such as Reich and Reichenbach, have attempted, in vain, to convince science that there is such a thing as a life force, known to the Hindus as *prana* and to the Chinese as *chi* (or *qi*), and that Reichenbach called the *odic force* and Reich called *orgone*. Although the existence of this force ought to be obvious to anyone who has looked at a living body next to a corpse, the so-called life sciences have refused to admit such a thing, and these pioneers were discredited and their research mocked. Reich, having fled the Third Reich to the United States, found the government in his new home scarcely more sympathetic than the Nazis and ended up convicted of quackery. Sentenced to federal prison, he died there in 1957.

To say any more about these figures would be to tell Walker's story for him. This is a readable, delightful, and highly compressed account of some of the most remarkable scientific findings of our age. Though Walker's tale is a fascinating one, it is also sobering. It reminds us that many of the truths we take for granted are little more than preconceptions and that supposedly proved facts about the universe are often little more than a tissue of guesses. Science has broken many limits and reached many new horizons; no one can deny that. But I suspect that it is about to charge into an impenetrable wall unless it has the humility to admit some of the truths that Walker so admirably describes.

—Richard Smoley
Wheaton, Illinois
February 2009

Richard Smoley is the author of several books, including *Hidden Wisdom: A Guide to the Western Inner Traditions* (with Jay Kinney), *Inner Christianity*, *Forbidden Faith: The Secret History of Gnosticism*, and *Conscious Love*. His latest work is *The Dice Game of Shiva: How Consciousness Creates the Universe*.

Preface

I began this project in 1995 at the age of forty. What started as a search for meaning after numerous business and personal disappointments became a profound spiritual journey as I explored more deeply. I completed the manuscript in almost exactly seven years. In 2004, I self-published it and in the next year acquired a literary agent and a book contract. Soon the book was scheduled for international publication. And then my world turned upside down.

One summer day in 2006, my twenty-five-year-old son Clint was diagnosed with cancer. One hour later, my agent called to say the publisher had dropped the book. Within weeks, two more family medical traumas followed. However, I'll just tell Clint's story and let the subsequent events speak for themselves.

That summer, Clint underwent two complicated stem cell transplants at Vanderbilt Medical Center. By August 2007 he was in full remission; the staff said they had never seen anyone do as well. Two months later, though, it was back. Conventional medicine had nothing left to offer, so Clint and I headed to Mexico for alternative treatment at the famed Hoxsey Clinic. Initially it went well, but in January he began to worsen. Another alternative treatment accelerated the cancer. Suddenly he was on his deathbed, fighting to breathe as he slowly drowned in his own fluids. It was St. Valentine's Day 2008.

I can't describe the heart-wrenching agony of watching my best friend, my only son, slip away. Twice, while on my knees sobbing at his bedside, I asked him to contact us if he could and let us know he was OK. He nodded affirmatively through the morphine haze. I marveled at his incredible courage, at how he was concerned only for the welfare of others, particularly me. He even joked with us. After a twenty-hour ordeal, Clint passed away.

My interest in spiritual experiences was a consuming passion, already deepened by those difficult years, but what happened next made the spiritual world the center of my existence. Clint kept his word. He stayed in touch.

There have been eighteen significant contact events to date. Some involved phone calls and texted photos. Others involved special dreams. Photos of Clint and of his beloved cat Simon tumbled over in mysterious circumstances. Electronic equipment malfunctioned, particularly at the start of his favorite television show. He physically touched some of us.

But the most amazing event of all happened just days after his passing. Cyndi was one of Clint's special friends, and she had kept a constant vigil at his hospital bed that final day. A few days later, she and her son Jeremy were playing Scrabble at home. Cyndi reached into the bag and rummaged around, grasping five of the wooden tiles. She arranged them on the rack, all the while conversing with her son. When she glanced down, her hair almost stood on end. *There, in perfect order from left to right, were the letters C-L-I-N-T!* The odds of this being chance were five million to one, and that doesn't include the *order* of the tiles.

Clint later came to me in a dream. He had a brilliant smile and looked fantastic, radiating the glow that some 50 percent of the population has reported during similar events. Later he came to his sister Rachel. During the dream, Rachel said, he was very happy and very excited by his experiences. When she reached out to hug him, her arms passed through him. It was exactly six months to the day of his passing.

It would be most difficult indeed to convince us these were only random events. That's why I feel so strongly, as you will see in this book, that attitudes about spiritual reality must change.

We've reached an important crossroads in human development. Clint's contacts were not meaningless or imaginary events. The ancients knew the truth: we live in a spiritual universe, and our familiar physical existence is only a tiny portion of that world. But in our modern world the truth is being ignored, even suppressed. Official minds remain closed to the reality of psychic phenomena, extrasensory perception, mediumship, natural healthcare, psychic healing, life after death, and vital energy. In the following pages we will explore such ideas and experiences in depth. We are on the very brink of rediscovering what has been lost since ancient times—our spiritual destiny. It is my sincere wish that, after taking this journey, you will agree with me that the Force *is* with us.

Introduction:
What's New Is Old

Unthinking respect for authority is the greatest enemy of truth.
—Albert Einstein

Modern cosmology states that everything we know and love accounts for only 4 percent of the universe. The remainder is composed of theoretical substances called *dark matter* and *dark energy*. The knowledge of modern science, all its wonderful studies and theories, explains only 4 percent of the cosmos. The rest, unseen by human eyes and undetectable by scientific instrumentation, forms the bulk of the world. This remaining 96 percent is the spirit realm of which the ancients spoke.

The key to it all is *energy*. However, the energy I mean is far different from what everyday science typically calls "energy." I'm talking about energy fields that are of a fundamental substance unlike anything in the everyday world.[1] The spirit realm is outside of everything we know and experience in our daily lives; it is a vast area of subtle energy and consciousness that creates and sustains our physical reality.

The qualities of this energy world can't be explained or discussed adequately through ordinary communication. This realm has to be experienced directly. These higher planes of reality are found, not in outer space, but in the inner space of human consciousness. That's the real secret the ancients knew. To discover the nature of these higher planes, one has to

1

journey *inward* and connect with the higher consciousness, the world of the spirit that is found in each of us.

Modern scientific instrumentation is beginning to scratch the surface of this realm, but the great primordial energy remains undetectable through ordinary means. For this reason, some question its existence. They agree in principle to the strangeness of subatomic reality as predicted by modern theory—accepting (but mostly ignoring) the existence of the quantum vacuum energy (also called the *zero point field* or *free energy*)—yet scoff at the idea of actually experiencing this realm through ancient religious practices or meditation.[2] The former is the hippest of modern science; the latter, nonsense.

Not all scientists feel this way.[3] Some are interested in spiritual practices as well as scientific theory. Some intuitively realize there is more to life, but they must be careful. Certain topics, as we shall see, are so taboo as to be unmentionable. In spite of this, a great deal of quality research has been conducted on such areas, and the results can be fascinating. One of the most surprising discoveries is the amazing similarity between ancient spiritual beliefs and modern physics. If we set the math aside, it sounds as though we're talking about the same thing. In his classic book, *The Tao of Physics*, internationally known physicist Fritjof Capra explored the similarities between the two in great detail. In his telling, they sound very much like two sides of the same coin.

In the summer of 1969, Capra was relaxing on the beach in Santa Cruz, California, when he had what the great psychologist Abraham Maslow called a *peak experience*. It was a beautiful late summer afternoon in a beautiful place, and as Capra watched the movement of the waves and the sparkling sunshine, he experienced a burst of insight, an emotional moment in which he perceived the rhythm and flow of nature's energy in a way that was difficult to put into words. It was a spiritual awakening. He instinctively knew of the great energy flow through the cosmos and through him at that moment.

Highly trained in theoretical physics, Capra was moved by the direct experience of this energy, something previously known to him only through graphs, charts, and mathematical formulae. He wrote, "I felt its rhythm and I 'heard' its sound, and at that moment I knew that this was the Dance of Shiva, the Lord of Dancers worshipped by the Hindus."[4]

Capra had studied Eastern mysticism. He had noticed the similarities between religions such as Buddhism and the New Physics. Before the experience in Santa Cruz, that knowledge was in his mind. Now it was in his heart. *The Tao of Physics* was the result.

Thus began a spiritual journey for Capra. He became convinced the ancient Eastern seers were aware of the deeper levels of nature and were also familiar with the difficulty of talking about such knowledge. He was struck by the fact that, although the methods of examination were quite different, their conclusions were nearly identical to those of his own discipline. The ancients knew what was going on. It was time for modern science to realize that not everything could be demonstrated in a laboratory. He writes:

> These changes, brought about by modern physics, have been widely discussed by physicists and by philosophers over the past decades, but very seldom has it been realized that they all seem to lead in the same direction, towards a view of the world which is very similar to the views held in Eastern mysticism. The concepts of modern physics often show surprising parallels to the ideas expressed in the religious philosophies of the Far East.[5]

For example, the ancients knew that the world was really energy. They also knew that the act of focusing our attention on this spiritual energy created "reality." They were fully aware of positive and negative charge and of how that polarity makes everything work. In fact, much of modern quantum theory was known to the ancients, including the idea of nonlocality and the power of intention.[6] Many sages believed that, through spiritual discipline and meditation, humans could connect with the energy of the higher order.

Such teachers held that, with the proper training and desire, knowledge could be experienced directly, intuitively. They knew that, while insights can be tested to some degree, the creative energies of intuition, of hunches and instinctive realizations, come from the world of the Spirit.

In our everyday world, many of us experience bursts of creative insight on a regular basis, whether it's a feeling we have in our hearts or a sudden realization of the answer to a vexing problem. Even science owes much to such realizations. The history of science is filled with tales of sudden bursts of knowledge and insight. For example, Einstein went to bed one night in the spring of 1905 and awoke with the answer to the problems of special relativity, the first of the mighty pillars of modern physics. This kind of direct experience of nature, of knowledge, was the primary goal of the great schools of Eastern mysticism, such as Chinese Taoism.

The early thinkers were "vitalists," people who thought a special vital force was active in the world, especially in living things. For thousands of years the vitalists prevailed, aided by the development of Western religions that agreed with a living, conscious energy from God. By the Renaissance era, though, things were changing. The new belief of materialism was in the works, and it provided an explanation that appealed to those who see the world as a series of objects. By the seventeenth century, the great philosopher René Descartes had split the world into matter and mind. The new concept of "dualism" began, and soon the idea of a vital force was considered to be an ignorant superstition, unworthy of scientific study.

Scientists began using a circular reasoning that would get them flunked in any freshman philosophy class. A vital force can't possibly exist, so it was unworthy of study. And because there were no scientific studies, it couldn't possibly exist! Phenomena that couldn't be seen couldn't be a part of our world. Everything was already known.

However, things run in cycles. New data began to suggest that many things exist that cannot be seen with the eye or detected with current technology. Newtonian physics was overturned by the exciting—and weird—findings of relativity theory and quantum mechanics. Suddenly the world was sounding far stranger than anything the vitalists suggested, yet anything of a spiritual nature was still considered absurd. Modern physics suggests the existence of other dimensions—the infamous "many worlds" theory—but let a philosopher or mystic mention something similar in the spiritual realm and they are considered lunatics.

There remains, however, the annoying (to science) fact that things of a spiritual nature are among the most common beliefs of humankind, something referred to as the *perennial philosophy*. Spiritual events are woven throughout our history. After decades of study in science, spiritual concepts, and the martial arts, I knew in my heart that the ancient beliefs represented a fundamental truth about the world. I began to research the evidence for a vital force. Since the force is said to be the mechanism behind psychic and spiritual phenomena, the search grew to include a lot of ground. I found two extremely significant things: the incredible amount of research supporting such data, and the staggering bias of orthodox science against such phenomena.

In the following pages I will present examples of data that demand a new model of reality. I will survey the startling findings coming out of studies in parapsychology, the paranormal, and the spirit. I will also discuss "psychoenergetics," the interaction of consciousness, matter, and energy. In fact, the evidence shows that the spirit world is more "real" than physical reality, something that would have been completely obvious to our forebears. After all, it's only been a few hundred years that modern science's mechanistic, reductionistic beliefs have captivated our minds. Slowly, under the force of evidence, we may begin to move toward a view that can integrate both new and old. A new paradigm is in the works. May the Force be with us.

The Force:
From Ch'i to the Cosmological Constant and Beyond

The intuitive mind is a sacred gift and the rational mind is a faithful servant. We have created a society that honors the servant and has forgotten the gift.

—Albert Einstein

There is a force in the world that makes things happen. Belief in it has existed since time immemorial. Like "The Force" in the *Star Wars* movies, it's an energy field that permeates the universe, forming and sustaining all things; it's an energy of consciousness that animates the world. It flows through living things in channels called *meridians* and is the basis for paranormal phenomena and alternative forms of healing. It is our connection with the higher planes of consciousness, the great beyond, the fundamental quantum reality that makes up the world. Once it has been accepted by the scientific community, it will rank among the greatest discoveries of all time.

In traditional Chinese belief, this force is called *ch'i*. The ch'i is the fundamental agent of the universe, the subtle energy, existing everywhere, that condenses out of the great field to form physical matter. It makes up material objects and is also the waveform that accounts for how objects interact. The term *ch'i* means "vital energy" or "ether," the continual flow of which maintains the balance between yin and yang, the great polar opposites.

7

In my opinion, it is the quantum field of modern physics, the fundamental entity of physical reality. We're all reading from the same sheet of music. In *The Tao of Physics*, Fritjof Capra quotes one of the greatest Taoist scholars of antiquity, Chang Tsai, describing it like this:

> When the ch'i condenses, its visibility becomes apparent so that there are then the shapes [of individual things]. When it disperses, its visibility is no longer apparent and there are no shapes. At the time of its condensation, can one say otherwise than that this is but temporary? But at the time of its dispersing, can one hastily say that it is then non-existent? . . . The Great Void cannot but consist of ch'i; this ch'i cannot but condense to form all things; and these things cannot but become dispersed so as to form the Great Void.[1]

Capra compared that description to the following statement by physicist Hermann Weyl:

> According to the [field theory of matter] a material particle such as an electron is merely a small domain of the electrical field within which the field strength assumes enormously high values, indicating that a comparatively huge field energy is concentrated in a very small place. Such an energy knot, which by no means is clearly delineated against the remaining field, propagates through empty space like a water wave across the surface of a lake; there is no such thing as one and the same substance of which the electron consists at all times.[2]

Yes, the ch'i. Like the fundamental concepts of physics, it is difficult to put into words. However, the ancient model works as well as that of modern physics to explain the mysteries of the universe. In both models, energy is said to be the fundamental entity. Polarity phenomena make the world work, adding the dynamics required for the cycles of growth and destruction. Only the terminology varies. What we call *charge* the Chinese knew as *yin* and *yang*. The ancients were also fully aware of the observer effect spoken of in the Copenhagen interpretation of quantum mechanics, namely, that reality is determined by the act of observation. We, through the use of intent and the act of observation, determine the universe, or at least "our" universe. This view is common to both physics and ancient cosmology. In fact, I can see little difference between the idea of the Great Void and dark matter, between ch'i and quantum fields, between the illusions of *maya* in Hinduism and the Copenhagen interpretation of quantum mechanics; yet, depending upon with whom you talk, one is considered absolute state-of-the-art science and the other ignorant superstition or myth. Clearly, the civilizations of the past were aware of the true nature of things. This is a fundamental truth we are just now in the process of discovering. In the rest of this chapter, we'll follow some explorations of the science of ch'i.

In 1979, a medical student named David Eisenberg took a break from his studies at Harvard Medical School to travel to China and research traditional Chinese medicine, the first Westerner to do so. Modern China had been a mystery to the West until President Nixon opened things up in 1972, restoring diplomatic relations and creating a flood of interest in the ancient land. Eisenberg had studied Mandarin as an undergrad at Harvard, so he was fluent in the language and had some knowledge of the customs. What he wasn't ready for was Chinese philosophy, particularly the concept of ch'i. He tells of his experiences in his book *Encounters with Qi* (an alternative spelling of *ch'i*).[3]

Eisenberg began by investigating acupuncture, a medical treatment entirely based on manipulating the flow of ch'i, usually by inserting needles at specific points in the skin. It was new ground for the young medical student and challenged all his belief systems. At the time, Eisenberg commented on the lack of documentation on vital energy, but in fact scientific research had already been done on ch'i and acupuncture.

In the 1960s, Professor Kim Bong Han had conducted anatomical research on animals to identify acupuncture meridians.[4] (Acupuncture works well on animals and even plants.) Using rabbits and other animals, Kim injected acupuncture points with radioactive phosphorus and analyzed the results using micro-autoradiography. They were astounding. A map appeared nearly identical to acupuncture charts from thousands of years ago. But that's not all.

Kim located a tiny series of unknown ducts, 0.5 to 1.5 micrometers in diameter, that followed the path of the classical acupuncture meridians. This tubule system was independent of the nervous or vascular systems of the animals. He found the tubular meridian system had further subdivisions. He called one of these the *internal duct system*. The tiny tubules were found to be free-floating structures within the vascular and lymphatic vessels of the animals, entering and exiting at various points along the vessel walls. A second series of ducts was found along the surfaces of the internal organs. This network was called the *intra-external duct system*. A third network ran along the outside of the blood and lymph vessels. Eventually Kim found two more duct networks, one in the superficial layers of the skin and one following the nervous system. Eventually, all five duct systems were found to connect, forming a continuous network throughout the major structures of the body. The minute terminal ends of the system were found to do something almost unbelievable: *they terminated in individual cell nuclei!* The discovery of this degree of interconnection in living things was unprecedented. Kim wondered what would happen if a tubule were cut.

He did just that, severing the liver meridian in a frog. In a very short time, microscopic degeneration could be seen. By three days, widespread vascular degeneration had occurred. The experiment was repeated, with the same results each time. Later he carefully severed the neural meridian ducts. Within 30 minutes, neurological changes were documented. Nerve function was grossly affected, with reflex times slowed by 500 percent, a condition that remained largely unchanged even after 48 hours. Later embryological studies showed the meridian system was formed during the first 15 hours of fetal development, well before any other organ system.

Kim Bong Han's conclusion was that the acupuncture meridian system is the most fundamental structure in living things.[5]

If much of acupuncture was mysterious to the young David Eisenberg, it at least involved physical needles. Imagine his astonishment when he encountered the ch'i kung masters, whose only instrument is their hands! Ch'i kung is an ancient Chinese practice for manipulating vital energy that is thousands of years old, predating other forms of martial arts. It is largely a rejuvenatory health practice of slow, precise movements and special breathing techniques, much like t'ai chi. Although ch'i kung has been known for at least three thousand years and was practiced by all the noted Chinese sages, including Confucius and Lao-tzu, true scientific studies of it have only been conducted by the Chinese since 1978.

Banished for a time in modern communist China, ch'i kung has recently made a comeback, and the Chinese are quite excited about it. They have conducted a great deal of research in this area in recent years, and, if the Western world will listen, significant knowledge might be added to the realm of human potential. Highly trained ch'i kung masters can do some pretty amazing things, as Dr. Eisenberg saw for himself during his two trips to China. He says:

> Qi Gong [ch'i kung] means the "manipulation of vital energy," and the term refers to an ancient practice, crucial in the development of Chinese medicine. The masters of this practice, originally Daoist or Buddhist monks, are said to manipulate Qi within their bodies through special breathing exercises, physical training, and intense concentration. Qi Gong masters claim to control their Qi absolutely, directing it through any portion of their body at will in order to perform seemingly superhuman feats.[6]

Eisenberg was impressed by these demonstrations; the feats were those often displayed in martial arts movies, but what he saw was for real. Even the aged masters were capable of amazing things, like breaking thick, unsupported stones with a bare fist. He also saw experiments that demonstrated ch'i kung masters projecting energy from their hands that registered on a standard oscilloscope. On numerous occasions he personally witnessed masters using psychokinesis, moving objects around or causing suspended items to move. When asked how they did it, the masters smiled graciously and uttered a single word: "Ch'i!"

Scientifically, the kind of ch'i to which the masters were referring has become known as *external ch'i*, meaning the ability to project energy from the body. *Internal ch'i*, on the other hand, is the energy that circulates *within* the body and is vital to life. All of us have that, as do animals and plants. However, external ch'i, the ability to project this same energy *outward*, is something only a small percentage of practitioners can do.

In July 1983, Eisenberg returned to China along with Herbert Benson, M.D., director of the Division of Behavioral Medicine at Harvard Medical School. Benson was considered an expert on meditation. He had developed his own version that he called the *relaxation response*, which had been shown to be effective in treating hypertension.

The first surprise for Benson was that researchers in Shanghai had conducted research along much of the same lines, using ch'i kung successfully to treat hypertension. After a tour of the facility and a discussion of some of the research involving ch'i kung, the American doctors visited Western-trained scientists at the Department of Acupuncture Research at the Shanghai Medical College. These scientists had seen for themselves the effectiveness of acupuncture, but when Benson and Eisenberg asked their opinion of ch'i kung practitioners and external ch'i, they remarked: "We are physiologists trained in physiology, so we do not believe in the emission of external Qi. It makes no sense to us on the basis of Western medical science." Eisenberg noted, "These physiologists shared the biases of their American counterparts."[7]

At the same medical college, the two doctors were presented with some startling results from the ophthalmology clinic. Eighty children had been chosen at random, precisely examined, and divided into four groups.

All were myopic (nearsighted). The first group received no treatment; the second, placebo eye drops. The third group was instructed in ch'i kung techniques to practice themselves, and the last group was treated by a ch'i kung master. The master treated each child for 20 minutes a day, placing his hands over the eye socket and behind the head and projecting his external ch'i into the eye.

The first two groups showed no improvement. In the third, two children showed marked improvement of vision. This response was small, but it was suggested that the children had been a bit young fully to understand the exercises. However, the fourth group was the kicker. *Sixteen of the twenty children showed marked improvements in vision*, as verified by extensive ophthalmologic testing.[8]

This study was not an isolated effort; another study presented to Benson and Eisenberg was particularly impressive. Dr. Fong Li-da of the Beijing Institute conducted a study of the effects of external ch'i on the common intestinal bacteria E. coli.[9] What was particularly interesting was that the ch'i kung master could use his ch'i either to promote the growth of the bacteria or to destroy it.

The study design was simple. Three test tubes with equal amounts of bacteria were given to the master, one at a time. The first was a control, so he simply held it for one minute and placed it in the rack. The second he subjected to his "lethal Qi," something he directed with his mind, for one minute. The third was treated with his "health promoting Qi" under the same procedure. Only his intent differed.

In forty trials, the results were the same. The positive ch'i caused a seven- to ten-fold increase in the bacteria. The lethal dose lowered the number of bacteria by a minimum of 50 percent. In the control test tubes, there was no change. Fong published this particular study in a local journal and met with the Americans during their visit. He was confident the study could be verified in any laboratory.

By the mid-1980s, studies with external ch'i had the Chinese scientists convinced that ch'i was real, an actual energetic entity, a part of physics unknown and unrecognized by the West. The Chinese researchers currently feel that they have proven the existence of ch'i scientifically and that it is the mechanism behind such psychic phenomena as psychokinesis and extrasensory perception (ESP), as well as the astounding claims of cures for serious diseases.[10] This evidence, along with the intense amount of study presently devoted to acupuncture, may prove to advance human potential in an unprecedented way. However, those who practice t'ai chi, ch'i kung, or kung fu have never doubted ch'i. They know it is true for the simplest of reasons: they can *feel* it.

The central questions for research on ch'i are now the following: is it a form of energy that was known in ancient times but has now been lost? If so, is this now rediscovered energy related to the known forms, such as electromagnetism? There's a fairly simple way to test this hypothesis: screen ch'i kung practitioners from all forms of electromagnetism and see if they can still practice effectively. That was exactly the idea in Dr. Elmer Green's "copper wall experiment."

First, why the term *copper wall*? It goes back to Michael Faraday, the great nineteenth-century British scientist, who discovered that a wire cage would absorb all forms of electromagnetism. The device is now called a *Faraday cage* in his honor and is used to eliminate interference from the vast amount of radio, TV, and other electromagnetic radiation that bathes the modern world. The cage is used in conventional research all the time, and parapsychologists have begun to use it for investigating psychic phenomena. It was only a matter of time before someone used it for the investigation of ch'i kung.

Elmer Green has long investigated the concept of subtle energies. In 1990, he and his team at the Menninger Foundation in Topeka, Kansas, designed a novel experiment to test the energies of ch'i kung masters and psychic healers. To eliminate possible contamination by outside electrical and electromagnetic energies, the experiments were done in a giant Faraday cage, one made of solid sheets of copper rather than just wire.

Measuring devices were placed in the four copper walls, in the aluminum outer coverings, and on the bodies of the test subjects. Both healers and patients insulated themselves from the copper surroundings by standing on glass blocks.

Data were analyzed by computer, polygraph, and electroencephalograph (EEG) monitors. Test runs were performed on the emission of external ch'i and on the energy of psychic healers, clairvoyants, and other psychic subjects. Although clairvoyants could function in the isolated environment, no electrical effects were noted. However, large voltage surges were recorded consistently in both the ch'i kung masters and the healers.[11] Repeated tests showed something strange. The healers and ch'i kung practitioners were consistently able to generate electrical-type surges that were more than a thousand times that of the normal galvanic skin potential of the body, all while effectively isolated from all outside energies.[12]

One particular healer, in a 30-minute session, registered fifteen separate surges, some that were "astoundingly large, 10^5 times" that of ordinary electrical voltages in the human body. It should come as no surprise that they were centered at the *tan tien*, the area just below the navel known since ancient times as the center of subtle energy in the human body. The only rational conclusion was that these enormous energy measurements were being generated by the test subjects. Green wrote up his findings in a paper, "Anomalous Electrostatic Phenomena in Exceptional Subjects," and it was published in the journal *Subtle Energies*, the official publication of the International Society for the Study of Subtle Energies and Energy Medicine.

The Chinese may be convinced of the scientific basis for paranormal phenomena and psychic energy, and Dr. Green and many others are making inroads in the West, but the real problem for further advancement stops at the gate of the recognized scientific establishment. Although many of the researchers interested in paranormal phenomena are members of "The Club," you don't shake up things with papers in *Subtle Energies*.

You need publication in a "high-impact" journal like *Nature* for people to sit up and take notice. A lot more study is needed, but things are moving in the right direction. For example, a surprising series of articles appeared in the January 1999 issue of *Scientific American*, that bastion of lay science. The articles posit the existence of a new form of energy, one that sounds very familiar. The new energy is implied by one part of the general theory of relativity, but the great Einstein would be surprised by its new usage.

Although Einstein's general theory of relativity predicted an expanding universe, he was never comfortable with the idea. To bring things back to the static state that seemed right to him, he added his famous "cosmological constant," representing an unknown, "constant" form of energy, with repulsive gravitation and independence from time or position in space. By adding this "fudge factor," Einstein could get his equations to match what he thought was correct: that the universe is static. Within a couple of decades, however, scientists knew for sure that the universe is indeed expanding, and at a rapid rate. Light from distant galaxies shows this to be true.

It's all a cosmic balance between the collective gravitation from the mass in the universe and the outward movement of everything from the Big Bang. However, the amount of mass available to stop the eternal expansion seems to be inadequate for the job, and recently cosmologists have found something even more startling—*the expansion of the universe seems to be speeding up!* This shouldn't happen with ordinary gravitation as we understand it, but it is. There appears to be a great repulsive force in the world, as well as the attractive one we know as gravity.[13]

In the *Scientific American* article "Surveying Space-Time with Supernovae," the authors propose a new type of energy to explain this unexpected phenomenon. The lead-in to the article reads as follows: "Exploding stars seen across immense distances show that the cosmic expansion may be accelerating—a sign that the universe may be driven apart by *an exotic new form of energy*" [italics added]. The authors comment:

A universe composed only of normal matter cannot grow in this fashion, because gravity is always attractive. Yet according to Einstein's theory, the expansion can speed up *if an exotic form of energy fills empty space everywhere*. This strange "vacuum energy" is embodied in Einstein's equations as the so-called cosmological constant. Unlike ordinary forms of mass and energy, the vacuum energy adds gravity that is repulsive and can drive the universe apart at ever increasing speeds. . . . Evidence for a strange form of energy imparting a repulsive gravitational force is the most interesting result we could have hoped for, yet it is so astonishing that we and others remain suitably skeptical [italics added].[14]

In a companion article, "Cosmological Antigravity," Lawrence M. Krauss writes: "The long-derided cosmological constant—a contrivance of Albert Einstein's that represents *a bizarre form of energy inherent in space itself*—is one of two contenders for explaining changes in the expansion rate of the universe [italics added]."[15] The author goes on to add:

But Einstein's cosmological term is distinct. The energy associated with it does not depend on position or time—hence the name "cosmological constant." The force caused by the constant operates even in the complete absence of matter or radiation. Therefore its source must be a curious energy that resides in empty space. *The cosmological constant, like the ether, endows the void with an almost metaphysical aura . . . like it or not, empty space is not empty after all* [italics added].[16]

Ironically, Einstein was always embarrassed by his cosmological constant and felt in later years it was his greatest mistake. Antigravity? Repulsive gravitation? Isn't this the stuff of science fiction? Initially he introduced the energy to balance his equations and show that the universe was in a "steady state." Later observations demonstrated the accelerating universe. Einstein was disappointed; perhaps he would be reassured to see how the qualities of his infamous "cosmological constant" are now being used to explain how the expansion of our universe can actually be accelerating, something not possible with the energies of the Big Bang alone. The great Einstein may have been correct about the existence of a "vacuum energy" that fills all space, but wrong about its effects. Rather than creating a steady-state universe, Einstein's vacuum energy may well be what is accelerating an already incredible expansion. *A bizarre form of energy that fills empty space—one with an almost metaphysical aura!* Doesn't that sound familiar? It's simple, really. The closer we look at the true, underlying nature of the world, the more it sounds like the teachings of the ancients from thousands of years ago. The ancient concept of ch'i may soon prove to be a cornerstone of modern science.

Einstein found equations that expressed a world that still looks pretty strange to most of us. William Tiller has found a way of looking at Einstein's world that may show us a mathematical way into a still stranger realm: the higher dimensions of human consciousness. Tiller has been a professor in the Department of Materials Science and Engineering at Stanford University since 1964; for some years he was also head of the department. Now a professor emeritus, he is internationally known and is probably the world's leading expert on crystals. Tiller is a professional scientist and a very good one—respected by his peers, the author of more than two hundred and fifty scientific papers, and the holder of five patents for his discoveries. He is also a movie star, as one of the experts appearing in the fantastic film *What the Bleep Do We Know?* He has done a surprising amount of study in paranormal areas as well, having published more than seventy papers in the field of psychoenergetics, the general topic of this book.

Tiller is above all a scientist, so he isn't satisfied with hearsay. He needs evidence and the appropriate scientific models. When he got interested in the field, no such models existed except for the hints provided in quantum mechanics, so Tiller created his own theories, backed up with mathematics.

Tiller believes that human consciousness is a force, an energy in the universe, just like everything else. He also believes that the speed of light is the barrier one must cross to reach new levels of existence. It is important at this point to mention that Einstein's special theory of relativity does not preclude an object from traveling faster than light. It just states that in theory it would take an infinite amount of energy to get there. And according to modern theories concerning zero-point and quantum vacuum energy, the cosmos is an infinite energy source.

Tiller has developed a scientific model of reality that uses the speed of light as a threshold. If we attempt to use Einstein's energy equations with values greater than the speed of light, we end up with the square root of a negative number, something mathematicians call an *imaginary number*, an entity thought not to exist in actuality. Some mathematicians, such as Charles Muses, call these *hypernumbers*.[17] Muses believes these numbers are required to develop equations to describe the behavior of higher dimensional phenomena. He also states that such hypernumbers are required for finding solutions to the equations of electromagnetic and quantum theories. Once again, although the math is there, the interpretation of the solutions to the equations is open to human opinion.

Tiller feels that the speed of light is the threshold between the spirit and physical worlds. If we graph the solutions to Einstein's energy equations, the positive values above zero yield a curve that increases toward infinity, with energy levels reaching an infinite amount with increasing velocities. This realm, with velocities less than light, is the physical world familiar to us all.

Below the value of zero, however, in an area Tiller calls "negative space/time," we see an area with velocities greater than light. This region is said by Tiller to be of a *magneto-electric* nature (the opposite of *electromagnetic* and not found in the physical world) and demonstrates negative entropy, the opposite of our everyday world. Tiller contends that this is the explanation for the magnetic nature of psychic phenomena, for the apparent instantaneous quality of ESP, and for clairvoyance.

Because it is backed with the appropriate mathematics and because it provides an explanation for much of the spiritual phenomena discussed throughout history, the theory is gaining ground. Tiller believes that the realm of higher energies, the area where velocities are greater than that of light, is the world of higher dimensions spoken of since the earliest historical writings, the unseen dimensions of the ancients. It is the world of psychic phenomena. And it seems to be connected in some unknown, fundamental way with human consciousness. It is the world of the Force.

New Dimensions: Perceptions beyond the Body

My own suspicion is that the universe is not only queerer than we suppose, but queerer than we can suppose.

—J. B. S. Haldane, British biologist

A funny thing happened to a woman named Vicki when she was thirteen years old. Vicki was scheduled for major surgery. After the anesthesia was administered, she found herself floating near the ceiling, looking down on the operating room table. It was almost like watching a movie; in a sort of detached state, Vicki viewed the procedures as though they were happening to someone else. She could plainly see her own body, draped on the table, as well as the surgeons and nurses as they ran through the complicated, though routine, activities of surgery. She felt no emotion other than mild curiosity about such an unusual event.

What happened to Vicki that day went beyond a garden variety out-of-body experience, however, for Vicki also experienced something much more profound: a near-death experience, or NDE. Even in our modern world, this phenomenon is fairly well known. Vicki's experience was typical. She comments:

In that near-death experience, I would describe it as going through a pipe or a tube type of feeling, and I was shocked, I was totally in awe, I mean I can't describe it, because I thought "So that is what it is like," and I saw my body, just before I got sucked into the tube. I was up on the ceiling and I saw my body being prepared for surgery and I knew it was me.[1]

Vicki also experienced the events typical of an NDE as described by the thousands of people whose cases have been studied: an overwhelming sense of love and happiness, like you'd won the lottery, your crippled grandmother could walk again, and you got to sit in for Keith Richards at a Stones concert, all rolled into one! She met other beings, even an extraordinary deity, and experienced knowledge of things not ordinarily known, a burst of consciousness. She described everything in minute detail, including the sensation of being whisked back through the tunnel and returned to her pain-wracked body in the operating room, which turned out to be a major bummer compared to where she had just been. Nothing new here, so what's the big deal?

It is simple really: *Vicki had been blind since shortly after her birth!* She was a premature infant, and—like so many others between 1947 and 1952, including musical great Stevie Wonder—she had been placed in an incubator with too much oxygen, which destroyed her optic nerves. Except for a brief interval after she was born, Vicki had never experienced sight. "I can't see anything. No light, no shadows, no nothing, ever," she said. "And so I have never been able to understand even the concept of light."[2] And yet somehow, from the vantage point of the ceiling, Vicki had seen her body being prepared for surgery.

What are we to make of this? The usual scientific explanation of an NDE is that the subject has experienced a particularly vivid hallucination brought on by the trauma or anesthesia. After all, people have been experiencing pretty wild drug-induced trips for a long, long time. A conveniently simple explanation is that it was all in Vicki's imagination. *But she was blind*, and she had been since the time she weighed less than two pounds! She had never seen any of the things most of us take for granted in life. She had nothing on which to base "imagination," and yet she was able to describe her event as well as a person with normal sight. Vicki's case is only one of many that provide evidence for the kinds of perception that this chapter explores.

Vicki's experience of observing her body from the outside is not unique to those who've had a brush with death. This unusual event has been reported throughout history and across cultures. The events are very similar regardless of whether they occur to a small child or a professor of engineering. Human consciousness seems to have the ability to separate from its physical body and travel through time and space: that is, to have out-of-body experiences, or OBEs.

Of course, this suggestion makes conventional scientists crazy! The late, great Carl Sagan, astronomer extraordinaire and Cornell professor, as well as author and media star, was an outspoken critic of paranormal events. He especially took exception to the idea of OBEs. In his opinion, it was all a process of hallucination or remembrance of the birthing process. In addition to being a world-famous scientist, Dr. Sagan was also a professional skeptic. In one of his popular books, he proposed a way of testing OBEs: Have the subject identify a random number hidden on a shelf high up near the ceiling of a tall room, and record the procedure on video to prevent cheating. If the subject could later report this number, it might—maybe—give credence to the concept of an OBE.

In an experiment well known within parapsychology, Charles Tart had already conducted just such a test, with his subject known as "Miss Z." She was one of those people who, for whatever reason, can have an OBE almost at will. Tart designed a test to see whether her mind, her consciousness, actually left her body during these events, or whether she was just the victim of clever imagination. He placed a paper with a randomly generated number on a shelf nearly to the ceiling. Miss Z was asked to memorize the number and time of day if she was able to "see" it with her astral form. With the tape rolling, the experiment began.

On all nights but one, though, she reported that while she had floated out of her body, she was not at the right position in the room, near the ceiling, to look at the target number, so she had no idea what it was. On the one occasion when she said she saw the number, she correctly reported that it was 25132. Now this is odds of 100,000 to 1 to guess correctly like that, by chance alone, on a single try. So Miss Z not only experienced herself as out of her body, floating near the ceiling, but she also gave a very impressive demonstration of seeming to perceive the physical room correctly from such a location.[3]

Interestingly enough, scientists outside the field of parapsychology had a novel explanation for the results of the experiment. The OBE was hogwash—Miss Z simply found out the number by using . . . *telepathy*! They used one paranormal event to explain away another, less acceptable one. Wait a minute, guys—telepathy isn't supposed to exist either!

Another persuasive study of knowledge obtained by "impossible" means was devised by Dr. Karlis Osis, a well-known figure in the field, and conducted at the American Society for Psychical Research in New York, where Osis was the director of research. The test subject was another gifted psychic, psychologist Alex Tanous. Their goal was to test something similar to, but not the same as, the OBE. They were investigating *clairvoyance*, the ability to project the mind through space and time, or the ability to receive knowledge from other levels of consciousness.

Osis went to a lot of trouble to devise a quality test. In addition to constructing a special viewing box, one that gave a different image of the object when viewed from different angles, around the box he also installed electrical strain gauges, which detect motion and electromagnetic fields. During the test, various figures were placed in the box, whose design allowed a unique optical illusion to form of each object when viewed from a special port in the side of the box. In this way, distinct images formed when the object was viewed from particular directions, adding another degree of control to the study.

Tanous was able, time after time, to describe the proper appearance of the test objects, strongly suggesting that he was viewing the test object as if he were within the box, that is, with some portion of "himself" other than his physical vision. His consciousness was able to move into the correct position to view the nonillusional aspect of the target he described. He could project consciousness into space, just as ancient cultures claimed. And what of the strain detectors? Each time Tanous stated he was viewing the test object, the instruments picked up fluctuations in energy output in that immediate area.[4] Consciousness was an energy form!

These phenomena—NDEs, OBEs, clairvoyance—are examples of *psi*, as psychic phenomena are known in the field. Surprisingly, psychic phenomena have been exhaustively studied in the West since the nineteenth century and continue to be the subject of intense scientific scrutiny. The evidence supporting the existence of psi is overwhelming. I was shocked when I realized just how extensive the evidence was. Mainstream science doesn't accept psi, so most of us, myself included, assume that no real research has been done on the topic, or that there has been research, and it showed only . . . imagination. Our assumption is wrong. Psi is a proven part of our world. Those who say otherwise are simply ignorant of the facts or find fault with the research, regardless of its quality. The real problem does not lie with psi, it lies with—*science!*

Generally speaking, the world of psi is part of a larger field loosely termed the *paranormal*. However, the scientists who study the world of *parapsychology*, that is, the world of psi, group their investigations into what I call the Big Four: three categories for extrasensory perception, or ESP—*telepathy, clairvoyance*, and *precognition*—and a fourth category for the ability to affect material objects with an unknown form of energy, *psychokinesis*, or PK. (Recently, researchers have begun to use the terms *anomalous cognition* for ESP and *anomalous perturbation* for PK, but I will stick with the more familiar terms.) Things like UFOs, the Loch Ness monster, hauntings, and the like all fall into the broader category of the paranormal. Before we dive into the evidence, let's look at the Big Four a little more closely.

With *telepathy*, information is obtained about the thoughts, feelings, or activities of another conscious being without using the normal channels so familiar to us all. Telepathy seems to defy physics. Studies show it to be instantaneous, faster than light, and unaffected by shielding methods, such as a lead container or a Faraday cage. As such, it is thought to involve an unknown form of energy. It also defies matter as well. Telepathy has been demonstrated during OBEs, when the physical body isn't even a player.

Unlike telepathy, which involves another consciousness, *clairvoyance* is defined as the paranormal acquisition of information about an object or physical event; that is, the data are derived from the physical environment and not from the mind of another person. The phenomenon seems to be unconstrained by time and space. Remote viewing, which I will discuss a bit later, is a modern example. Conventional science has no explanation for how a person can obtain knowledge from a distant source, or how human personality can travel there or tune into it from a distance, or what energies are involved.

The third form of ESP is *precognition*, the awareness of a future event that cannot be deduced from data we currently know in the present. Remote viewers, psychics, and mediums often display this type of awareness. If time is linear, how can we explain this ability? How can we know something that hasn't occurred yet? The answer is easy, though no less confusing. Space and time, as Einstein stressed, are constructions of the human mind, the game board upon which we make sense of life with our rational minds. They are *not* a fundamental aspect of nature. Both facts have been demonstrated in particle physics, where things are nonlocally connected, and particles have been shown to move backward in time.[5] Even though these results are well established, scientists still bristle at the thought of the same thing occurring on a macroscopic level. However, startling evidence exists showing that it does.

While all the three types of ESP involve the ability to sense matters beyond the range of ordinary perception, the fourth major psi activity forms a category of its own. Psychokinesis, or PK, involves not information, but matter. It is defined as the influence of mind on a physical system that can't be entirely explained by any currently known energy. In other words, under certain circumstances, some people can move things with their minds, or, in the case of ch'i kung masters, by the projection of an unknown form of energy—unknown to conventional science, that is. The masters serenely state that they are using ch'i.

Serious study of psi began in the mid-nineteenth century, when mediumship was all the rage both in America and across the Atlantic. Much excellent early work was done by members of the British Society for Psychical Research, who forged the path for true scientific investigation of psi phenomena. Their interests covered the entire range of paranormal activity, from hauntings to precognitive dreams, from seers and séances to poltergeists. However, it took the groundbreaking work of the wizard of Duke University, J. B. Rhine (1895–1980), to establish the true science of parapsychology.

Joseph Banks Rhine originally planned to become a minister. However, J. B. was a scientist at heart, and he dropped out of seminary, stating that he "saw no logical ground for the role of a minister."[6] As he left his religious training, he commented on his reasons to his psychology professor:

> In my course on religion we talked about man's soul as if it were the most real thing in the world, and over here in psychology we talked about the brain reactions as if that is all we know about human beings. The word "soul" doesn't appear in any of the textbooks we have read. You don't even use it in the classroom. Thus in one classroom I am a living soul; in the other, a brain machine.[7]

Rhine never fully gave up on religion, however, and the modern science of parapsychology grew from his attempt to find a common ground between theology and science. Rhine had been greatly disappointed with both disciplines as a young man, and he set out, with his wife Louisa, to find the link he intuitively felt bound the two. The young couple enrolled together in a graduate biology program at the University of Chicago.

By the 1930s, the Rhines had settled at North Carolina's Duke University, where they would soon establish a program to test scientifically the strange spiritual phenomena that have accompanied mankind throughout history. It was there, in their history-making ESP lab, that the first real, statistical scientific study of psi began. It was about this time that J. B. Rhine first designed his now-famous ESP card tests, which have even starred in a movie.

The film *Ghostbusters* opens with a psychology professor (played by Bill Murray) using a version of the Rhine test. A young male student attempts to guess the symbols on a special deck of cards—all fairly standard procedure, except for the radical form of the reward. If he guesses incorrectly, he gets zapped with electricity! A beautiful young coed misses right and left with her guesses, yet the wily Murray lets her slide, while the poor guy gets shocked even if he guesses correctly. The cards used were designed by J. B. Rhine decades before the movie became a smash hit.

The basic version of the test used a series of five cards, each with a simple symbol: a circle, a star, a cross, a square, and three wiggly lines in parallel. The subject attempted to guess the correct card that Rhine or one of his associates was holding up, and the number of correct guesses and misses were tabulated.

One of the first things Rhine realized was that for this test to have any merit, the order of the cards had to be *random*. This was achieved in a simple but effective way: the cards were thoroughly shuffled. This step is vital for two reasons. First, it kept the subjects from guessing correctly on the basis of logical inference alone; second, and even more importantly, with a random sequence of targets, *it was possible to work out exactly what the average number of correct guesses would be from chance alone.*[8]

Of course, getting more hits than predicted is an exciting result. But it may come as a bit of a shock to realize that getting *less* than the predicted number of hits is very significant as well. That outcome is known as *psi-missing*. It works both ways, folks! If probability theory states that there should be a given number of correct hits due to chance alone, then a smaller number is also of significance. Psi-missing is now a well-documented phenomenon in the world of parapsychology.

In the mid-1950s, Rhine commented,

> The conclusion is inescapable that there is something operative in man that transcends the laws of matter and therefore, by definition, a nonphysical or spiritual law is made manifest. The universe, therefore, does not conform to the prevailing materialistic concept. It is one about which it is possible to be religious; possible, at least, if the minimal requirement of religion be a philosophy of man's place in the universe based on the operation of spiritual forces.[9]

From the 1934 publication of Rhine's great introduction to the world of psi, *Extra-Sensory Perception*, to the end of his decades-long career, his hundreds of carefully crafted experiments to investigate the paranormal resulted in very strong evidence for the existence of psychic phenomena. But they also shed light on some other interesting aspects of psi as well. His experiments, and work in other labs by independent researchers replicating his studies, produced a cumulative probability of 10^{-24}, or only one chance of error in a trillion, trillion.[10]

One surprising fact was that the qualities of the target involved—things like size, shape, or color—didn't really seem to matter. Even more important, however, was the startling fact that time or space didn't seem to make a difference, either. This is perhaps the thing that most riled the orthodox scientific community. Renowned parapsychologist K. Ramakrishna Rao comments:

> Any hypothetical relationship of distance to ESP must assume that there is some energy transmission between the subject and the targets that is inhibited by the distance factor. But if precognition is a fact, and we have

strong evidence to believe that it is, what is the nature of this transmission that occurs between the subject and the not-yet-existing target? Thus, the evidence for precognition and the success of ESP experiments over long distances lead one to believe that *space and time are not constraining variables as far as psi is concerned* [italics added].[11]

The wise ones of traditional societies understood the value of overcoming time and space. In nearly all such societies, prophets, shamans, oracles, or medicine men or women had a central role, providing a valuable service to their community. They cured the sick; they gave guidance to rulers; they provided intelligence in time of war. Their abilities usually included astral projection and clairvoyance, among other things. Of course, psychic ability can be nebulous and unpredictable, even among the very best. It doesn't always work. But sometimes it does—even in the most modern lives.

Our government knows this. So do the various intelligence agencies and the U.S. Army. So guess what? One traditional role of the psychically gifted is still alive and well—and well hidden: psychic spying. Federal operatives have been up to their eyeballs in psychic espionage and intelligence activity since the 1970s. They've just given it a new name: *remote viewing*.

It sounds so innocuous, like taking a look from a distant mountaintop. That's good, because that's what the name was intended to convey. You can sell the concept of remote viewing . . . maybe. You can't when you call it by its traditional name, *clairvoyance*. In modern society, educated people flip out when you talk about psychic phenomena, particularly if they've totally bought into the trendy aspects of science. They think of those ridiculous TV commercials for psychic hotlines. Among the scientific elite, it's not chic to be spiritual.

But remote viewing turned out to be hip for a couple of reasons. One was the name. It successfully gave clairvoyance and astral projection a squeaky-clean new image, removing the stigma associated with the psychic world. It worked. And second, *it worked*; people could actually be trained to separate their consciousness from their physical bodies, letting it travel through time and space.

Imagine the excitement of Army Intelligence and the Central Intelligence Agency (CIA) when they finally realized the potential of this new modus operandi. It was a spook's dream, to be able to spy on the enemy using only an operator's consciousness. Heck, with luck you might be able to read your enemies' thoughts, maybe even kill them with mind-vibes! Yes, in spite of the scientific scorn toward remote viewing, the government went with it. They weren't interested in academic theory; they wanted results. Remote viewing delivered the goods.

It all started in June 1972. Harold Puthoff, Ph.D., had been recently hired by one of the world's top think tanks, the Stanford Research Institute (SRI). He was an expert on lasers and quantum mechanics, with a doctorate in physics—a man on the move. He was also very interested in psi and creativity, because he thought they might provide an insight into the mysteries of quantum physics.

SRI brought him on board to help with a laser project, and later he began to examine psi phenomena in an effort to advance his work with quantum mechanics. On June 4, 1972, he met the great Ingo Swann: artist, psychic, and eccentric, cigar-chomping New Yorker . . . in short, the man who started it all. Puthoff was in for a wild ride that changed his life forever.

Puthoff felt the future of quantum physics might possibly lie with psychic phenomena. He eventually found funding to pursue his ideas: Bill Church, founder of Church's Fried Chicken, agreed to finance some of Puthoff's research. Puthoff put out the word that he was looking for gifted psychics. The appeal netted him a letter from one Ingo Swann in New York. After a few more letters, Puthoff agreed to fly Swann to sunny California, to the headquarters of SRI. He arrived on June 4 and immediately blew their minds.

Puthoff wanted to see if Swann could affect sensitive equipment with his mind. The two men drove over to Stanford University, to the basement of the physics building, Varian Hall, where one of the most specialized sensing devices in the world was housed. It was an experimental magnetometer, built with money from the Office of Naval Research. The instrument was designed to look for quarks, the proposed fundamental particle of matter, and in fact this very machine would eventually find them.

It was an exceptional piece of equipment, specially shielded from all forms of radiation by copper, aluminum, and custom alloys, all designed to detect the tiny magnetic field perturbations that quarks are said to make. It even contained a supercooled superconductor, an expensive device that allowed electricity to flow without resistance.

Puthoff briefly explained the device to Swann, and then hit him with the big one: could he alter the magnetometer's output while it was specially shielded and buried in the concrete floor? Swann was briefly puzzled by such an unusual request, but he agreed to try.

Swann concentrated, and something wild happened. The buried magnetometer's chart recorder suddenly changed! *Just like that.* Puthoff noticed that the recorder's data correlated with Swann's efforts. The other scientists scoffed, thinking it was just a coincidence. Swann repeated this effect several times and even sketched a diagram showing the internal mechanism, something the designer later agreed was completely accurate. As soon as Swann left the room, the data returned to normal. Here was one of the most sophisticated sensing devices in the world, shielded from all known forms of electromagnetic radiation, yet Swann had affected it with his consciousness.[12]

Puthoff was hooked. He prepared a brief description of Swann's success, along with copies of the data, and went fishing for more funding. Within a few weeks, Puthoff landed the biggest fish of all: the U.S. government. So began one of the strangest arms races in history, and both Puthoff and Swann were key players. Psychic research and activity were officially on the map—and the Soviets officially on notice.

The Soviets had always been interested in psychic phenomena—it's almost a national heritage with them—and they displayed great interest in the United States' supposed psychic experiments when they got wind of them. Until then the Soviets thought they had a monopoly on psychic military activity. At about the same time, the book *Psychic Discoveries Behind the Iron Curtain* became a best-seller.[13] Then suddenly, in a kind of circularity of effect, the American spooks became very interested in the potential for psychic intelligence activity, if for no other reason than that the Soviets were so into it. If there was anything to it at all, the United States had to get on the ball. Next, word circulated that the Soviets were working on a program to mentally affect the trajectory of intercontinental ballistic missiles (ICBMs). Suddenly, psychic phenomena were red hot. The powers-that-be decided it was time to act. They came to see Hal Puthoff at SRI after his report concerning Swann and the magnetometer made the rounds.[14]

By October 1972, Puthoff and his partner Russell Targ, Ph.D., also a laser physicist, were conducting experiments in ESP with Swann. One day, two strange-looking dudes showed up at SRI. They wanted to see for themselves if Swann could actually do anything of value. They brought an object with them and had Puthoff place it in an experimental box. Using ESP, could Swann tell them what it was? Swann got into the "zone" and described the object. "I see something small, brown, and irregular, sort of like a leaf, or something that resembles it, except that it seems very much alive, like it's even moving!" The test object was a large, brown moth, its appearance being very leaf-like to blend in with its environment.[15]

Swann had done it, at least to a degree. The men left. A few weeks later they presented Puthoff with a check for $50,000 to continue the research. The men were from the CIA. The government was in. Continue the research, come up with something really useful (that check said), and more money would follow. Puthoff, Swann, and Targ were ecstatic! At last, official, government-sponsored psi research was on. Now, what could they do that might be of value to the intelligence community?

For a while they did standard ESP-type stuff, having Swann guess the identity of hidden objects and the like. The results were mediocre. The program was off to a slow start, just when everything seemed to be on the line. Swann was pretty sharp, though. He knew exactly what the CIA wanted. They wanted psychic spies, people who could mentally investigate an important military or intelligence target and tell them what was going on there. Swann was eager to comply, yet puzzled by how to proceed.

You'd think that Puthoff and Targ could simply instruct Swann to check out a certain room at the Kremlin and report on what was said or who was there, but it wasn't that easy. Once Swann heard such data, his imagination was bound to become involved, either supplying an interpretation and thus limiting the value of the information or drawing his attention on a tangent so that he missed the target altogether. Swann developed a strict protocol to avoid the problems of imagination; it called for trained viewers to be coached through the session by monitors who were also blinded to the target. That helped, but a more exact method was needed. Swann hit upon it one day while lounging in the pool. A voice told him, "Try coordinates." That was it! Geographic coordinates could be used to identify a target without actually naming it.

It took a lot of convincing for Puthoff and Targ to agree, but after they saw the results, they became believers. Swann wasn't the only one who could do it, either; other remote viewers learned to replicate his success. As difficult as it may be to accept, by simply naming a set of coordinates, a trained remote viewer could view the target in question. Eventually it was found that simply associating a set of randomly generated numbers could do just as well. It was suggested the human collective consciousness was at work.[16]

Granted, this sounds absurd, but it worked. Say, for example, the CIA wanted more information on a suspected weapons-manufacturing plant in the Soviet Union. A randomly generated series of numbers would be assigned to the task and faxed by secure line to SRI, or later to Fort Meade, in Maryland. These numbers would represent that particular target. The handler would brief the remote viewer by giving only the coordinates themselves, perhaps adding the statement that it was a "place." The viewer would relax, get into the "zone," and enter the "ether" with his or her consciousness.

Following a strict protocol developed by Ingo Swann, the remote viewer could actually see the scene in question, as though his or her spirit were floating right there. And the information collected went beyond visual data. The viewer could also pick up smells and sounds, and sometimes thoughts, from people at the target. Swann's strict protocol allowed the team to distinguish between actual relevant data and the viewer's personal impressions. It seemed crazy, but it worked.

Sometimes the viewer would describe a scene that sounded incorrect until the analysts checked out the history of the target. The remote viewer had described something from the target's past! As difficult as it was to believe, human consciousness could traverse both time and space. The ancients were right again. The remote-viewing team had no idea how it all worked, but the results were reproducible; other viewers got similar data from the same coordinates.

In the formative stage of psi research at SRI, Puthoff and Targ tried almost everything. Remote viewing was attempted from small submarines. They used Faraday cages to block known forms of energy. These variations seemed to have no effect at all. The viewing proceeded as usual, with the same results. Whatever was at work here was outside of the conventional world as we know it.

Similar procedures were repeated thousands of times over the next few years. The phenomenon was reproducible. Trained remote viewers could transcend time and space with their consciousness and report what they saw. One of the very best was a middle-aged gentleman named Pat Price, a former police commissioner of Burbank, California, and a Christmas tree farmer, among other things. A couple of Price's early efforts suggest that he was indeed viewing the scene from another level of existence, with another aspect of himself rather than his physical senses. In fact, Pat Price's astonishing abilities eventually led Puthoff to focus exclusively on clairvoyant activity and to coin the term *remote viewing*.

In those formative years, the CIA remained unconvinced that the viewers were not being coached to the targets. Their CIA contact was a man named Richard Kennett, Ph.D., M.D., a research analyst who investigated psi for the CIA. At Puthoff's request, Kennett got a colleague to give him the geographic coordinates of a target that was unknown to him or Puthoff. They were precise coordinates, down to the minute and seconds of latitude and longitude.

Initially, Ingo Swann was given the task. He described a government facility, with sketches and maps of the target. Puthoff didn't know how accurate Swann had been, but he prepared the report to send to Kennett. Before he could finish, fate played a role, and he got a call from a man who identified himself as Pat Price. They were acquainted slightly, having met at a lecture in Los Angeles. On impulse, Puthoff decided to give Price a go at the mystery target and read him the coordinates. A few days later, Puthoff received Price's description of the target in the mail.

Price described the same scene as Swann, except in much greater detail. He began by describing the target as viewed from above, giving precise data about the terrain, such as the exact height of surrounding peaks, as well as an in-depth weather analysis. Then Price went "into" the facility itself. He described the interior in great detail and even, amazingly, mentioned the nameplate on a desk, a Master Sergeant Long. Puthoff sensed that Price was on to something big and called him to ask if he could reveal even more detail about the target. Puthoff wanted to knock the socks off the CIA; he wanted something that would leave no doubt as to the capabilities of remote viewing.

Price went back into the ether and described the scene in unbelievable detail, doing something almost unheard of in remote viewing: he was able psychically to enter secure file cabinets and read the names off the files! He also provided the names of documents on the desktops. Puthoff typed up his report and forwarded it to Kennett. He, in turn, gave the written description to the man who had chosen the coordinates, a CIA officer named Bill O'Donnell. "Rick, this isn't even close," said O'Donnell apologetically, once he had read the descriptions. "I gave you the coordinates of my summer cabin. I just took the maps out of my car, found out where my cabin was in the woods, and that's what I gave you. This," he said, pointing to the descriptions by Swann and Price, "is bull."[17]

Kennett didn't quite know what to make of all this, but he was struck by the fact that both Swann and Price had described essentially the same place. He decided to check it out. The next weekend he drove out to the site and found the cabin. He also found something else. Nearby was a secret government facility, complete with satellite antennae and "no trespassing" signs.

Kennett checked it out further with someone at the Agency who knew what the site was, out in the West Virginia woods. He gave the official the descriptions. All hell broke loose. The site was a secret National Security Agency underground facility called Sugar Grove, and some very important people wanted to know how Kennett and the team at SRI got such sensitive information. They were furious. The investigations began. Finally, when no evidence of a leak could be found, the hoopla faded away.

Price made it all up to the Agency in the summer of 1973 by remote viewing a similar site in the Soviet Union. He provided details of a site in the Ural Mountains and commented that the secret facility had a disproportionate number of female workers. The CIA later confirmed all of Price's information. Ironically, the National Security Agency would eventually become one of the largest users of remote viewing, working extensively from facilities at SRI and Fort Meade.

Puthoff and Targ's program was starting to gain momentum. One day the team decided to see if a moving target made any difference. Rick Kennett chose a random, three-digit number, wrote it down on a piece of paper, and placed it in his shirt pocket. The goal was to see whether Price could determine the number while Kennett soared around the sky in a glider.

Kennett's glider was towed aloft, while Price and Puthoff remained on the ground. Price concentrated. He had no problem determining both the three digits and their correct sequence, but he did complain of something strange. He started getting queasy, like being seasick. An object kept swinging back and forth while Price was trying to read the paper in Kennett's shirt pocket. The oscillations were nearly making Price physically ill.

He sketched the object. It looked an awful lot like an Egyptian *ankh*, the ancient key of life. Both Price and Puthoff were puzzled.

After touching down, Kennett confirmed that the number was correct. Price had done it again. When Price mentioned the unusual side effect of his viewing session, Kennett laughed out loud. He reached under his shirt and pulled out an Egyptian *ankh* on a cord around his neck! The pendant had been swinging back and forth with the movement of the glider, interfering with Price's view of the paper in his shirt pocket! We're beyond telepathy with this. Price was *there*—his consciousness had viewed the cockpit of a moving glider and had been distracted by the oscillating pendant. Some aspect of Price had transcended space and entered that glider.

Later on, remote viewers at Fort Meade would often be affected by the presence of water, smoke, or noxious chemicals while remote viewing. It became something the monitors had to watch for. Sometimes the viewer would actually vomit while investigating a target, or become so upset the session would have to be terminated. To people like Puthoff, Targ, Swann, Price, and the dozens of remote viewers subsequently used by the military, remote viewing was not a figment of human imagination. It was real. They were there. New dimensions, indeed.

Eventually, the word got out. Various government agencies and the military became intensely interested in what the boys at SRI were doing. Further tests were very promising. The funds were rolling in. In 1978 the Army initiated a new unit to conduct remote viewing for intelligence purposes; code named Grill Flame, the unit was based at Fort Meade, Maryland. Guys like Ingo Swann were beginning to take on freelance work. Puthoff and Targ were excited, although I'm sure they were surprised by the cards fate had dealt them. They were laser physicists, after all! Now they found themselves deeply enmeshed in psychic espionage. However, it was also cutting-edge stuff.

In November 1974 they struck pay dirt. Amidst great controversy, *Nature* published their work.[18] But the triumph was mixed with disappointment.

The editors had fixed the match beforehand. In an accompanying editorial, they made it quite clear that they were unconvinced by the work of Puthoff and Targ. They made a big deal out of minor negative points raised by the referees of the paper, points that had already been addressed by the authors in the published version.

Eighteen months later, amid the ongoing controversy, Puthoff and Targ managed to get a more in-depth paper published in the prestigious journal of the leading electrical engineering professional society, the *Proceedings of the IEEE*.[19] The editor, a Bell Labs scientist named Robert Lucky, had initially wanted to turn them down, but when Puthoff and Targ appeared in person to answer questions from a panel of scientists, Lucky was impressed. He even did a little remote viewing himself and became a believer. He was later quoted as saying, "Psychic stuff is really not much more far-fetched than some of the physics behind the laser."[20]

In early 1974, *Time* did a cover story on psi research.[21] Author Leon Jaroff was quick to mention that Puthoff and Swann were both members of "the bizarre and controversial cult of Scientology." Indeed they were, for a while. This wasn't terribly unusual in the sixties. Both men later dropped out of Scientology, and Puthoff eventually joined a group of anti-Scientologists. However, the damage had been done, and despite their high-profile publications, Puthoff and Targ's work was not followed up by mainstream researchers.

Still, they continued their work at SRI. Times change, though, and by 1995 the remote viewing programs at both SRI and Fort Meade had been halted because of slashed budgets and leaks to the press. The work had lasted almost twenty years, with incredible success. Some believe that it just went deeper underground, a logical conclusion considering the amazing potential of the technique. When the program ended, Russell Targ had already left SRI. However, Hal Puthoff continues to this day exploring the quantum concept of zero point energy, the vast amount of energy filling all the world predicted by modern physics, yet ignored by most scientists.[22] Puthoff already has several patents for his work, and he may be on to one of the most important scientific discoveries of all time.[23] Many of the remote viewers who participated in the work began making their knowledge public. Today you can take courses in remote viewing and even order DVDs that teach it.

As for Ingo Swann, he retired back to Manhattan, where he still roams the cosmos, to startling effect. A few years ago, before the first space probes explored the solar system, Swann remote viewed Jupiter and other planets. He made several wild claims that sounded like fantasy, among them that Jupiter had a subtle set of rings and radiated more energy into space than it received from the sun. It was all a joke to the astronomers, until the probes sent back their data. Swann had been right on the money! Everything he said about Jupiter was found to be correct.[24] Even so, the scientific community still insists remote viewing doesn't work.

CHAPTER THREE

More Dimensions:
The Body beyond the Body

Nothing is too wonderful to be true, if it be consistent with the laws of nature.
> —Michael Faraday, nineteenth-century British physicist

Since earliest times it has been recognized that there are higher planes of existence. The ancient sages insisted that our consciousness could separate from the physical body and explore these other realms. They were just as certain about something else. Our *bodies* exist in other dimensions as well. In Theosophical writings, this concept is sometimes called the *human multidimensional anatomy*. The ancients said frequency is the key, and modern researchers are beginning to agree. Human multidimensional anatomy is said to be a function of harmonics. The higher-frequency bodies are a condition of octaves, much as in music.

According to ancient teachings, the first of these octaves is the one most closely associated with the physical body, the *etheric body*. The etheric body, also called the *etheric double*, is intimately bonded with the physical structure of living things and is the first of the so-called subtle energy bodies. It has been said for eons that illness and disease show up first in the etheric body, until the energy balance becomes altered and disease manifests in the familiar physical vessel. Because of the intimate connection between these two bodies, they are sometimes seen as a unit, the physical-etheric complex.

When Kim Bong Han experimented with acupuncture meridians in rabbits and other animals in the 1960s (see chapter 2), he believed he was altering the energy flow from the etheric body. Cutting the vital link between the etheric and physical bodies imbalanced the flow of ch'i, with disastrous results for the test animals. Of course, modern science scoffs at such claims, but a review of the work of Dr. Harold Saxton Burr and the Kirlians might prompt some rethinking.

In the 1940s, Harold Burr was a neuroanatomist at Yale. He had been studying salamanders for quite a while for several reasons, not the least of which is that salamanders are one of the very few animals that can regenerate new limbs as adults. To his surprise, Burr found that salamanders have an electrical energy field nearly identical to the shape of the animal itself. He also found this field to be aligned with the animals' brain and spinal cord. This was exciting new ground, to say the least.

The next question was a natural one—at what point in embryological development did this strange field begin? After a bit of study, Burr was shocked to find that the *electrical energy-field axis originated in the unfertilized egg itself*. It was inherent in the very germ cell of the organism! To Burr, it seemed logical to assume that this primordial field was the one that later became apparent in the alignment of the central nervous systems of the salamanders.

Salamanders have eggs that are big enough to observe under a conventional microscope. Burr injected a tiny amount of indelible ink into the electrical energy-field axis of an egg, then sat back and waited. In every case, the ink spot eventually became incorporated into the brain and spinal cord of the growing organism. Something profound was happening here: an energy field that predated the physical body of the organism.

He began to study plants as well. He observed the energy templates around tiny seedlings. To his surprise he found the electrical field resembled, not the seed, *but rather the shape of the later, adult plant into which it would develop.* What had traditionally been referred to as the *etheric body* had been found in animals and plants.[1]

In these studies, Burr used a sophisticated new voltmeter of his own design, one that drew no voltage from the subjects. As a result, the instrument reflected the energy characteristics of the mysterious fields. He conducted research for more than twenty years and made further startling discoveries. For example, the alteration of a single gene within a plant's DNA would cause profound changes in the voltage readings. Burr went on to find that the future health of the plant could be predicted from the energy field surrounding its seed.

On a hunch, Burr began to study the trees around the Yale campus, organisms that are obviously stationary and live to be quite old. Using instruments of his own design, he found some intriguing things. The energy fields around the trees, studied over a twenty-year period, showed definite signs of being influenced by lunar and solar cycles, as well as by sunspot activity.[2] Again, old knowledge is rediscovered: for generations farmers planted their crops by what they called the "signs," based on the lunar and solar cycles of nature as recorded in the almanacs. They swore by them, insisting they worked. Modern botanists snicker at such "nonsense," but Burr's work gives credibility to this ancient belief. The energy fields of living things can be affected by the cycles of the moon and sun.

And then there's the fabled aura, the glow said to emanate from the higher energy bodies of living things. It has been reported throughout history and across cultures. There's hardly a painting from the Middle Ages that doesn't show an individual with an aura—or, if you like, a halo—beaming around his or her head.

In fact, many people can see the portion of the aura that emanates from the etheric body. It is usually bluish-gray, extending a few inches from the physical body. It is most easily seen against a light-colored background. To see the other aspects of the aura, the radiations from the higher-energy bodies beyond the etheric body, additional skills are required. Some claim to see vivid colors and detect aspects of a person's emotional state and physical health in the aura. Advanced practitioners claim to be able to see actual "thought forms," the spiritual manifestations of thought in the aura. Modern researchers are confident at least that the etheric body glows. Semyon Kirlian certainly thought so.

In 1939, Semyon Kirlian was considered the best electrician in the Soviet city of Krasnodar, the capital of the Kuban region of Russia near the Black Sea. One day a nearby medical research institute needed some electrical instrumentation repaired; someone mentioned Kirlian. They contacted him, and he agreed to come over and take a look. Then, as so often happens, fate intervened.

While at the institute, Kirlian noticed patients being treated with electrotherapy. Suddenly something caught his eye. Tiny flashes of light were visible between the electrodes and the patients' skin. Kirlian wondered if this phenomenon could be photographed. He decided to try it on himself by placing a photographic plate between the electrodes and his skin. The pain was excruciating, but he held on long enough for an image.

As the photo developed in his darkroom, he began to see something odd. He saw his hand and fingers, but they were surrounded by a luminescent glow! Flares of energy could be seen radiating from certain areas of his hand, areas he would later find were the classic acupuncture points of the ancient Chinese. He found that the phenomenon was already known to science. They called it *corona discharge*, the so-called cold emission of electrons. The effect is based on the fact that electrically grounded objects in high-frequency fields, between 75,000 to 200,000 cycles per second, usually demonstrate spark discharges between the object and the electrode. By placing a piece of photographic paper between the two, the phenomenon can be recorded on film. The method came to be known as *Kirlian photography* or *electrophotography*.

Kirlian didn't disagree with the science, but he intuitively felt there was much more to it. He and his wife Valentina continued with their research.

Ordinary objects, like a metal coin, just demonstrated a uniform glow around the edges. Living things were another matter. They pulsed with eruptions of energy flares, some in vivid colors. Dots of energy were apparent at intervals across the surface of the object.

They found the same sort of thing with a leaf plucked from a plant. It positively glowed, with turquoise and reddish-yellow energy flares surrounding the edges of the leaf, along with innumerable tiny dots of energy. Some of the energy flares emanated from specific areas of the leaf, almost like tiny volcanic eruptions. Further studies with human hands and fingers showed similar patterns. Living things were *alive* with this energy, something an ordinary camera couldn't see.

Kirlian knew he was on to something big. He and his wife eventually developed a device that could record an object in motion. A whole new world was revealed to them. The human hand looked like a fireworks display of sparkling energy patterns, some that were constant and some that faded and returned. Flares of multicolored energies streamed out into space from certain areas. It was breathtaking. Again they tried a fresh leaf from a plant. It also displayed the same types of beautiful energy patterns. Things began to really get interesting, however, when they placed a withered leaf in their new device. There were almost no energy patterns at all!

The Kirlians became convinced that the instruments could revolutionize medicine and a host of other areas, and gradually word of their method spread.[3] Over the years, hundreds of scientists and technicians visited their small home and laboratory. They were impressed, but official wheels turn slowly, especially over something that was likely to smash the current paradigm. One day in 1949, an important-looking gentleman appeared with what was to be an official test, although the Kirlians didn't know it at the time.

He was the chairman of a major scientific research institute and had with him a container that housed two identical plant leaves, both taken from the same species of plant at the same time. He wanted them photographed with the new device. Kirlian immediately set to work on what was now a routine procedure. He knew from years of experimentation that each particular plant species produced a unique type of electrophotographic image. What he found with this sample puzzled him. One leaf was as expected, with the now-familiar patterns of colors and energy flares. The other, however, showed something strange—tiny geometric figures distributed sparsely across the leaf.

Kirlian immediately blamed his equipment. Something must have gone wrong with the damn circuits! He and Valentina tried again and again, actually working throughout the night to obtain the proper exposure. Nothing worked. One leaf was normal, and one kept producing the distorted image. Kirlian was both disappointed and worried. This was the Soviet Union. They had labor camps in unpleasant places. It didn't take much to become an official guest of one.

Wearily they showed their results to the botanist, expecting the worst. "You've found it!" exclaimed the scientist. It had all been a blind test to examine the efficiency of the Kirlians' device. The leaves had come from identical plants except for one important point. One plant was healthy. The other suffered from a serious disease that would soon terminate it, although it still appeared perfectly normal at the time. The scientist was ecstatic.

The Kirlians were on the map.

The couple continued to demonstrate their device, even encouraging visitors to gulp down a shot of vodka and watch the effect on their own energy patterns. (It was almost instantaneous, and the ripple could be seen throughout the energy field.) For all its potential for healthcare, however, the Kirlians discovered something even more profound with their instrument. One day Kirlian took a photo of a fresh leaf, then snipped it in half and took a second photograph. What he saw raised the hairs on the back of his neck. There, clear as day, was the *entire* leaf, with the usual glow and energy flares. What remained of the missing portion was mind-blowing. There, in the photograph, connected to the actual leaf fragment, *was a ghostly image of the missing part, perfect in all detail,* with the texture, patterns, and veins of the leaf! Kirlian had photographed the energy template, the etheric body, which remained of the missing half of the leaf.

They had documented for the very first time what would soon become known as the *phantom leaf effect*, the most famous aspect of Kirlian photography. It would make them famous around the world—and the subject of immediate controversy, much of which continues to this day.

The first suggestion was that the moisture pattern of the missing leaf fragment had caused the phantom appearance. This explanation was quickly refuted when California State University researcher Keith Wagner used a clear Lucite block to cover any traces of moisture left behind by the missing portion. Clear, excellent examples of the phantom leaf effect were still obtained.[4] Another researcher, Allen Detrick, later successfully photographed both sides of a snipped leaf, obtaining separate, distinct phantom images of both sides in full detail. Residual moisture would certainly *not* explain this effect.

Kirlian continued throughout his life to advance his discovery. He was able to invent a coupling device that allowed Kirlian photography through an electron microscope. He and his wife invented all sorts of specialized optical equipment. The Soviet Union eventually sanctioned their work, giving them a nice apartment and a pension. Word of their discovery spread around the world. One of the people who began to experiment with it was a Rumanian named Ion Dumitrescu. He advanced the idea of the phantom leaf effect even further, making it all the more mysterious. He found evidence of a *hologram* in living things.

One of the amazing qualities of a hologram is that when a small portion of a holographic picture is removed, the entire image appears in that fragment. Dumitrescu cut a small hole in a fresh leaf and made a Kirlian photo of it. He was in for a shock. In the photograph, visible in minute detail through the hole, was another full image of the entire leaf, complete with a tiny hole in the appropriate place! It was almost like looking at the reflection of a mirror in another mirror.[5]

For years freethinkers had suggested that living things have a holographic nature, particularly in aspects of the brain. Some went so far as to suggest that the universe itself was just a giant hologram, an infinite energy interference pattern, an unimaginable area where all of the information is contained in every part of it. The concept in physics of nonlocality, which has been experimentally verified, is suggested as evidence of this. Now the new findings of the phantom leaf effect further supported it.[6]

Dumitrescu's work was first reported in the West in *Psychic Discoveries behind the Iron Curtain*, the book that got the CIA moving on remote viewing. By the 1980s, Kirlian photography was second only to X-rays as the most common medical diagnostic tool in Russia. It remains the subject of controversy in the United States, although it has also generated a great deal of interest.

It eventually began to appear in Western research on the early diagnosis of cancer and cystic fibrosis, with some success. Psychic healers have been photographed, revealing huge, brightly colored energy flares emanating from their hands when they are in a healing mode. Dr. Dumitrescu continues his work in Paris, where he has computerized the energy fields of patients. He feels that such energy field analysis could revolutionize internal medicine, permitting detection of illness well before it manifests in the physical body.[7]

The next subtle energy body is the fabled *astral body*. It is the first of the higher-frequency bodies that can detach from the physical form for periods of time. This body is responsible for the strange phenomenon of astral projection, now called *out-of-body experience* (OBE). It is also *the seat of human emotions*. Sometimes the astral body separates from the physical-etheric complex. Many researchers believe that this separation happens every night, during the process of dreaming.

Strangely enough, dreaming is a vital process of life. Deny a person the ability to dream, as can be done with certain drugs, and health rapidly breaks down. Sleep deprivation is bad, but dream deprivation can be fatal.

Particularly important is REM sleep, the stage of rapid eye movement when dreaming occurs. Deny a person sleep, and what little they can grab will be REM sleep, as shown in studies involving the military elite, such as Navy SEALs and Army Special Forces, all of whom soon learn the pleasures of going without proper amounts of sleep. Obviously, dreaming plays a vital role in our lives, but why?

Many believe that dreaming is the time when the astral body separates from the physical-etheric interface and travels elsewhere, at least temporarily. It is said that if the astral body stays gone too long you won't come back, that the so-called silver cord described in the esoteric literature will separate from the physical body. In the related phenomenon of an OBE, many people are terrified by a feeling that they can't get back into their bodies. It seems as though the expanded astral consciousness has a hard time cramming itself back into the constraints of the humble physical body.

Another unusual aspect of astral consciousness is *lucid dreams*, that is, dreams in which the person knows that he or she is dreaming and can change the dream to suit him- or herself. Lucid dreams have been the subject of a great deal of study. They are unique in several ways. For starters, the dreamer retains full consciousness, yet is dreaming. The dreams are unusually vivid, more real than real, you might say. But what really makes lucid dreams unusual is the dreamer's ability to *control* them. In ordinary, run-of-the-mill dreams, we are passive participants. In a lucid dream, the dreamer guides the dream, changing a nightmare into a pleasurable experience, for example.

And everything is so *real*! Colors are more vivid. Floors and walls are solid. Emotions never felt so strong. A lucid dream with a romantic overtone can be better than the real thing! Some researchers feel that normal dreams are a virtual phenomenon, like a hologram, but that lucid dreams originate in another level of reality. Physicist Fred Alan Wolf, another star of *What the Bleep Do We Know?*, believes that lucid dreams are visits to parallel universes, worlds inaccessible to our everyday consciousness.[8] If this is the case, then why are dreams so vital to our existence?

In some belief systems, our lives here on the physical plane are said to be a learning experience, a time in which events can be actualized in the world of ordinary matter, a time for growth and development. During dreaming and events such as OBEs, the astral body enters other realms, perhaps to retain an ongoing contact with the higher planes of existence, the higher aspects of ourselves.

However peculiar these higher-dimensional bodies may sound, they are still connected to the physical body. The connection is made through energy centers called *chakras*. For example, these energy centers join the emotions of the astral body to the physical body, particularly to the endocrine system. Chakras are ancient and mystical, but recent studies have shown that they are also quite literally measurable.

Dr. Valerie Hunt, a physical therapist and researcher at the University of California, Los Angeles, was investigating the effects of Rolfing, a system of vigorous massage and realignment, on the human body. What she found went far beyond Rolfing. Hunt was using a sophisticated, computerized electromyograph (EMG) system that measures the electrical potential of muscles through the skin. (I often used a similar device in my chiropractic practice as a diagnostic tool.) Valerie Hunt's results were anything but routine.

As she scanned the test subjects, she began to notice readings in certain areas of the body that were far higher than those typically reported. Brain waves usually fall in the range of 0 to 100 cycles per second (cps). Muscle readings are typically up to about 225 cps, with the special cardiac muscle of the heart running as high as 250 cps. Hunt's readings were registering as high as 1000 cps in particular regions of the body. Readings in this range were unprecedented in the scientific literature.

Here's why: no one had ever bothered to check the solar plexus area or the top of the head. Hunt was familiar with the concept of chakras, and it suddenly dawned on her that these were the areas that were giving such high readings. Maybe there was something to the ancient theories after all.

She brought in a psychic, Rosalyn Bruyere, who was said to be able to see the auric radiations and the chakras.

Hunt was curious to see whether there was any correlation between her EMG readings and what Bruyere reported from her psychic vision. Bruyere was not told which areas Hunt was recording; she simply reported her psychic perceptions. What they found was amazing. When Bruyere reported a particular color in the aura or the chakras, Hunt's equipment correlated *exactly*.[9]

When Bruyere reported pure white in a chakra, the readings were the highest of all, over 1,000 cps, the highest ever recorded in the human body. Hunt was both amazed and puzzled. "The results were so exciting that I simply was not able to sleep that night. The scientific model I subscribed to throughout my life just couldn't explain these findings." Repeated studies proved to be remarkably consistent. "It was the same right down the line."[10]

Hunt became deeply impressed with her findings. As she continued her work, she found evidence of individuals' talents and personality in their energy fields. In subjects who focused on the material aspects of life, Hunt found low-frequency readings of just a bit above the normal biological range of 250 cps. Psychics and natural healers had frequencies in the range of 400 to 800 cps, substantially higher than average. On rare occasions, however, Hunt found individuals whose energy field levels were off the scale, some as high as 200,000 cps. These people were labeled "mystic personalities." Hunt found these subjects to be spiritually advanced, with psychic and trance-like abilities, yet also grounded and aware of their place in the universe and the interconnectedness of everything.

Hunt next began to look at how the chakras and fields were affected by external stimuli. After decades in the martial arts, I have personally experienced the sensitivity of the energy fields. I can *feel* a strike before it is executed. And during the practice of ch'i kung, many people can feel the chakras. In some of the exercises, the hands cup around invisible balls of energy during the movements. When the energy ball moves near a traditional chakra, distinct feelings of fullness or volume can be detected. Although this sensation is very subjective, it happens. On days when I feel good and energetic, or when I practice with advanced people, the energy balls feel much larger. I can feel the energy in the room and around the chakras. Valerie Hunt and others have measured this kind of awareness.

In one test, Hunt measured the EMG of the energy field and the EEG readings of the brain at the same time. She administered the stimulus, such as a bright flash of light or a loud noise, and watched the show. What she found was almost scary. *The energy field registered the stimulation well before the brain did!*

Similar findings have been verified by others. Neurophysiologists Benjamin Libet and Bertram Feinstein at San Francisco's Mount Zion Hospital found that electrical stimuli were registered by the brain and prompted a reaction by the test subjects well before the subjects were aware of the required reaction, such as pressing a button. Their subconscious mind made the decision to react before they were consciously aware of it. Surprisingly, the subjects thought *they* were making the decision.[11] Hunt comments:

> I think we have way overrated the brain as the active ingredient in the relationship of a human to the world. It's just a real good computer. But the aspects of the mind that have to do with creativity, imagination, spirituality, and all those things, I don't see them in the brain at all. The mind's not in the brain. It's in that darn field.[12]

The etheric and astral bodies and the chakras are only a small part of what is called in Theosophy the *human multidimensional anatomy*. The Vedas of ancient India, the earliest known writings, discuss such ideas in significant detail. The philosophers of classical Greece, Plato in particular, also believed in similar concepts. In 1875, world traveler and renowned mystic Madame Helena Petrovna Blavatsky began the Theosophical Society in New York City and reintroduced the idea of subtle energy bodies to the West. Later members who modified and added to the knowledge of Theosophy included Annie Besant, C. W. Leadbeater, and A. E. Powell, all of whom wrote extensively on spiritual topics. In fact, Theosophy is considered to be the leading influence of the New Age movement in general. As such, its model of human multidimensional anatomy is widely accepted in New Age accounts of psychoenergetics and warrants a brief overview here.

According to Theosophy, seven is a sacred cosmic number, as it is in Christianity and many other religions, and there are seven energy bodies in human multidimensional anatomy. There are also seven planes of existence. The lowest plane, the seventh, has the slowest vibrational rate. It has two components: 7a, the physical body; and 7b, the etheric body. The sixth plane contains the astral body, the first of the subtle energy bodies that can detach from the physical body for periods of time. It is also the seat of emotion.

At the next higher frequency is the fifth plane, which has three components. The most advanced is 5a, the higher mental plane, which contains what is known as "mind," the world of pure thought. This is where inspiration, imagination, and invention are said to originate. Next in line is 5b, the causal body, which is said to be the domain of abstract thought. The causal body is the area associated with discovering the essence of things. It is here that intuition begins. The causal body is the vehicle of consciousness that gets to the heart of things, that can arrive at the total "gestalt" of an idea. The causal body has its own chakra system, distinct from that of the physical body. The third aspect of the fifth plane, 5c, is the lower mental body, where we find the individual personality. Here, thoughts are transformed into energy vibrations; the term for when others can detect or interpret these vibrations is *telepathy*. This lower mental body is also the source of reason and logic. It is also superimposed upon the physical form, like the others described so far, all of which can occupy the same space because they have different frequencies.

Of course, there is much more to human beings than emotion and thought, even abstract thought of a higher order. We are creatures of spirit as well. *We have a soul.* According to the Theosophical model, there are planes for this aspect of our being. The fourth plane is that of the soul, appropriately called the *soulful plane*. This plane carries the eternal essence of the individual. Number three is the spiritual plane, containing pure spirit. Here we begin to see the higher energy of the individual meld with that of the cosmos. Plane number two is the oversoulful plane, which is characterized by the Holy Spirit. Above that, at the pinnacle, is the highest plane, the divine plane, said to be that of Deity. Thus, the seven bodies and planes of ancient knowledge link us with the cosmos and the highest intelligence of all.[13]

According to William Tiller, what we call *consciousness* is the soul, that aspect of the divine energy that resides in each of us, manifesting into dense matter of the physical world. We are, in his words, "multiplexed in the Divine." Our four higher bodies deal with the soul, territory that is difficult for us to relate to. We all understand emotion. We see it and generate it every day. Intellect is also easy to understand. Man is a creature of logic, of reason. Even intuition, as mysterious as it seems to be, is part of our common experience. But when we reach the area beyond these aspects, we are in an entirely different realm.[14]

There are concepts in science, like quantum theory and relativity, in which language is insufficient to describe what our hearts and minds tell us. The same is true of the spiritual realms of the soul. There are advanced people around who could tell us, but I'm not sure we could understand. Some things have to be *felt*, experienced, for us to comprehend them fully. The Yaqui shaman don Juan used to tell his student Carlos Castaneda that talking about such things was an exercise in futility. Only when one has accumulated enough personal power through spiritual practices and self-discipline do the higher mysteries of life become available to us. Once again, it's all a matter of energy. The Force must be with us.

CHAPTER FOUR

Where Do We Go?
Arguments for an Afterlife

Is not short pain well borne, that brings long ease,
and lays the soul to sleep in quiet grove?
Sleep after toil, port after stormy seas,
Ease after war, death after life does greatly please.
—Edmund Spenser, *The Faerie Queene*

Ah, the mysteries of life. . . . Is there a purpose to it all, or is life as science would have us believe, just an accidental occurrence, a random event, the result of a handful of organic compounds that got together a few billion years ago? And if there is meaning behind our existence, what is it?

We are sentient beings, you and I, and we sometimes ponder the adventure and disappointment that we call *life*, searching for some meaning to justify our existence. I'd like to think there's a purpose to it all, some master plan for our lives, something to validate the daily grind. It would be nice to think that all the pain and boredom are not pointless. And if there is some grand master plan, if life is not just an evolutionary happenstance, then what happens when it's over? Is this great adventure just a one-time shot, something that transpires over a few decades and vanishes forever, at least for the individual in question?

These are the really big questions in life, folks, and the biggest one of all is the toughest one to answer: if our souls really are immortal and there is indeed an afterlife awaiting when this earthly repose ends, then, when it's all really over, when the old ticker finally stops and the brainwaves cease, tell me—*where do we go?*

Yes, ladies and gentlemen, that's the really Big Question. We hope the answer is a nice, pleasant place, and certainly not an overly warm one, if you catch my drift. The Big Question has been around for a long time. Gravesites from thousands of years ago, long before written history, show us that ancient man was as nervous and puzzled about it as we are today. Even the Neanderthal graves were nicely done up, with stones carefully arranged and such things as flowers and ordinary items included with the deceased, much as we do today. Ancient peoples obviously believed in an afterlife; they went to an awful lot of trouble to prepare for it. Their written records and oral legends are filled with details about what happens when we shuffle off this mortal coil.

If you follow the majority line, then you believe in an afterlife. Most of the world's population believes we continue on in some fashion after death, and a large percentage of those asked—something a bit over half—say they have been contacted by departed loved ones through voices, visions, or dreams.

Belief in life after death is the kind of thing most of us feel in our hearts. We may believe that death is not the end, but we're not too sure about what lies ahead. Of course, intuitive knowledge and feelings don't carry much weight with the scientific crowd, leaving open the question about whether there's truth to the "survival phenomenon," to use the parapsychological term. Let's look again at the phenomenon of the near-death experience (NDE).

An NDE is distinguished from the out-of-body experience (OBE) by the fact that the subject is clinically dead. Heart and respiratory functions have ceased, temporarily at least. In some cases, brainwave activity has ceased as well.[1]

Of course, the NDE is far from an exclusively modern phenomenon, nor is it limited to the Western world. In fact, the aspect of the NDE that first attracted the attention of modern researchers was its universality. The phenomenon is just too common to be meaningless. Nowadays it is probably hip to claim having had such an experience; it's all part of being "with it." But until the late 1970s, NDEs were given little official credibility—unless you were a student of ancient literature.

Near-death experiences are mentioned by Plato in Book X of *The Republic*, when he recounts the story of a Greek soldier named Er, who awoke just in time to avoid being roasted on his own funeral pyre and who then described a classic example of an NDE. Such occurrences are also mentioned in detail in the *Book of the Dead* from both the Tibetan and Egyptian traditions. Smith College professor and former Harvard researcher Carol Zaleski wrote a book on the subject called *Otherworld Journeys*, and she reports that medieval literature is full of accounts that resemble NDEs. However, it took Dr. Raymond Moody, Jr., M.D., Ph.D., to really bring the idea to the forefront with his best-seller, *Life After Life*, in the late 1970s.

Moody, whose doctorate is in philosophy, worked as a psychiatrist for years, and he began to take note of a strange event many of his patients related. It struck him as both odd and fascinating. He began formally to interview people who claimed to have experienced an NDE and found an amazing degree of reliability. There were cultural differences, of course, but the main elements were very much alike. How could we be assured that these were genuine journeys and not the kind of hallucinations that his colleagues laughed about? Moody began to analyze his data for hints of proof. He found some interesting stories.

Sometimes NDEs involve more than one person, a really spooky thought. In one instance, a woman was traveling through the tunnel (one of the canonical elements), grooving on it all while approaching the light (another canonical element), when she actually saw someone coming from the other direction. *It was a woman she knew!* The friend telepathically transmitted the idea that she had been there, in the light, and was now being sent back. After the woman recovered, she looked into the case of her friend. It had been real! Her friend had suffered a cardiac arrest at the same time as her own near-fatal event.[2]

In other cases, people have traveled into the light, only to be greeted by someone they knew whom they believed to be alive. Although the subject was unaware of it at the time of the NDE, the person had in fact died. Numerous examples of this kind are recorded in the research literature.

The opinion of the scientific establishment, when it deigns to comment, is that naturally NDEs are only hallucinations, products of the fertile, though silly, human mind. There is one big problem, though. How do they explain the EEG?

The electroencephalograph (EEG) records brain waves through small electrodes glued to the scalp. It is a common instrument for medical diagnosis, widely used and extensively studied. Scientists will be quick to tell you that much has been learned about the brain's activity through the use of the EEG, but they are stumped by the findings in some NDEs. The reason is simple. Clinically dead patients, *with flat EEG readings, indicating no brain activity at all*, have nevertheless frequently returned to consciousness and reported detailed near-death experiences. It may come as a shock to find that many patients have recovered fully after being declared "brain dead," but the diagnosis of brain death is just an *opinion*.[3] By the 1990s, where NDEs were concerned, it was beginning to seem that the case for hallucinations was crumbling. After all, a dead brain is incapable of hallucination or anything else. Yet patients declared brain dead often experienced elaborate NDEs and lived to tell about them. It was beginning to look as though NDEs were . . . *real*.

In the literature on NDEs, Raymond Moody shares the stage with Kenneth Ring, Ph.D., a University of Connecticut psychologist. Of the two, Ring was the first to apply statistical analysis and standardized interview techniques to his investigation of NDEs. After a great deal of study, Ring, like Moody, published a book on the subject, *Life at Death*.

Ring states outright that NDEs are a genuine phenomenon and that the people involved actually travel to another dimension, another level of consciousness where energy and frequency are the key. His conclusions are based upon data from the subjects themselves. Ring became convinced that what was happening to these people was real, at least as real as the ordinary world. In fact, Ring believes that the reason the people see stunning landscapes and flowers is that the human mind continues to process energy-interference patterns in the higher realms just as it does on earth. He wrote:

> I believe that this is a realm that is created by interacting thought structures. These structures or "thought-forms" combine to form patterns, just as interference waves form patterns on a holographic plate. And just as the holographic image appears to be fully real when illuminated by a laser beam, so the images produced by interacting thought-forms appear to be real.[4]

People who have experienced an NDE report some strange things. Their own physical appearance is one such thing. Many report that after they separate from their physical body, they take the shape of a cloud of energy, of consciousness, or of some other amorphous shape that still retains the essence of "them."

In one humorous example, a man left his body and became "something like a jellyfish," a bubble-like energy form that gently sank to the floor. After a brief time, he suddenly assumed the ghostly three-dimensional shape of himself . . . naked. Two women were in the room at the time, and although they couldn't see him (as he found out later), he was acutely embarrassed by his nakedness; so in a flash, he became a *clothed* 3-D ghostly image of a man! The clothing was so complete that he could even see the seams in the pants and sleeves of his shirt, astral tailoring at its best.

Several people reported that, when they weren't thinking about themselves, they were just a cloud of energy that merged with the great cloud around them. Then when they began to think, their thoughts gathered them together once again to form their own personal energy cloud.

One man scrutinized his hands and arms during a near-death moment and reported being able to see the ghostly detail of everything, including "the delicate whorls of his fingerprints and tubes of light up his arms" (the acupuncture meridians, perhaps).[5] In a surprising turnabout, many elderly people found themselves in youthful bodies during their time in the higher realm. Even more shocking is that children often found themselves appearing as adults, giving credence to the belief that our souls are much older than we think. And then there is the business of the "life review"—better known as Judgment Day.

Judgment Day: traditionally believed to be the day of reckoning, when all of our sins, as well as our good deeds, are accounted for and appropriate actions taken. However, those who have died and returned tell things a bit differently than most of our religions teach.

According to most religions, we will all experience a life review soon after we arrive in the next world, a sort of cosmic video that details the important points of our existence. Those who have experienced it describe it as a total review of one's entire life. One person commented, "It's like climbing right inside a movie of your life. Every moment from every year of your life is played back in complete sensory detail. Total, total recall. And it all happens in an instant."[6]

Yes, there is a judgment, but in this telling, it is we who do the judging, and we have to get it right. Advanced spiritual persons are usually with us, the so-called luminous beings, but only in a loving, accepting way. We bring on the guilt trip, not them. They only intercede to show us key points and give us a cosmic overview, but they do it in a kind, benevolent way. And, of course, it's all a learning experience, which is the point of physical existence to begin with.

In this guidance, the first key of the luminous beings is to love. Loving is a conscious energy all its own, a method of bonding with the energy of the universe, which all emanates from the divine source. To be loving is also the way you should treat others. Although the luminous beings admit that love can be a difficult undertaking, they hint from time to time that our spiritual and biological existence is in jeopardy without it.

The second key is knowledge. Human life is a *learning experience*, a time to develop in the material world, where emotions and growth are more concrete than they are in the immaterial world. We are here to take care of one another and to learn. It is all a matter of spiritual maturation.[7] During the NDE, knowledge is given a lot of emphasis, particularly during the life review. Some people are instructed to begin a quest for knowledge when they return to earth, especially in areas where they will achieve self-development and learning that will help others. And we retain the knowledge that we have accumulated during our life when we pass over to the "other side." One person was told, "Knowledge is one of the few things you will be able to take with you after you have died."

These two principles—love and knowledge—help explain why some people have a *near*-death experience and not the real thing: they return from the experience for a reason. In one of Raymond Moody's cases, a man who was scheduled for the real thing arrived in the next world. When he was told his time was up, he started to cry. He was upset and concerned about his nephew, whom he and his wife were rearing. He was afraid his spouse couldn't handle the job by herself. When the luminous being saw this reaction, he made a snap decision and granted him the ability to return, but only because the man was selflessly worried about the boy.[8]

In another instance, a woman remarked to the light being that she had to return because she hadn't danced enough in life yet! Apparently the luminous being was in a generous mood. He gave a belly laugh and allowed her to return to her body.[9]

Although all of the spiritual and esoteric sources maintain that ours is an existence of free will—that our future is not predetermined and that we have the ability to make certain decisions about it—in some instances a potential future is revealed to those in the near-death state. Kenneth Ring calls this glimpse of our own future the "personal flashforward."

Some years ago a boy experienced an NDE. Certain aspects of his future were shown to him in a vision. He was told he would marry at twenty-eight and would eventually have two children. He was shown a holographic virtual image of future scenes from his life, including one that showed him and his family sitting in the living room of the house he would eventually have. As he gazed at the scene, he noticed something strange on the wall, an unusual device he didn't recognize. He returned to his body, and the years passed. Every prediction shown to him came true. Eventually he found himself in the exact scene shown to him decades before. There on the wall was a forced-air heater, something he had failed to recognize when a boy, for the simple reason that it hadn't been invented yet![10]

In another case a lady experienced an NDE and was shown a picture of Raymond Moody. She was even told his name. The luminous beings told her that when the time was right she would meet him and tell her story. The year was 1971, and Moody wouldn't publish his groundbreaking book until 1975. Four years later, in early 1975, Moody and his family happened to move to the very same street as the one on which this lady lived. That Halloween, Moody's son was out trick-or-treating, and while he was at the lady's door she asked him his name. The lady was astounded, and she instructed the boy to tell his father that she just *had* to talk with him. She related her near-death experiences to him, and the prediction was fulfilled; her tale joined the others in Moody's first book, *Life After Life*.[11]

Whatever the true nature of an NDE, it is one of the most awesome experiences a human being can have. Maybe death isn't so bad after all, if we get to spend eternity in such a great place. But it may not be that simple. We may have to earn our place there, by having to return to earthly life again and again, until we get it right, in a kind of spiritual apprenticeship program. I'm talking, of course, about *reincarnation*.

Like most matters of a spiritual nature, the idea of reincarnation predates written history. The Vedas describe it at length, and it has become a cornerstone of Hindu thought. Among traditional societies throughout the world, reincarnation is considered to be a fact, something that is just a natural process of human life.

If the ancient beliefs are true, then the purpose of reincarnation is a noble one. We are divine, eternal creatures, made in the image of God. Our purpose is to grow and experience, to learn and develop spiritually. One lifetime is not enough. The process of experiencing multiple lifetimes over many, many years, in many situations and as either sex, allows us to develop in a way far beyond what would be possible in a single trip. Suddenly pain and disappointment become a learning experience, rather than just bad luck in an unfortunate existence that leads to nothing. As Nietzsche said, that which does not kill us makes us stronger. Maybe that which *does* kill us makes us stronger still.

In general, reincarnation, if it is true, goes something like this: the unique entity that I call "me" was created eons ago. We are—in reality— our higher energy bodies, the eternal aspects of our nature.[12] The physical body is a temporary vessel for consciousness, a vehicle that allows us to experience life on the physical plane—in the *simulator*, as William Tiller calls it.

Throughout many lifetimes, the experiences we have are stored in the higher bodies, where they result in growth and change. At death, we review and critique our most recent life along with help from higher spiritual beings, and eventually we plan our next life, with specific purposes and goals in mind. It has been stated that this belief is one of the few that explains all the misery and suffering in life, giving meaning to all the illness, disease, and heartbreak we experience.

It would be the ultimate tool for development: a lifetime here and a lifetime there, as different races, in different times, as the opposite sex— what a trip! But it wouldn't do any good if we could remember our past lives while we were living our current one. It wouldn't seem as real, as genuine.[13] No, we have to wipe the slate clean each time and start anew, having forgotten—temporarily—the experiences of our previous lives. We have to forget.

Someone who is challenging that amnesia is Joel Whitton, a professor of psychiatry at the University of Toronto Medical School. He is an expert in clinical hypnosis and has a degree in neurobiology as well. As a psychiatrist, Whitton has a burning curiosity about the subconscious mind. Many in that field believe that the subconscious is the key to understanding much of what makes us human and the emotions and personality that make it all real. Whitton found some strange things while working with hypnotized patients. Many of them recalled memories of prior existence on earth. In fact, studies have shown that over 90 percent of hypnotizable people recall past lives.[14] One of the premier texts on hypnosis, *Trauma, Trance and Transformation*, warns the fledgling hypnotherapist to be prepared for their clients' memories of past lives.

Whitton was initially struck by the amount of agreement among his patients. All of them had memories of past lives. Some recalled as many as twenty-five, although most reached a point where their primitive past lives seemed to merge into one, in what he called their *caveman existences*, in which one lifetime seemed indistinguishable from the rest. All had experienced at least one life as the opposite sex, and all stated the purpose of it all to be growth and development.[15]

One of Whitton's test subjects stated that he planned his next life as "a sort of clockwork instrument into which you could insert certain parts in order for specific consequences to follow."[16] This perspective explains, to a degree, the meaning of NDEs. All the spiritual and esoteric literature insists that you have free will. But suppose a freak accident seemingly takes it away, and you find yourself in heaven a bit ahead of schedule. Who knows? Maybe the NDE itself was part of the master plan, something designed to change your path and possibly, through you, the paths of others you encounter.

In some of Whitton's cases, the test subjects supplied oddly accurate historical data. Some of the best-known examples involve languages, specifically ones the subject should not have known. Some of these languages were so rare that they were known by only a handful of linguists in the world.

One man, a thirty-seven-year old behavioral scientist, recalled a life as a Viking. While experiencing this life under hypnosis, he shouted out several words that were foreign to Whitton. However, his trusty tape recorder caught the phrases, and Whitton forwarded them to linguistic specialists who analyzed the tape and recognized the words. They were Old Norse, the language of the Vikings.

Later, the same man was hypnotically regressed to an older life in ancient Persia. He asked for a notepad and pen and began to write in an unknown language. Whitton later had the sample analyzed by experts. It was eventually found to be an example of the Sassanid Pahlavi language, an ancient tongue of Mesopotamia that existed from 226 to 651 AD. It has long been extinct.[17]

These examples lead us toward the belief that there is definitely something to reincarnation. Of course, they don't constitute scientific proof, but, given the circumstances, what could? It would be extremely difficult in a laboratory to prove that someone has lived before in a different body, as a different person. All we have to go on is the anecdotal evidence. Still, we need physical evidence to really sink the hook and get the scientific crowd to listen.

Another professor of psychiatry, Dr. Ian Stevenson of the University of Virginia, has given that evidence to us. Ian Stevenson was perhaps the top researcher of reincarnation in the world until his death in 2007. He decided to choose subjects who were relatively untainted by life and would not need hypnosis. Accordingly, he chose children, specifically ones who talked of strange existences in another body. His studies extended over thirty years and included thousands of cases from around the world. [18]

One of the first things Stevenson found was how common spontaneous past-life recalls are. They are extraordinarily common among small children. In fact, the number of credible cases far exceeded the time and resources available to investigate them. In a typical case, a child of between two and four suddenly begins to talk about memories of the "other life," often complete with reams of actual data, such as names, descriptions of the location and appearance of their homes, what they did in their past life, and even details about how they died. In some cases involving murder, the children could even identify their killers.

In many instances the children could correctly identify their former parents, family members, and friends and could rush through their former homes with ease, identifying the various rooms, especially their own, as well as nearby places where they had played. It was positively spooky. The phenomenon was so uncanny that it became difficult to understand in any other way than the most obvious . . . that the child in question had been there before.

Stevenson would go on to study the phenomenon for years, compiling thousands of case studies. Many of his findings corroborated Whitton's data. He also found that many of the subjects were reborn with others that they had known in past lives, as though their destinies were interwoven. In some cases, the motivation for returning together seemed to be affection; in others, a sense of guilt or indebtedness.[19]

In addition, Stevenson found an amazing correlation of the basic personality of the test subjects across lives. Although the material aspects of their lives varied greatly from one existence to another, the basic attributes that made them unique remained unchanged from life to life. Caring, loving people seemed to retain these characteristics in each incarnation. By the same token, criminals and those with character defects also demonstrated like behavior in later incarnations. How rich or poor they were didn't seem to be a factor. The basic human personality stayed about the same, perhaps requiring many incarnations into the future to change and refine.

Stevenson did great stuff, paradigm-smashing research, but the most shocking, and the most compelling, evidence of reincarnation was the *physical evidence* he found. Stevenson's data were so complete, and his research so detailed, that he was often able to correlate current physical evidence with the encounters of the former lives.

In one example, a boy who had the misfortune of having his throat cut in a former life still retained a thin red line in the exact spot of the slash.

In another, a boy who had committed suicide by shooting himself in the head had two scarlike birthmarks in the exact locations of the entrance and exit wounds! Another had a birthmark that looked exactly like a surgical scar, complete with suture marks, in the precise location of his surgery in his former life. All of these past-life details were confirmed with official records. In many cases Stevenson was able to obtain hospital and autopsy records demonstrating that the deceased had indeed experienced trauma to the precise area indicated by the present birthmarks. He also found evidence that certain facial features and deformities carried over from one life to the next. He eventually compiled so much data that he completed a four-volume set on this one mind-boggling phenomenon. He also compiled six volumes on his reincarnation cases in general. With this mountain of evidence facing it, even the scientific establishment sat up and took notice.

Stevenson's findings were published in some highly distinguished journals, such as the *American Journal of Psychiatry*, the *International Journal of Comparative Sociology*, and the *Journal of Nervous and Mental Disease*. Even the American Medical Association, the famous AMA, gave him a glowing review. In a report from *JAMA*, the *Journal of the American Medical Association*, the editors stated that he had "painstakingly and unemotionally collected a detailed series of cases in which the evidence for reincarnation is difficult to understand on any other grounds. . . . He has placed on record a large amount of data that cannot be ignored."[20]

The facts make for a strong case that we survive physical death, retaining much of our knowledge and even our individual personalities. It is even possible that we live again as another person throughout our spiritual development. For all this, however, the realm beyond death remains the great mystery of life.

Why doesn't someone, just once, come back and tell us what it's all about? Many cases have been reported where so-called ghosts return and reveal the location of something of importance to the family, like the location of hidden documents, or occasionally, the identity of a murderer. Of course, throughout human history there have been those who claim to be mediums—that is, able to communicate with the dead (and also with angels, demons, and other immaterial entities). Many are frauds, milking distraught folks out of their hard-earned bucks, but some really do have something going on. Today, mediumship is suddenly hip again. It is even featured on TV, which, in the modern world, is definitive evidence of having "made it." With popularity has come a measure of scientific interest. Studies at the University of Arizona focusing on some of the top mediums in the world, including George Anderson, considered the most accurate medium active today, John Edward, of TV's *Crossing Over*, and Allison DuBois, upon whom the hit TV show *Medium* is based, have demonstrated remarkable evidence of life after death. Mediums in the studies were capable of astounding accuracy with their psychic readings, all without knowing the subject or even without being in the same building with them during the reading. Statistics showed the odds to be literally trillions-to-one that the results were the work of chance alone.[21]

These studies were conducted by Dr. Gary Schwartz, a Harvard Ph.D. and former Yale professor of psychology. As they progressed, Schwartz tightened the protocols to prevent any hint of fraud. The amazing accuracy continued. Allison DuBois gave a reading for famed author Deepak Chopra that involved his beloved deceased father. Her accuracy was astounding. But what finally convinced Schwartz of the readings' authenticity was a simple reading by John Edward. As Schwartz states:

> If there is any one single piece of mediumship data that led me to accept the living soul hypothesis, it is a brief and seemingly silly incident that occurred in a John Edward reading on television.
>
> He was speaking with a woman who appeared to be in her early thirties and was receiving information about one of her older deceased relatives. He then said something like, "She is showing me a little dog. Did your relative have a little dog?"

The woman looked confused. She did not know whether her relative had a little dog or not.

Then John said something that truly surprised me. He said, "She's telling me that the dog was named after a food. A food name."

After the reading, the lady called an aunt who confirmed that the deceased had owned a small dog. Its name was "Popsicles," for a simple reason. The dog loved Popsicles. Schwartz commented:

> Being the enthusiastic agnostic that I am, I ticked off the skeptical possibilities about detectives . . . or some deceit off camera to make it look as if John had done something remarkable when he was really cheating . . . or reading the mind of the audience member . . . or an amazing guess.

After reviewing all the possibilities a skeptic might consider, Dr. Schwartz concluded with:

> Here's what I think, as a scientist: The probability that John is the real thing—and that Laurie [Campbell], Suzane [Northrop], Anne [Gehman], George [Anderson], and certain other mediums are engaged in something honest and truly spiritual—is as great as the probability that the light from distant stars continues in some form, forever.[22]

Given that, as Schwartz knows, light from distant stars *does* continue forever, his statement is a clear endorsement of the living soul hypothesis.

Mediumship, like many of the other topics we have discussed, is an ancient practice. For centuries, the Greek and Roman governments employed psychics in official capacities. Long before psychic bureaucrats were working in Rome, however, there was the Witch—or Medium—of Endor, who is discussed in the Bible (1 Sam. 28:3–25). Her story is one of the best-known examples of mediumship in early writings: after the death of the great prophet Samuel, King Saul of Israel banished all magicians and necromancers (mediums) from the kingdom. There were problems with the neighboring Philistines, however, who were massing for an attack. When Saul was unable to communicate with God about a plan of action, he disguised himself and slipped away to the Witch of Endor for advice. She conjured up the spirit of Samuel, who offered no advice but predicted the downfall of Saul as king. He was killed in battle the next day, along with his sons.

In another famous example of mediumship, Socrates went on record as being guided through life by a discarnate entity he called his *daimon* (a kind of personal god or higher Self), and at the end of his life he only drank the infamous hemlock potion because the entity failed to object. When he was sentenced to death, he commented: "My approaching end is not happening by chance. I see quite clearly that to die, and thus to be released, will be better for me; and therefore the oracle has given me no sign [that it is not to be]."[23]

Socrates' student Plato held similar beliefs. Eventually necromancy, the conjuring up of the dead, became so common that both the Greeks and Romans outlawed it, with death as the punishment. Even the Bible warns us not to communicate with the dead (see Deut. 18:10–11).

Still, the early Church was quite tolerant of psychic phenomena. Many of the early popes were mystics themselves. In early Christianity it was acceptable to be a healer, magician, psychic, or shaman. By the thirteenth century, the Church officially recognized the Beguines, a female organization of mystics. In the same period, however, as competition from various "heretical" viewpoints increased, the Church changed its policies. In the mid-thirteenth century, Pope Gregory IX initiated the Inquisition, which would later include torture, and spiritual practices began to be persecuted. Thus began the dark centuries of witch hunts. By the fifteenth century, the Council of Vienna proclaimed the Beguines heretics, and they were burned at the stake in large numbers throughout France.[24] Between the fifteenth and nineteenth centuries, approximately forty thousand "witches" and "heretics" were executed, usually in a most unpleasant manner. During this time, with the sanction of the Church, most of the information on psychic phenomena and mediumship from earlier eras was destroyed. The only reason knowledge of psi survived in the West was that it was such a common occurrence and well-known aspect of life.

Times change. Mediumship exploded in America and Europe during the nineteenth century, and by the early twentieth century there was a medium on every corner, hoping to make a quick buck playing on the emotions of those who longed to communicate with lost loved ones. There were even training courses on how to practice phony mediumship, complete with plenty of props to fool the gullible public. Séances were given in the dark, where wires could be used to move things about and assistants were more easily hidden. They used every trick in the book and gave mediumship a terrible reputation. With all this spirit-mania brewing, along came the world-famous magician, Harry Houdini, the greatest escape artist in history.

Houdini the escape artist remains a household name today. Less well remembered, however, is his interest in mediumship. He knew all the tricks, because in his early days, when he was all but starving, he was a phony medium himself. He was also very close to his mother, so attached that he was never the same after her death, which happened at the height of his fame. For nine years after she died, Houdini employed mediums extensively, not to debunk them as he later would, but in hopes of receiving a message from his departed mother. He became good friends with Sir Arthur Conan Doyle, the author of the famous Sherlock Holmes mysteries. Conan Doyle had lost a son in 1915 and a brother-in-law the next year. Both Conan Doyle and Houdini thought spirit communication was possible, and both were obsessed with getting to talk with their loved ones again. Conan Doyle and his wife Jean began giving séances and lectures.

In 1922 it all ended when Conan Doyle's wife claimed to have received a spirit message from Houdini's mother through the technique of automatic writing. The message wasn't to his liking, and Houdini became enraged. In his profound disappointment at failing to receive what he considered to be a genuine message from his beloved mother, he began a holy quest to debunk all mediums.

The feud between the Conan Doyles and Houdini raged for years, with Houdini rushing around like someone possessed, debunking every medium in sight. Today it is generally thought that the great Houdini debunked every single medium he investigated. This is not true. Several defied every attempt to explain their ability away as a trick. And when all else failed, Houdini resorted to the tricks he used as an escape artist . . . he cheated!

Houdini was an amazing man. He could actually escape from a standard straightjacket—his hands and fingers were so strong that he could unbuckle the device by pinching through the heavy canvas—but for more advanced stunts, he routinely used trickery. Handcuffs were rigged to open when jarred, keys were hidden in trunks, and escape panels were employed. Houdini could, through years of practice, swallow a key or other item and regurgitate it at will. He was incredibly muscular and athletic and able to tolerate high levels of pain, but he freely used props as well. And in 1924, while investigating a medium for *Scientific American*, he cheated again.

The magazine had offered a reward to anyone who could demonstrate actual ability to communicate with the dead. A well-known psychic, Mina Crandon, known professionally as Margery, was on the verge of receiving the cash as a result of her impressive physical and spiritual mediumship. Houdini became enraged over having been excluded from the panel of judges and later used his expertise to demonstrate how Margery could have managed all the physical occurrences using various props. However, Houdini remained unable to explain Margery's spiritual demonstrations, which involved direct-voice communication with her dead brother Walter. In fact, in one reading, Walter verbally abused Houdini for his zealousness.

In the pivotal reading, Houdini had an assistant hide a folding ruler near Margery, something that could be used to move objects. He then gladly tipped off the officials. Both Margery and Houdini denied hiding the ruler, but the committee had more trust in Houdini, the famous magician, than in a humble medium, although some committee members later went on record stating that they were suspicious of Houdini's over-zealousness and true motivations. Years later, his assistant admitted to hiding the ruler, but it was too late. *Scientific American* had denied Margery the prize.

Houdini's death matched his life. He was a little dude, but exceedingly tough. He was famous for his ability to take a punch to the abdomen. While he was performing in Detroit in 1926, a young college athlete asked him to demonstrate this ability. The athlete drove a punch into Houdini before he was properly set. Houdini's appendix ruptured and peritonitis set in (something that is still dangerous today). Perhaps synchronistically, he crossed over on—of all days—Halloween.

In one of the ultimate ironies in life, Houdini has since become the object of mediumship himself. It is important to understand that in spite of his actions, Houdini never stopped believing that communication with the dead was possible. He said so in his book on fraudulent mediumship, *A Magician among the Spirits.* He also left a secret message with his wife, Beatrice, shortly before his death, a message he promised he would find a way to deliver from beyond the grave. It was a ten-word code for a simple statement: *Rosabelle Believe.* Only Beatrice knew the message.

About a year after Houdini's death, Arthur Ford, one of the best-known mediums in modern times, made his public debut at a lecture given by Conan Doyle. Ford's messages were said to emanate from a spirit called Fletcher, a pseudonym for a man he had known who died in the butchery of World War I. On February 8, 1928, Ford officially announced that Houdini's mother had been in communication with him about a secret message, one Beatrice would understand. Beatrice was astounded; she confirmed it was indeed the message and arranged a private séance with Ford. Afterward, she announced to the world that her husband's spirit had delivered to her the secret message! Houdini had accomplished in death what he failed to do in life: achieve genuine communication from the other side.

The public went insane! There remains little doubt that the code was given. Only the circumstances remain unknown. Little is known about the actual séance with Ford. However, Beatrice did go on record as stating that is was "the correct message prearranged between Mr. Houdini and myself."[25] This is not the end of the story, however.

Some years later, for reasons that have never been fully explained, Beatrice retracted the statement, denying Houdini had delivered it. Why she would have lied if the story were untrue is unknown, as is why she would have risked public humiliation by retracting the story if it were correct. Pressures from family, church, and government have all been suggested, and all are unproven. The mystery remains.

So, do we live on after physical death, as the ancients have insisted for eons, or does consciousness end along with our last breath? Certainly those who have experienced an NDE believe we live on. Many believe that reincarnation affords one of the best explanations for the crippling diseases and illnesses and other forms of massive human suffering on this planet. In a way, reincarnation answers the age-old question of *theodicy*: why would a loving, caring God create such misery for his children? Once we accept the reality of reincarnation, all misery becomes just a part of the big picture, necessary for the growth we are required to achieve in order to progress to the next level of consciousness. And from a rather practical point of view, albeit a morbid one, we must experience death on the physical plane to enable us eventually to start the incarnation cycle anew, to kick-start the Wheel of Life again. We have to die in order to finally, fully, *live*.

Exciting evidence points to the fact that we do live on, that each of us is an eternal soul. Perhaps someday soon the scientific establishment will listen to the studies done on survival phenomena. Ironically, the spirits report through mediums that, even after their own deaths, skeptical scientists remain skeptical. Even in the afterlife, they still don't believe in life after death. *They insist instead that their physical life was only a dream!*

Regardless, it is difficult to review the literature with an open mind and *not* agree that something extraordinary occurs.[26] On the other hand, maybe the whole issue just doesn't matter. In a few short years we will each know for ourselves anyway. As Don Juan used to say in his famous conversations with Carlos Castaneda, there are no survivors on this earth.

Paranormal Panache:
Superstars of Psychokinesis

Miracles are not contrary to nature, but only contrary to what we know about nature.

—Saint Augustine

In my youth I was a science fan. I even won a regional science fair as a high-school freshman with a project on Einstein's theories of relativity. However, during this time I remained curious about ancient spiritual teachings. Science was so opposed to them, yet they seemed such an important part of human history. It struck me that scientists were a little quick to dismiss spiritual concepts that had remained such an important part of the human experience. Many of these ideas were far older, and significantly more widespread, than modern scientific concepts. Although popularity didn't make them correct, it did suggest that they might have some significance.

I kept thinking about psychic phenomena again and again. Widely reported throughout human history and in all corners of the globe, things like clairvoyance and ESP sounded pretty far out, but then, so do relativity and black holes. Were the leaders of science so sure that psi was such utter nonsense that it didn't even deserve an earnest look? Are so many of the world's people, now and in the past, that dumb? The orthodox scientific community would answer that question with a resounding . . . yes!

A couple of decades later, when I began to examine the psychic world in detail, I was in for a surprise. Most people I talked with were open to some forms of psi, and most had personally experienced things that seemed kind of . . . well . . . *strange*. Dreams of things that later actually happened, almost imperceptible feelings about things that turned out to be true, siblings who could read each other's thoughts—the list went on. When I seriously began to examine the ancient belief in subtle energy, it seemed likely that this strange energy, the Force, was the mechanism behind psychic phenomena.

While many people were open to the possibility of psi having some validity, they were put off by the nonsense surrounding it and the self-proclaimed psychics who so often appear in TV and magazine ads. Most intelligent, educated people I talked with put such personalities in the same category as that of the worst of the television evangelists, and with good reason. Both were tapping emotion-laden spiritual beliefs to fleece unsuspecting folks of their hard-earned bucks. Some folks thought psychic phenomena might be genuine but were skeptical about it because orthodox science refused to accept the research that validated it. As a result, many kinds of psi continue to operate quietly in the shadows. There is one phenomenon, however, that seems positively to thrive on limelight—psychokinesis. We'll look first at three psychokinetic superstars and then visit some labs where this glittery gift is being quietly tested.

Every few hundred years or so, someone really, really special comes along, one of those significant beings who challenges the paradigm of the times. Daniel David Home was such a man. Born in Scotland in 1833, D. D. Home relocated to the United States at the age of nine. As is so often the case with psychically gifted people, Home was a sickly child and would remain so as an adult. Home's mother was said to have the gift of "second sight," and it seemed her offspring did as well.

At the age of thirteen, Home saw the ghost of a close friend. The apparition whirled through the air and made three large circles. Home intuitively took this to mean the boy had been dead for three days. News traveled slowly in those days, but within a day or so the family got the word. At the time Home had reported seeing his spirit, the young boy had been dead three days. From that point on, D. D. Home was a free spirit himself.

Home's career spanned decades, and he was studied by several respected scientists of the era, particularly Sir William Crookes, an internationally known British physicist and developer of X-ray equipment. He demonstrated his talents for the emperor Napoleon III and Tsar Alexander II in their courts. Everyone was amazed by Home's strange abilities, and in spite of the efforts of many, including Napoleon III and the poet Robert Browning, he was never found to be using fraud in any fashion whatsoever. Of course, it was natural to assume he was. Home could do things that would blow people's minds.

For starters, Home nearly always conducted his séances in bright daylight. He would often give them in a home or office he had just entered, without needing to prepare things in advance as some of his colleagues did. It is also of great significance that Home *did not accept money for his work*. Although Home was frequently broke during his life and often had to give literary readings to feed himself, he never charged for demonstrations of what he considered a gift, in spite of the fact that he could have easily become a rich man, considering his extraordinary abilities and the thirst for spiritualism at the time.

One of Home's great talents lay in levitation and poltergeist activity. In séances, items would levitate, and often strange knocks and sounds would explode throughout the room. Unlike most of his psychic colleagues, Homes could produce these effects in a brightly lit room to which he had just been introduced. Once, during a séance in the court of Napoleon III, under very bright lights, Home levitated a tablecloth from a heavy table a good distance from where he stood. One of his envious enemies, Prince Metternich, dived beneath the table to expose the trick. Metternich was shocked to find the strange bumps and knocks were coming from within the table itself. William Crookes was present at a later séance where the entire house shook so badly he feared it would fall down around the witnesses.[1]

One of Home's favorite demonstrations was to make his accordion float around the room playing the song "Home Sweet Home." Crookes was flabbergasted when he witnessed this, but he was determined to explore the phenomenon at length. He purchased his own accordion, locked it in a cage, and showed the device to Home. With a wry smile on his face, Home proceeded to make *it* float around within the cage and play several tunes anyway, all with the slack-mouthed Crookes watching within the well-lighted room!

But it was Home's strange abilities at *human* levitation that really got people excited. On many dozens of occasions, D. D. Home was seen by credible witnesses to have levitated both himself and others, often in spectacular fashion. It was common for Home to levitate himself, more than once rising all the way to the high ceiling of a large building into which he had just stepped a few minutes before.

On one memorable occasion Home was seen to rise more than twenty feet into the air and float out through an open window in a horizontal position. After a few moments he came floating back in through another window, to the shock of the surprised crowd, and then gently eased back down to a standing position on the floor! This particular event was witnessed by more than a dozen prominent people. On other occasions Home was seen to levitate others, seemingly at random. Crookes saw Home levitate a seated woman at one of his brightly lit séances, chair and all! Crookes was later to perform an in-depth study of the wonders of Home, and he calculated that more than one hundred people had witnessed Home's levitations. On some occasions people were seen to jump and grab on to Home's legs as he rose into the air in plain view. The stowaways rose right along with him![2]

Of course, with the exception of Crookes and Lord Adare, who investigated him extensively, the scientific world of the day was adamantly skeptical of Home, although it was said they were too afraid of him actually to test him! Most explanations of Home included something to do with "mass hypnosis," since he performed his feats in broad daylight and often before prominent citizens. Had they been in the dark, trickery would have surely been forcefully suggested. That didn't keep a writer in the prestigious journal *Nature* from using mass hypnosis as an explanation of Home's incredible abilities. At least that made more sense than the writer's other explanation. He also meekly made the suggestion that Home was . . . *a werewolf!*

Nina Kulagina was a war hero. As a teenager during World War II, she had fought in the great siege of Leningrad and was proclaimed a Soviet national hero. She was also one of the most skilled and documented practitioners of psychokinesis in history. Perhaps no other person has been so extensively tested. On thousands of occasions until her death in 1990, Kulagina demonstrated her exceptional ability to anyone who wanted to observe. All of them came away totally mystified. Thousands of people have seen her move ordinary objects like matches, bread rolls, cigarettes, fruit, pitchers of water, and dinnerware, all with the power of her mind. She was tested to the extreme, in dozens of laboratories, and was never found to be using the slightest form of trickery.

The tests were varied, ingenious, and sometimes silly. She could separate the yolk from a raw egg while it floated in a container of saline solution. On some occasions, if she really concentrated, she could make it join back again with the egg white! She could form letters in a smoke-filled glass container and could even cause specific letters to appear on undeveloped photographic paper. One scientist was blown away when she caused a dinner roll to slide toward her on the table, vibrate a bit, and then leap into her open mouth! For all her extraordinary ability, however, Nina Kulagina paid a personal price.

It required intense concentration to perform her kind of PK, and she often became ill after a substantial test. She usually lost three or four pounds of water weight after a difficult session. It could take as much as two hours before she could perform her exceptional feats in any given session, even if everything went well. With profound skeptics, it could take as long as seven difficult hours of intense concentration, including moments during which her pulse would race to 250 beats per minute.

Why did the sessions with skeptics take longer? Because hostility and negativity have a profound effect on psychic functions. Sensitives like Nina feel these attitudes acutely, and they interfere with the performance of psychic tasks, something the critics never seem to consider. Although it may not be a factor in a chemistry experiment, human intention can have a strong effect on psychic activity. But Nina had fought the Nazis for three years as a teenager. She wasn't about to give up. After a difficult session she would be totally exhausted and wiped out, with a feeble, nearly absent pulse. Her health suffered as a result. In spite of all this, she always went out of her way to demonstrate her remarkable gift. She felt the possibility for human growth was worth the price.

And then there's the best-known psychic in the world, Uri Geller. Controversy continues to surround Geller even today, for, although he has stumped scientists on many occasions, he is sometimes unable to perform his feats, and his style is so erratic that it casts doubts on whether he's an expert practitioner of psi, a master stage magician, or both. In any case, he stands in a class by himself.

Geller is an Israeli, with a six-foot-three frame and movie-star looks, which he put to good use as a young man in his home country, becoming a model for shaving cream, among other products. His story goes like this: at the age of four, while playing in the family garden, Geller had a visitation from a luminous being. Shortly thereafter, Geller began to exhibit paranormal abilities. He never had an OBE or anything like that. Rather, Geller's abilities tended toward telepathy, clairvoyance, and PK, particularly the ability to bend metal. This last is by no means unique to him, but he remains the world's most famous spoon bender.

When he was ten his parents separated, and Uri went with his mother to Cyprus, where his psi abilities apparently continued to develop. Geller returned to Israel in 1967, at the age of seventeen. He chose a fateful time: the Six-Day War was looming on the horizon. It was the "summer of love" in the United States, but the Middle East was in turmoil. Geller, like a good Israeli, enlisted in the army and volunteered for the paratroopers just in time for the action. He fought with valor and was wounded in combat.

After his recuperation, Uri was advised by friends to put on performances of his psychic abilities, and, being a natural showman, he began to perform at private parties. He must have been very good, because in a short while he found himself performing for the great Golda Meir herself. A bit later, the prime minister was asked about the future of Israel. She quipped, "I don't know—ask Uri Geller!" In just two short years after going airborne with the paratroopers, Geller found himself a household name in his native country. World fame was just around the corner.

Geller came to the attention of former Apollo astronaut Edgar Mitchell and his newly formed Institute for Noetic Sciences, which studies human consciousness and potential. Rumor had it that the Soviets were very interested in Geller and were tailing him. The CIA had to find out if he had genuine ability. They took him to . . . you guessed it . . . SRI, where Hal Puthoff and Russell Targ were tearing apart the current paradigm. Geller was about to blow some minds.

Geller states that at the time he was still controlled by his handlers in Mossad (the Israeli intelligence service) and was instructed not to do certain tasks at SRI, although he refuses to be more specific. On the other hand, SRI security required that he be kept away from some of the things that Ingo Swann and Pat Price were doing there. Then there was the problem of ego. Swann wasn't too happy about this Israeli pretty boy stealing the show, and Geller wasn't known for modesty.

As a result, Uri was kept on a short leash, but it didn't matter. He was about to demonstrate some aspects of psi that have yet to be explained by conventional science. In November 1972, he was tested at SRI. During this time he was continuously filmed and videotaped as scientists and professional magicians scrutinized his actions for any type of sleight of hand or magical techniques, and double-blind methods were used whenever possible.

In the first experiment, a verified die (one of a pair of dice) was placed in a sealed container, shaken extensively, and placed on a table. Geller had to guess what number was up on the die, a test for clairvoyance. During the ten test runs he performed, he was not allowed to touch the container in any way. On two of the runs, he stated that he wasn't getting a clear impression and refrained from guessing. That's allowed. However, on the other eight tries, he was 100 percent correct. The odds against this happening by pure chance alone are in the range of *a million to one.*

The next test was a different version of the same concept. Ten identical aluminum film canisters were used to house a variety of ordinary objects. With no physical contact allowed, on twelve out of twelve attempts he correctly chose the only container that housed an object, and once again the odds are in the neighborhood of a million to one. Geller had quite successfully demonstrated his abilities with ESP.

The next step was PK. An electronic precision balance was used, with the output electronically recorded by specialized, sensitive equipment. A 1-gram weight was placed in an aluminum canister, which was arranged on the scale. The entire device was then covered with a glass jar. After the initial weight was recorded, Geller was asked to change the reading of the equipment psychokinetically. He was able to do so on two attempts. Each attempt lasted about one-fifth of a second. On one run he decreased the weight by 1.5 grams, and on the next he increased it by a gram. To put it another way, his first trial negated the weight entirely, and his second attempt doubled it.[3] All was captured on tape for posterity.

In the final experiment performed during the initial series of tests, Geller was once again called on to demonstrate a form of PK, this one involving a sensitive device that measures magnetic fields, a gaussmeter. All the usual precautions were taken to guard against fraud, and everything was videotaped. Geller got set and began to pass his hands over the instrument. He was not allowed to touch it in any way.

The needle on the gaussmeter began to move each time he passed his hands over it. On several attempts he demonstrated a magnetic field, presumably from his hands, that was about 50 percent as strong as that of the earth. This was an incredible event and beyond any rational explanation. The earth's magnetic field is fairly weak, all things considered, but it is still a massive presence when compared to the tiny amounts that have been measured in the human body.

The boys at SRI were mightily impressed, notwithstanding that, in spite of all the filmed evidence, some were still suspicious of Geller because of his manic behavior. However, the fact remains that they found no evidence whatsoever that Geller was cheating or guilty of any type of fraud. Like it or not, Uri Geller was for real. The only problem with Uri was this: where did his genuine psi stop and his magical skills, if any, begin?

To start with, a review of some facts is in order. When it comes to telepathy and clairvoyance, there is no doubt: Geller is one of the very best around, and he's genuine. It's his metal-bending antics and other examples of PK that raise doubts, not because he can't do them, but because he rattles on with a patter that appears close to what magicians do to distract an audience.

My response is . . . *so what*? That's all a matter of style. He's being judged by standards of personal taste. If he's videotaped, which of course he has been many times, and careful scrutiny of the tapes reveals no sleight of hand or other magical tricks, then what does all the showmanship matter? However, a real problem does sometimes arise with Uri: when he is under pressure, such as he was during his famous appearance with Johnny Carson on *The Tonight Show* in 1973, he can fail badly.

But that failure is simply an example of the problem that has plagued paranormal research from the very start: phenomena aren't always repeatable at a specific moment in time. Sometimes they happen and sometimes they don't. Once again I comment . . . so what? We're not dealing with a chemistry experiment here. Human behavior is always difficult to study; it's an inexact science if there ever was one. This is new territory. We're learning the rules as we go along. We don't know the mechanisms behind psi . . . *that's precisely what we're trying to find out!* You can't attempt to get repeatable results until you find out a bit about what's going on to start with. We can't even agree when it's about psychology, never mind psi; the major theories lie scattered all over the place. It is time to quit judging studies of human consciousness and behavior by the standards of chemistry and physics. Time will show psi to be much more profound than that.

Geller did not stop with SRI. Great Britain's John Taylor and his associates of King's College, London, had a chance to examine him in 1974. Once again, they went to great lengths to use every method available to rule out any type of fraud or trickery. Taylor was also aware that he was delving into areas that much of science frowned on. Things had to be tight. Taylor even had special metallurgical samples prepared by the experts at King's College and sealed in glass containers. Geller was not allowed to touch the samples in any way. In the presence of other scientists besides Taylor, Geller was able to bend these, too, even though the samples had been completely sealed and untouched by him, at any time, both before and after the experiment. So much for the widely held belief that Geller must touch an item in order actually to bend it.

At the end of the tests, Taylor devised an experiment he was excited about. Could Geller use PK, mental energy, or whatever it was to change the readings of a standard, professional Geiger counter? Taylor was aware of the test results with the gaussmeter at SRI, but he wanted to take it a step further. The following is Dr. Taylor's own description of the event:

> At first nothing happened, but by extreme concentration and an increase in muscular tension associated with the rising pulse rate, the needle deflected to 50 counts per second for a full two seconds, and sound effects heightening the drama of the occasion. By means of a small loudspeaker each count produced a "pip," and before Geller affected the machine the sound was a steady "pip . . . pip . . . pip." . . . In his hands the sound suddenly rose to become a wail, one which usually indicates dangerous radioactive material nearby. When Geller stopped concentrating the wail stopped and the

apparent danger with it. This wail was repeated twice more, and then when a deflection of one hundred counts per second was achieved, the wail rose almost to a scream. A final attempt made the needle deflect to a reading of one thousand counts per second, again lasting for about twelve seconds. This was five hundred times the background rate—the machine was emitting a scream in the process.[4]

As amazing as these accounts might be, the good Dr. Taylor himself did something just as puzzling in its own right. After his studies of psi, he went on record as supportive of paranormal phenomena. He even wrote a book about it called *Superminds*. Then, a few years down the pike, he did a 180-degree turnaround—no explanations offered—and denied all his findings about Geller.

Geller has his own U-turn story. At the height of his fame, he announced that he gained his powers from a massive computer on a UFO, a controller called *Spectra*. He said Spectra was controlled in turn by a superpowered entity called *Hoova*, the supposed ruler of Earth on behalf of some far-flung galactic federation. People were turned off. A few years later Geller recanted the Spectra story, saying it all resulted from sessions of regression hypnosis he had received. However, there's a little more to the story than that.

By 1974, word had leaked to the outside world about Geller's work at SRI. He could affect sensitive devices with his mind. SRI's government sponsors saw this ability as a potential security risk. What if his secrets could be learned? The Soviets might be able to disrupt the flight of an ICBM, or maybe even cause it to explode prematurely! Scientists at Lawrence Livermore National Laboratory decided to test Geller in their spare time. The tests went on into early 1975, and then some strange things began to happen.

One day, as was the usual protocol, Geller's sessions were being tape-recorded. In the background could be heard a strange, metallic voice. Most of what it was saying was unintelligible, except for a few strange words.

The scientists were spooked, especially when crazy things began to happen to them.

It was scary. For example, the scientists would be talking together in the lab, just intellectually shooting the breeze, when out of the blue would appear an almost comically stereotypical flying saucer, a gray shape about eight inches across that whizzed around the room and vanished. They couldn't help but think about what Geller had said about Spectra. Huge animals would suddenly appear and scare the bejesus out of the scientists. The incidents weren't limited to the Livermore site. Once a huge black raven popped out of nowhere and stared at prominent Livermore researcher Mike Russo and his horrified wife while they relaxed in bed. But it would get stranger still.

Another Livermore physicist named Don Curtis and his wife were sitting in their living room one evening when, with no warning at all, a phantom arm suddenly appeared hovering in the room! The arm was dressed in the sleeve of a man's plain gray suit and, instead of a hand, had a large metal hook. The hook twisted around for a few moments, then faded from view. Enough was enough.

They contacted Rick Kennett at the CIA, the same man involved in many of the remote viewing projects. When Kennett listened to the tapes, he felt a chill run up his spine and the fine hairs on the back of his neck stand on end. The only intelligible words were top-secret code names for high-security government projects! None of the scientists knew of these, nor did Geller. Kennett later said he had the feeling the message was left just for him! He called Puthoff and demanded that he meet with him and Targ the next time they were in Washington.

By coincidence, Targ and Puthoff were scheduled to be in Washington for a fund-raising tour within a few days. Kennett met them at their hotel room. Although it was close to midnight, he went into the stories anyway, secretly hoping the scientists could shed some light on all the craziness. In an excellent book on remote viewing, *Remote Viewers: The Secret History of America's Psychic Spies*, author Jim Schnabel tells the story:

"And so the . . . arm—" said Kennett, winding up the story. "The thing was rotating, with this gray suit on, and it had a hook on it. It was a false arm. What do you think of that?"

And as Kennett pronounced the word *that*, there was a sharp, heavy pounding on the door to the hotel room, as if someone were intending to knock it down. Kennett had a mischievous streak. Was he playing some kind of practical joke here? Puthoff and Targ didn't think so. The pounding was so loud it was frightening. After a moment, Targ went over to the window and hid behind the curtains. Puthoff stood inside the bathroom. Kennett went over to the door and opened it.

Standing in the doorway was a man who at first glance was remarkable only for his unremarkableness. He was nondescript and unthreatening, somewhere in middle age. He walked past Kennett very slowly, with a stiff gait, to the middle of the room, between the two beds. He turned around, and said in an oddly stilted voice, "*Oh! I guess . . . I must . . . be . . . in . . . the wrong . . . room.*"

And with that he walked out, slowly, stiffly, giving all of them time to see that one sleeve of his gray suit, pinned to his side, was empty."[5]

Eventually things quieted down and life returned to normal at Livermore, but only after one more strange occurrence. Mike Russo received an odd phone call one day from an unusual, yet familiar, metallic voice. The voice warned them to stop the research into Uri Geller. They did. Within a month, all the unusual phenomena stopped.[6]

Geller's powers may be doubted by the scientific world, but the business world is a bit more pragmatic. All they want are results. Geller has delivered. Working with mining companies to find valuable mineral ores, he has made fortunes for both himself and the companies. Today he travels the world, continuing to wow audiences, as well as heads of state, with his abilities. Occasionally someone will comment to him, "If you're so good with psychic powers, then why aren't you rich?" Geller always gives the same reply: "I am!"

While Geller's flamboyant metal-bending exploits provoked controversy, in the quieter experimentation of recent years, metal bending has gained a certain credibility. John Hasted of Birkbeck College in London, as well as two French professors, Charles Crussard and Jean Bouvaist, have taken this kind of testing to an entirely new level, documenting cases of so-called "impossible PK."[7]

One case investigated by Hasted was particularly interesting. Certain alloys are capable of being bent only if they are gradually and carefully bent over a period of time. If the action is any faster, the bar simply snaps. This characteristic is a physical quality of the metal, inherent in the crystalline lattice of the metal itself. The bar can only be bent by a process known as "creep," a slow force focused on the bar for a period of time. Hasted has successfully tested and recorded individuals who could bend the bar in much less time than normally required—something that is, in everyday terms, impossible.

The French researchers Crussard and Bouvaist have documented numerous times that French metal-bender Jean-Paul Girard can indeed bend a metal strip that is contained in a sealed glass tube. His ability has been fully and comprehensively documented. Girard has also been capable of bending enormous bars that are beyond the range of even the strongest human—feats that have been recorded on videotape. In one of Crussard's laboratory videos, Girard is seen lightly stroking one of these rods, which soon bends significantly. Tests demonstrated it would take three times the limit of human strength to have caused such deformation.

The French scientists took exceptional pains to document their studies. The metal samples were processed through a battery of tests that included careful measurement. These tests included micromeasurement of the hardness of the sample, residual strain profiles, electron micrograph analysis, and chemical analysis of areas throughout the sample, as well as the use of hallmarks that were permanently embossed into the metal's surface to prevent sleight-of-hand substitution. Still, the amazing PK continued.

In some of Girard's tests, samples of the aluminum strips used appeared to have been subjected to temperatures of over 600°C, something that could only be seen through special analysis. The scientists also documented a case in which a metal sample was bombarded with radioactive cesium atoms before the tests, so that the cesium atoms became part of the sample. Analysis afterward revealed a change in the distribution of the cesium atoms in such a way that the very molecular pattern of the metal appeared to have been changed in some strange manner.

J. B. Rhine and his team also conducted quite a bit of research into PK. It all got started when Rhine happened to meet an avid gambler. Many crap shooters have the feeling that they can, at least some of the time, mentally influence the roll of the dice. Rhine met such a man, whose tales got him to thinking. It would have been easy for Rhine to dismiss them as the boastings of a party guy, but something told Rhine otherwise. He would spend the next nine years investigating the possibility of PK and dice before he felt confident enough actually to publish his work. His monumental work with ESP had stirred up a lot of negativity, so this time Rhine wanted to be sure.

He was once again clever with his testing. Commercial dice are not "true." The higher numbers are lighter, so they tend to roll up more often. Rhine corrected for this difference by specifying that the subject should "aim high" or "aim low" for the number on the dice or by instructing the subjects to attempt to roll a "seven," just as they would in an actual game. Later he even used a machine to toss the dice rather than the conventional cup to gain additional control.

The results did indeed show an above-chance scoring, but what really got his attention was something else. Very consistently, performance declined as the tests continued through the time periods, or quarters. This so-called *quartile decline* was of great significance. *Chance does not become fatigued during the course of an experiment, but humans do*. It was this decline, more than anything else, that demonstrated to Rhine that the subjects were in fact influencing the tests. Since nothing but PK was a reasonable explanation, the evidence was very strong that PK was being used. Of course, there was also the fact that the odds of this quartile decline occurring by chance were *in excess of 100 million to one!*[8]

When it comes to the sheer volume and quality of work on PK, however, no one can match the work performed by Dr. Robert G. Jahn of Princeton University's fabulous Princeton Engineering Anomalies Research (PEAR) program.[9]

It all started innocently enough. Jahn was a distinguished scientist of national prominence, a man at the pinnacle of his career. A former consultant for the National Aeronautics and Space Administration (NASA) and the Department of Defense, Jahn's original specialty was space propulsion. He even authored a definitive text on the subject, *Physics of Electronic Propulsion*. Jahn eventually became a full professor of aerospace science at Princeton and later the dean of the School of Engineering and Applied Science at that much-respected university.

As an engineer, Jahn was put off by tales of the paranormal, as any orthodox scientist would be, until something happened that changed the course of his life. As so often happens in the course of events, he never saw it coming.

An undergraduate student stopped by one day to seek advice on a research project concerning, of all things, psychokinesis. Jahn was mildly disgusted by the topic, yet the young woman was such an outstanding electrical engineering student that his curiosity got the better of him. The project involved testing whether electronic random-number generators could be influenced mentally. Jahn told the student that as long as her scientific controls and technology were first rate, he would help her. He became fascinated by the student's results, which seemed to suggest that there might be something to PK after all, something that all of his careful study and research would indicate was just not possible. Yet the data were staring him in the face. The study was so surprising that by the second year of the project Jahn was as involved in it as his student was. By 1979 he had founded PEAR, along with clinical psychologist Brenda Dunne, and soon they were immersed in a vigorous study of psi.

By this time technology had improved a bit since the days of J. B. Rhine. The random-event generator the PEAR folks used was an electronic device that generates random binary numbers based on the phenomenon of radioactive decay, a natural random process. As in other PK tests, the subjects were asked to influence the machine remotely. The operators were not instructed in any method but were simply told to relax and attempt to get the machine to shift in the requested direction. In short order the team found that the harder the operators tried, the worse their results were. Team member Brenda Dunne stated that at first, nearly everyone had some success, but once they grew in confidence and began to "try," the success was usually short-lived. Still later, though, most were again able to perform as they had been instructed, influencing the random-event generator or other devices in a statistically significant way.

The numbers were not at all large. In the initial runs, with a chance level of 50 percent, the operators scored above the base 61 percent of the time, and below it 64 percent of the time. These were small, but significant, effects. The really important thing, though, was that these tests were conducted with ordinary people, not with psychic superstars as in so many of the early experiments in parapsychology.

Over time Jahn and Dunne conducted thousands and thousands of test runs, and the results were nearly always the same: people could influence the machine! Later studies found that they could do it from thousands of miles away, which made the critics look silly when they insisted that the machine had been shaken or touched or exhaled upon, thus skewing the results. Eventually Jahn and Dunne accumulated a vast amount of data, enough to fill several phone books, and demonstrated the amazing fact that, yes, people really do have PK ability.

In time the PEAR researchers realized that some of the operators even displayed consistent patterns they termed *signatures*. For example, certain operators consistently scored above or below the baseline. These operators performed in similar patterns on different machines and on different tests. Some were simply amazing. The now-famous "Operator 10" just blew everyone away. He (or she) could score above chance at a rate of 300 to one and below chance at 100,000 to one. When these scores are factored together, they produce odds against chance alone of more than *three million to one.*

Later studies demonstrated that pairs of operators who were "bonded" (romantically involved) got even better results than single operators. Eventually the team got into activity similar to remote viewing, successfully of course. They even designed a mechanical robot in the shape of a frog that could be commanded by psychic signals from the operators, as well as a drum machine that could beat on psychic command.

Jahn and Dunne found the same basic response with another famous study design for testing macro-PK. It used a large device with 9,000 "marbles" that were released to roll down a pinball-like board, passing 330 nylon pegs and collecting in a series of 19 bins. Usually a type of bell curve would result, with most of the marbles landing in the middle bins and fewer toward the ends. Operators were instructed to attempt to change this pattern. The results were once again small, but at the same time spectacular. People could indeed influence the fall of the marbles. The studies at PEAR went on for years and have just recently—after a quarter century—reached their conclusion. To appreciate the findings fully, we have to backtrack just a moment and briefly discuss statistics.

Most findings in psi are very small, often just a little above chance, which is something the numerous critics of psi love to point out. However, when many thousands of tests are conducted involving large numbers of people, these small amounts become most important. The issue of statistics in psi research changed completely in the 1970s when a psychologist at Colorado University named Gene Glass developed a new statistical method called *meta-analysis.*[10] Meta-analysis is a technique that takes into collective consideration the vast numbers of studies addressing the same basic phenomenon, even though the actual tests might vary significantly. Dr. Glass realized that this new method might make a vast difference in the acceptance of parapsychology. The many studies, when taken individually, show the probability of psi, but not in a spectacular way. *But what would happen*, Glass wondered, *if we did a cumulative study of the individual studies?*

The findings changed everything. Because the PEAR studies were so extensive, in both time and number of subjects, they are supremely well suited to meta-analysis. The method was of such groundbreaking importance that it is now a standard statistical procedure in science.

Two Princeton researchers were quick to realize the possibilities. In December 1989, Dean Radin, a Princeton psychologist and an authority on parapsychology, along with Roger Nelson, one of Jahn's assistants, published a paper on the meta-analysis of the micro-PK findings. It had enough merit to get published, not in one of the many parapsychological journals, but in the big-league *Foundations of Physics*.

The paper was titled "Consciousness-related Effects in Random Physical Systems," and it shook up some people, to say the least. Radin and Nelson investigated 152 reports describing 597 experimental studies and 235 control studies by 68 distinct investigators; all the studies involved the influence of consciousness on microelectric systems, such as the random-event generator. When the smoke had cleared, they found the odds of these collective findings occurring by chance alone at one in 10^{35}—which is a one with 35 zeros after it![11] In the words of science investigator Richard Milton, "This is as close as anyone in the scientific world ever comes to a 'racing certainty.'"

Another important statistical method developed only recently addresses the so-called file-drawer problem. Harvard's Robert Rosenthal conceived it as a method to further investigate psi data. For years, critics of psi (basically the whole of the orthodox scientific community) have assumed that any study that was not positive for psi would be stuffed away in a file drawer to avoid embarrassment. Of course, this is not at all true; many studies that were unclear or negative concerning psi have been published, but the suspicion remains. The fun begins when we realize that by using meta-analysis, the exact ratio of these "file-drawer" studies to successful, published studies can be accurately calculated.

In other words, meta-analysis shows that in the study of PK-controlled dice throwing, for example, there would have to be nearly 18,000 "file-drawer" studies for the successful ones to be anything but chance occurrences. Since this number is many thousands more than have ever been conducted, it is clear evidence, along with the results of the studies themselves, for the existence of PK.

Radin and Nelson calculated that with the micro-PK evidence on hand, there would have to be 54,000 failed, unpublished tests for the micro-PK results to be a chance happening. This number far exceeds the number of studies ever conducted, period, on any aspect of psi, given the under-funding of parapsychology. The evidence is crystal clear. Psi is a genuine phenomenon.

CHAPTER SIX

Magnetically Magnificent: Exploring the Human Energy Field

More secrets of knowledge have been discovered by plain and neglected men than by men of popular fame. And this is so with good reason. For the men of popular fame are busy on popular matters.

—Roger Bacon, English philosopher and scientist (1220–1292)

The name of Dr. Franz Anton Mesmer is a household word, but for entirely the wrong reasons. Today the word *mesmerize* is synonymous with *hypnotize*, but Mesmer was not a hypnotist—far from it. He was a successful physician of the eighteenth century who used the vital force of life for the treatment of illness, a practice he called *animal magnetism*. He had various methods for charging patients with vital energy, but as far as I can tell he never practiced anything close to hypnosis. However, hypnosis was in fact developed by one of his students, which may explain why the misunderstanding of his name persists widely, even among parapsychologists who should know better.

Born in Germany in 1734, Mesmer graduated with a medical degree from the University of Vienna. His thesis, written in 1766, was titled *De planetarium influxu*, which was translated into English as *On the Influence of the Planets on the Human Body*. In those days, as his thesis title shows,

Mesmer was an avid student of the works of the ancients and the great medieval physician Paracelsus.

During his early practice in Vienna, however, Mesmer discovered that strategically placed magnets seemed to have healing powers. He began to reconsider his original belief concerning the effects of the moon and planets on the body and instead started to think in terms of the forces involved, convinced they were of a magnetic nature.

Due no doubt to the early influence of Paracelsus, the first physician in the West to discuss vital energy seriously, Mesmer concluded that the life force was of a magnetic nature, much like the mineral magnetism present in lodestone and associated with ferrous metals, but he felt that it was of a different order than those ordinary forms of magnetism. Since it seemed to have an important effect on living tissues, especially in humans, he named it *animal magnetism*.

The actual force itself he termed *fluidum*. Mesmer felt he was on the verge of something big, the link between living things and the cosmos, the correspondence among electricity, magnetism, and the living. He stated that living matter had a property about it that could be affected by "earthly and celestial magnetic forces."[1] After learning the techniques of healing touch from a Swiss priest, J. J. Gassner, Mesmer was ready to experiment a bit more.

By 1776, Mesmer ceased using magnets at all, preferring instead to transmit the healing energy to the patient directly through the palms of his hands or indirectly through a *bacquet*. This device was a container of water "charged" with fluidum from which iron rods or strands of silk protruded so that they could be grasped by the patients. Mesmer was ready to tell the world about his discovery. He started with the Viennese Medical Society.[2]

Unfortunately, the society was not impressed; by then, the new beliefs of materialism were beginning to seep into medical and scientific thought in a big way. They promptly expelled Mesmer from the medical faculty and forced him to close his medical practice. In 1778 he decided to move to Paris, a place where the citizens were "people more enlightened and less indifferent to new discoveries."[3] There he had the good fortune of meeting Charles Deslon, a professor in the Faculty of Medicine of Paris (part of the University of Paris) and the personal physician to Count d'Artois.

Deslon was captivated by what Mesmer had to demonstrate and became his student and eventually his medical partner. Deslon went on to proclaim Mesmer's "contribution one of the most important of our age" at a meeting of the medical faculty of the University of Paris. Things began to heat up from there, and in a short time Mesmer and Deslon found themselves treating the cream of Parisian society, apparently with a great deal of success. Mesmer excitedly prepared a paper and sent copies to the Royal Society of London, the Académie des Sciences in Paris, and the Academy of Berlin. Of the three, only Berlin bothered to reply, and then only with the statement that it was all just an illusion.[4] Mesmer was crushed.

However, Mesmer and Deslon continued working. In 1784, according to Deslon's notes, they treated eight thousand patients. That's when the real trouble began. They were getting too big, and the medical establishment of Paris was not happy. They were losing too much business to the pair. Something had to be done.

The doctors had enough clout to influence King Louis XVI to assemble a committee to investigate Mesmer; the group included Benjamin Franklin, who was in Paris at the time to beg funds for the American Revolution, and Antoine Lavoisier, the famous French chemist. The committee was quick to condemn Mesmer, stating that, since this new "force" could not be detected with the senses or with the instruments of the day, any success the doctors had had was attributable only to their patients' imagination, in what today we would call the *placebo effect*.

After the fiasco of 1784, things started to go downhill for Mesmer. His practice began to slide, and he eventually became the subject of public ridicule. Finally he gave it up, retiring to Switzerland to enjoy his last years and write down his thoughts.

In 1815, one year before his death, Mesmer completed his greatest work, *Mesmerism, or the System of Reciprocal Influences; of The Theory and Practice of Animal Magnetism.*[5] He would have likely remained a footnote in history if his name hadn't become such a common term—as in to *mesmerize*—even though, given that Mesmer was an energy healer and not a hypnotist, the word is used incorrectly. (The connection is not entirely misplaced, however, as one of Mesmer's disciples, the Marquis de Puységur, did develop hypnosis.) Sadly, Mesmer's name also connotes charlatanism.

It is interesting to note the findings of a later committee on Mesmer. Several years after his death, a committee from the Medical Section of the Académie des Sciences examined animal magnetism. The year was 1831. After a significant amount of study, the prestigious committee concluded that . . . *Mesmer was indeed correct!* It is a shame that the man didn't live long enough to see his discovery recognized.

Approximately fifty years after Anton Mesmer's success and ruin, another German scientist was well on his way to becoming the top chemist in all of Europe. Baron Karl von Reichenbach was the first to explore the chemistry of coal-tar derivatives, discovering, among other things, paraffin oil and creosote.

The discovery of paraffin, in 1834, was a major accomplishment. In those days, electric lights hadn't even been imagined yet. Paraffin served as a cheap, dependable source of material for candles. The newfangled type of candle made life better for a lot of people on both sides of the Atlantic. Reichenbach was well into what appeared to be a stellar career and award-winning stuff. Then, in 1844, he met Maria Novotny.

Reichenbach was introduced to the young woman by a Viennese surgeon who was treating her for neurasthenia, an emotional disorder involving fatigue and other psychosomatic symptoms. The surgeon stated that the twenty-five-year-old patient was hypersensitive and a little odd. In particular, Maria said she could perceive a force emanating from magnets and, sometimes, from people. Reichenbach was a chemist, a solid scientist, so he was naturally skeptical about what the young woman claimed to perceive. He suggested a test.

As Maria rested in bed, Reichenbach had an assistant go into an adjoining room and uncover a large magnet placed just opposite Maria's bed on the other side of the wall. The assistant complied, noting the exact time. It was later determined that, at the very instant the assistant exposed the magnet, the girl became uncomfortable, sharply declaring that there was a magnet around somewhere.[6] Reichenbach became more curious than ever.

Further tests demonstrated that Maria could determine when the armature was removed from a magnet while she was blindfolded. At another time, when she was unconscious during a neurasthenic episode, Reichenbach approached her with a magnet. It reportedly stuck to her body as though to metal. Later, as she responded to treatment, Maria seemed to lose her strange ability. Reichenbach found four other young female neurasthenics and discovered that they too had the ability to some degree.[7] Reichenbach was hooked. He had come upon something that deserved looking into further and could lead to a major discovery of immense importance.

In the beginning, Reichenbach, like Mesmer, thought he was dealing with ordinary magnetism. He began a series of investigations of magnetic phenomena. Try as he might, though, he was unable to find a connection, other than the fact that some people claimed to see strange vapors and energies associated with magnets.

Falling back on his training and experience as a chemist, Reichenbach decided to try nonmetallic substances, like crystalline sulfur and alum, and nonmagnetic metals, like copper and zinc. He was surprised to find the neurasthenic subjects claimed to see specific colors associated with these substances and to experience different subjective feelings with each substance, particularly when touched with them.

As Reichenbach began to examine his findings, he concluded, as Mesmer had, that he was dealing, not with electricity or magnetism at all, but rather with a specific new form of energy that seemed to permeate crystalline structures and influence biological tissues. He decided to call it the *odic force*.[8]

He found that with odic fields, like poles attract, opposite to the behavior of ordinary magnets. The energy could be conducted through a wire, like electricity can, but at a much slower rate, about 13 feet per second. Unlike electrical flow, which is determined by the conductivity of the material involved, the odic force depended upon the material's *density*. He also found, as so many others have, that the force could be used to charge objects, in a sense storing the energy for later use.[9]

Reichenbach continued his research, finding that some aspects of the force could be focused through a lens, much as light could. Other aspects of it seemed to flow around objects, much as the flame of a candle will, and could even be affected by air currents, behaving like a strange, ethereal gas. (Modern researchers tend to think that this behavior is evidence that the odic force, like other, more familiar forces, obeys the wave/particle duality predicted by quantum theory.) He also found associations between odic force and sunlight. The largest concentration of force seemed to lie at the red and blue-violet ranges of the electromagnetic spectrum.[10]

In 1845, Reichenbach published a book on his findings. It caused a sensation in the German-speaking world and again later when translated into English. *Researches on Magnetism, Electricity, Heat and Light in Relation to the Vital Forces* became a best-seller among the common citizen yet was shunned by the scientific world.[11] Reichenbach's principal opponent in England, Dr. James Braid, who coined the term *hypnotism*, said it was all just a phenomenon of suggestion, à la Mesmer. Disappointed by the response to his discovery by the scientific establishment, Reichenbach decided to return to his work in chemistry and physical science. However, the damage had already been done. Rather than being considered one of the greatest scientists of the eighteenth century, Reichenbach has just become a historical oddity, another crank interested in the nonexistent "vital force."

By the turn of the twentieth century, another scientist began to make claims for an unusual energy field in humans. This time it was an English physician named Walter Kilner. The good doctor was successful early in his career, accepting a teaching post at London's prestigious St. Thomas's Hospital in 1869. He also invented a sterile preservation jar that bears his name, and Kilner jars are still common in British kitchens today. When X-rays were discovered in 1895, St. Thomas's Hospital was quick to employ them. Because Kilner was so highly respected, he was named head of the new X-ray department.

X-rays occupy only a tiny portion of the electromagnetic spectrum, although one of a much higher energy level than ordinary light. Kilner became curious about how other portions of the spectrum might look if they could be made visible to the human eye. He began to experiment with the chemical cyanine blue, a compound that occurs naturally in plants and is responsible for the purple and blue color of many flowers. Cyanine blue was already used in the photographic industry because it made photographic plates sensitive to all parts of the visible spectrum. Kilner coated glass screens with it and then began to observe things around him.[12] He was in for a shock.

Kilner found that when he viewed humans through the special filter, he saw what appeared to be an energy field surrounding them, very much like the aura described in the old metaphysical literature. The energy field was a thin, blue-gray outline of the organism, although its appearance depended upon, among other things, the physical and emotional health of the subject. He continued his research, finding that he could eventually predict the health and disease states of the subjects by the appearance of their aura.

Kilner was fascinated by his finding, but also guarded about what it meant. He felt certain he was seeing the human aura, visible through the special cyanine blue filter, but he was a physician and scientist, not a psychic. He knew the dangers of being associated with the paranormal. As a result, he decided to call the energy field the *human atmosphere*, a name he hoped would distance him from the occult and, thereby allow science to take it seriously. In 1912, he published a book by the same name, summarizing his research findings.[13] In his mind, he had stumbled upon a discovery of vast importance to mankind, opening up a new horizon in human potential. Instead, in the words of science investigator Richard Milton, "publishing the book proved to be an act of professional suicide."[14]

The book can still be found in bookstores today, and it has earned Kilner a place in history within the realm of the paranormal, but it ruined his medical and scientific careers. The *British Medical Journal* published a review of it in the January 6, 1912, issue. They were not kind, stating, among other things, that "Dr. Kilner has failed to convince us that his aura is more real than Macbeth's visionary dagger."

Few reputable scientists have done more work on subtle energy in recent years than Dr. William Tiller, whose work I introduced in chapter 2. After reviewing a great deal of information about paranormal topics, Tiller became directly involved in research himself. One of the things he developed was an instrument that could detect energy radiations from humans.

Drawing on some related Soviet research, Tiller and two of his Stanford students built what he termed a "biological radiation detector." The device consisted of two lead-glass plates, sealed into the form of a box, with a combination of xenon and carbon dioxide gas filling the box. It was powered by a transformer and connected to both an oscilloscope and a pulse counter.

After calibration, the detector was set at a baseline of zero, and a subject sat quietly in front of it for five minutes. After that, the subject placed his or her hands on either side of the box, about two inches away from the glass plates. They were instructed to focus their intent on the machine, and the data were recorded. A cool-down period followed, during which the subject again just sat by the machine.

From 1977 to 1979, Tiller ran thousands of tests with the device. He found some interesting things. On some days, everyone tested could achieve a positive, significant result. On others, almost no one succeeded, although most got better with practice. No correlation was found with lunar or solar events, or with rain. Extensive testing was carried out to see if the machine could be shielded against the subjects' energy. Tiller found that it could not. Nor could he determine that any form of conventional energy was the causative agent. Although the experimenters got the best data when the subjects held their hands near the glass plates, they also got very good results when the subjects simply concentrated their intent on the detector.

In another session, Tiller placed the subject in a Faraday cage, 10 feet away from the device, which was also in a small Faraday cage. It still worked! From this and similar studies, Tiller concluded that, in addition to the PK effects of the human mind, other energies were at work outside the realm of electromagnetism.[15] Tiller also commented on the relationship between magnetism and the paranormal. When a Faraday cage is used to remove electromagnetic interference, psi is often stronger, but when a subject is *magnetically* shielded, the effects of psi are all but cancelled.[16]

For hints of a possible explanation, we can look to another unusual finding concerning magnetism: there are no magnetic monopoles. That is, there is never north without south in the same entity. With electricity, however, there *are* monopoles. The existence of separate positive and negative charges is a fundamental aspect of nature, one of the things that make the world work. In general, nature is wonderfully symmetrical, displaying a grand balance that many people believe demonstrates a connection with higher energy and consciousness. However, although magnetism is closely associated with electricity, no magnetic monopoles equivalent to positive and negative electrical charges have ever been found in nature. James Clerk Maxwell's famous equations *predict* the existence of magnetic charges and currents in nature, and the fact that none have actually been discovered is an asymmetry that troubles many scientists. Tiller thinks that these missing aspects of magnetism, so important to subtle energy and paranormal phenomena, are to be found in higher realms of consciousness and other dimensions of greater frequencies.[17]

Tiller also reminds us of another gap in our thinking: although great attention has been given to the chemical aspects of living things, very little has been focused on the fact that we are also creatures of *light*. The human body, for instance, is an extraordinarily complex network of chemical reactions governed by enzymes, the chemical catalysts that create living functions as we know them. Yes, these are chemical processes, but they are activated by photons—by light.

Tiller also comments that the photoreceptor found in the human eye, the chemical flavin, is found in virtually every cell in the body, as are carotene, melanin, and heme molecules, all of which demonstrate photoactivity. Light appears to be essential to life in ways far beyond stimulating carbohydrate synthesis in green plants, which is the source of all food on earth.

Living things not only absorb light, they also *radiate* it. Studies show that mammalian tissues emit one photon per cell about every 30 minutes. It should come as no surprise that the source of the radiation appears to be the mitochondria, the cell-within-a-cell energy factories that contain their own, distinct DNA. Studies in China showed that humans, too, are literally radiant. From 1975 to 1985, a Chinese researcher, Dr. Zheng, studied the emission of photons from human fingertips. She found some interesting things. Light was radiated at different times during the seasons and was especially high for a time during illness or injury. In general, her data demonstrated that an increase in photons at the blue end of the spectrum indicated a loss of vitality or a growing pathology in the subjects.

Zheng is herself a ch'i kung master, and, after moving to San Francisco, she participated in a study that measured energy emission from her hands. Tight controls were used to eliminate background light. Zheng was found to radiate substantial amounts of blue and red photons from her fingertips, and later studies showed average individuals radiated in the same spectrum, but in lesser amounts. Tiller was involved in that study, and he feels that Zheng's ch'i kung training was responsible for the increased energy emissions.[18]

Vital energy has long been thought to be associated with electro-magnetic radiation. Tiller believes that the evidence is strong enough to conclude that we are light machines as well as chemical ones. Studies by German scientist Fritz-Albert Popp have validated much of Tiller's work.[19] Of course, the ancients have said that we are beings of light all along.

CHAPTER SEVEN

Orgasmic Outcast: Was Wilhelm Reich Right?

Perfectly exact physics is not so very exact, just as holy men are not so very holy.

—Wilhelm Reich, physician

As we've seen in several cases, a scientist who chooses to join the search for the Force takes a huge risk. One twentieth-century physician and scientist dedicated his entire life and career to the quest, and it cost him dearly. Wilhelm Reich, heir to the work of the great Sigmund Freud and director of his famed clinic in Vienna, spent decades searching for the vital force. What he found was astounding and remains the source of great controversy. This chapter tells his story.

Imagine this grim picture. It is 1956. Reich's papers are being confiscated—for the third time in his life. His books and other written materials are gathered up by government officials acting on a court order. The author's atrocities have gotten too far out of hand. A proud, stubborn man, true to his beliefs to the end, Wilhelm Reich has refused to give in to the government's orders. As a result, he languishes in a grim prison cell, a man in late middle age, while the work of a lifetime is collected and burned.

By the mid-twentieth century, this government had become particularly adept at rigid enforcement of laws and quick discipline for those who fell into disfavor. But burning books? The accumulated work of a lifetime by an internationally known researcher? Even materials on topics unrelated to the court order were thrown into the incinerators. The enforcers went about their work with great enthusiasm; it was obvious they enjoyed it. One could easily picture them in black uniforms, complete with armbands.

One would be wrong. It wasn't Nazi Germany. That was earlier: Reich had already suffered the same fate under the Nazis in 1935 when his books and scientific papers were burned on a grand scale. He had barely escaped the Fatherland with his life. It wasn't the Russians, either, although the Soviet officials had done exactly the same thing in 1933.

No, in 1956 the confiscation of Reich's work was taking place, not at the hands of a Hitler or Stalin, but in the last country on earth where you'd expect such a thing to happen. That's right: the land of the free and the home of the brave, that flag-waving, apple-pie-eating bastion of free speech, history's model of democracy, all red, white, and blue. Reich's books were being burned in the U. S. of A.

Thus did Dr. Wilhelm Reich gain the dubious distinction of being the only person in history to have his books burned by the Nazis, the Russians, and the Americans alike. It was an honor he could have done without.

Wilhelm Reich was born on March 24, 1897, in the German-Ukrainian area of Austria, the son of a wealthy farmer. Privately tutored in his early years, he excelled in high school and graduated with honors. After the death of his father when Wilhelm was just seventeen, he managed the family estate until World War I burst on the horizon. Like most able-bodied young men of the time, Reich entered the military, eventually serving as a lieutenant in the Austrian army until 1918. He saw action on the Italian front three times during the Great War, serving his country with distinction.

Shortly after his discharge, Reich decided on a medical career and entered the medical school of the University of Vienna, completing the rigorous six-year course in just four years. He was an outstanding student, graduating with an "excellent" rating and supporting himself as a tutor to undergraduates. He received his M.D. degree in July 1922, at the age of twenty-five.

While a medical student, Reich displayed an interest in psychiatry and joined the Vienna Psychoanalytic Society under the great Sigmund Freud in 1920. After receiving his degree, he enthusiastically jumped feet-first into psychoanalysis, taking postgraduate courses in hypnosis and advanced psychotherapy. He later completed a two-year residency in neuropsychiatry at the university.

Apparently Reich was very good at his chosen field and rose rapidly through the ranks under Freud. By 1928, just six years out of medical school, Reich was the director of Freud's Psychoanalytic Polyclinic. He was in the big leagues, on the track to superstardom—something he would achieve, but not in the manner he imagined.[1]

Deeply interested in human neurosis, Reich believed that much of the problem sprang from various social ills. Impressed by the ideas of Karl Marx, he became a socialist in 1924 and a communist in 1928, hoping to combine the social analysis of Marx with the depth psychology of Freud. His goal was a noble one—to vanquish mental illness as a plague of mankind. However, a trip to Russia in 1929 put an end to those dreams. Reich quickly became disgusted with the Soviet bureaucracy and its moralistic attitude toward sex. He would eventually be expelled from the Communist Party in 1933, although the stigma of Communism would follow him for the rest of his life.

Essentially, what Reich had observed in his practice was that undischarged emotional or sexual energy seemed to become bound into the patient's body as tension, muscular contractions, tense facial expressions, and inhibited breathing. He called this *muscular armoring* and invented his own psychoanalytical technique for dealing with it, something he called *character analysis*. He eventually published the definitive text on the subject under that name.

By 1930, Reich's unusual theories caused a falling out with Freud, but it didn't matter. He was becoming a star in his own right. He relocated to Berlin. Unfortunately, his Austrian countryman, Adolf Hitler, was fast rising to power in Germany.

By the winter of 1933, Hitler controlled Germany, and Reich wisely decided to move on, first to Norway and later to the United States, as Freud and Einstein would do (like them, Reich was Jewish). However, in the meantime, Reich made a monumental discovery, or so he claimed. His work with armored, neurotic patients eventually led him to speculate about the nature of the sexual energy that was inhibited by muscular tension. Reich found that, if the energy flow could be released through massage or bodywork, or through satisfying sexual activity, the patient's neurosis dissipated as well.

Reich came to the conclusion that this energy was something more than just repressed sexual desire. It was an energy force all its own, and, because it was felt coursing through the body at the moment of orgasm and appeared to be so strongly associated with the sexual function, he decided to call it *orgone energy*.[2]

Reich became convinced that the neuroses of sexually dysfunctional people was a direct result of a blockage in the flow of psychic energy, largely due to muscular armoring, the thick bands of contracted muscle and connective tissues that Reich saw again and again in practice. That is, *chronic muscular tension is what was inhibiting the flow of psychic energy*. The body and mind were interconnected. Freud called this energy the *libido*. The great psychologist C. G. Jung said this energy was the very life force itself. Really good sex, the kind that results in spine-tingling, toe-twitching orgasms, released the tension, along with the neurosis. Human neurosis was due to the damming up of psychic energy.

The search was on. Reich began investigating the nature of this energy, the orgone. He was crossing a line between disciplines, from psychology to biophysics. His life would never be the same.

From 1934 to 1939, Reich developed much of his orgone theory while lecturing at the Psychological Institute of the University of Oslo. Things were heating up in Berlin, and, at least for a time, Norway was a welcome haven from the madness of the Nazis. Just before leaving Germany in 1933, however, Reich made what he considered to be the turning point in his work, the discovery of the biological function of tension and charge.[3]

The name he gave this process, consisting of tension and relaxation, charge and discharge, was *biological pulsation*. He considered it the most fundamental aspect of living things. To him it demonstrated a basic principle of the living: the need for gratification, or, in biophysical terms, "the discharge of surplus energy in the organism by way of fusion with another organism."[4] Reich found this process to have four components: mechanical tension; bioelectric charge; bioelectrical discharge; and, finally, mechanical relaxation. The question that struck him was this: What was the nature of this energy? Was it truly electricity, or was it something entirely different and unique?

Reich entered the next phase of his search by examining ordinary matter under high magnification. Using the best microscopes and other equipment he could obtain, Reich began looking for the border between living and nonliving, something that might give him a clue to the nature of orgone. Initially he saw nothing out of the ordinary when he viewed inorganic substances like soil, humus, and coal dust or organic matter like bits of common foods. After he added simple chemicals, such as potassium hydroxide or water, and allowed the samples to soak for a few days, he tried again. Everything looked soggy, but normal. Then he switched to high power, adjusting the eyepieces and objective lenses until a magnification of two thousand times was achieved.

At first he saw nothing, but as he kept looking, he began to see odd blue flashes in the viewing field. As he looked more closely, he noticed small vesicles, tiny objects that shimmered with a blue light. They seemed to assume different shapes and sizes, and they moved about and merged with one another, almost as if they were . . . *alive*. Reich was intrigued, but not overly impressed.

He did notice, however, that different substances seemed to be associated with distinct forms of the strange blue vesicles. He was puzzled, of course, and his initial thought was that the samples had been contaminated by something in the air or by mixing solutions. The answer to that was simple. Reich aggressively heated the next samples in an autoclave to ensure no biological contaminants were left in the resulting mix. Then he turned up the viewing power.

Imagine his shock when he found the viewing field jammed with the blue vesicles, moving about as if they had volition! Instead of destroying the strange objects, the high heat of the autoclave appeared to have produced more of them; and if they were as alive as they appeared to be, then some basic concepts of biology desperately needed to be amended. Reich had just discovered what he would call the *bion*, which he considered to be the link between the living and the nonliving.

Reich found that the vesicles contained fluid as well as a strange type of blue radiation. They appeared to lose their biological activity over time, and as this loss occurred the shimmering blue color faded away. He also noticed something else: his eyes began to bother him. He developed conjunctivitis, an eye irritation, from viewing the bions. When he switched to a monocular eyepiece, only the observing eye was affected.

Eventually the eye trouble became so annoying that Reich had to see an ophthalmologist. The doctor was puzzled by what he found, but he did tell Reich that his eyes had been irritated by some form of radiation. Reich was astounded. The bions were radiating some unknown form of energy, something powerful enough to cause significant irritation to his eyes. What could account for this phenomenon?

Reich also noticed other odd things. Although he was viewing the specimens during winter in a darkened room, he began to develop a nice, impressive tan. He also began to notice a bluish-gray vapor surrounding his lab coat, his shirt sleeves, and, when he happened to glance in a mirror, even his light-colored hair. What's more, his energy levels went through the roof: Reich found himself charged with a boundless and strange vitality, often continuing his research for many hours on end without fatigue.

After a great deal of experimentation, Reich found the blue-energy bions would develop from most types of matter, both organic and inorganic, if the samples were heated and allowed to swell in solution. He became convinced that he was witnessing the spontaneous generation of the link between living and nonliving matter. The bions moved about, fusing and pulsating as they went, with very fine vibrational movement of the blue substance within the vesicles. Reich noticed his basic premise of charge and discharge at work within the bions.

More surprises were in store, however. Reich began an aggressive series of experiments. He found that the presence of bions would destroy bacteria and small protozoa added to the samples. He obtained cancer cells from laboratory mice bred for that purpose. *The cancer cells were also destroyed by the blue energy of the bions!* Even more strangely, Reich found that protozoa and cancer cells developed spontaneously from the "vesicularly disintegrated matter," the source of the bions. Obviously such growth was in opposition to everything known to biology. Reich rechecked his experiments, ensuring that everything was sterile and properly autoclaved.

The bions always appeared eventually, especially if a chemical like potassium hydroxide was added to accelerate the swelling of the sample along with heat from the autoclave. Without the added heat, the bions still formed, although it took much longer, in some cases several days. High levels of heat made them form almost at once. Human red blood cells, erythrocytes, showed especially high levels of orgone energy, particularly if the host was healthy. Reich became convinced that he had found the fabled life energy itself, the biological energy postulated for so long by the fringes of Western science and the energy at work in the orgasm.

Thus Reich came to a stumbling block that has surfaced before in the search for a vital energy: the old forest-and-tree problem. If everything in the world is composed of some sort of fundamental energy, then how *can* we see the forest for the trees? How can we isolate and study something that is all-pervasive, that may not be readily apparent to our normal senses? How can we separate the subtle energy fields that make up our world from those that make up us? And what of the known energies in our world? How can we know that the subtle energy Reich sought is not just an electromagnetic property?

Reich did the best he could in his investigation, constructing a Faraday cage in his basement with a small opening to allow sufficient air for breathing. He turned out the lights, closed the cage, and sat down to wait. After about 30 minutes or so, he began to perceive a vague shimmer of moving blue-gray vapors within the cage. When he fixed his eyes upon a particular spot, he saw again the moving light particles that were now familiar to him. Then a puzzle presented itself. When he closed his eyes, the particles remained in view. It was just an afterimage of the retina after all. But wait! The cage was totally dark. What could irritate the retina enough to cause an afterimage?

As Reich sat in the cage, a thought suddenly occurred to him. He pulled out his handy viewing scope and peered into the darkness. The bluish-gray or violet light particles became magnified—in a totally darkened room!

Reich noticed more. Some of the dots seemed to pulsate as they moved toward him. The violet dots seemed to radiate from the walls in a rhythmic sequence. They formed moving spirals through the air. Once again, the optical tube magnified the effects. After a couple of hours in the cage, Reich noticed a blue-gray shimmer from the fabric of his white lab coat, the same thing he had seen before while in the presence of the bion cultures. He stated, "The radiation seems to adhere to substance, such as cloth or hair."

As he carried out his experiments over time, he again noticed the effects of humidity. The energy appeared stronger on bright, sunny days, weaker on rainy or humid days. Reich was convinced he was onto something. He had discovered an energy flow in living things that was obtained from inanimate matter. The bions were the link between the two. Now, the next question was how could it be harnessed and used to benefit mankind? At his institute in Maine, he got down to work. Orgone might be the secret to effective cancer treatment. Reich was a physician. Curing cancer mattered to him, and he was determined to find a way to use orgone energy to do it. The year was 1942. Wilhelm Reich was forty-five years old.

Reich began his experiments by constructing a box large enough for the patient to sit in comfortably. He used alternating layers of organic and inorganic materials for the structure, which he called an *accumulator*. He included a seat and a viewing port and started the experiments.

The patients were instructed to sit quietly in the accumulator, relax, and attempt to breathe fully and deeply. Standard medical blood tests and X-rays were used to monitor the patient, as were special tests unique to Reich, ones that tracked the amount of orgone in the red blood cells, for instance. Reich began his initial research with terminal cases, people referred to him who had no other recourse within conventional medicine. The time spent in the accumulator varied depending upon the deficiency of orgone in the patient, but a typical time was 30 minutes. The patients sat and relaxed. Reich watched. Then it happened. They began to get better.

Reich did not cure everyone, and some patients improved for a while and then regressed, but he was onto something of great potential value. As his success with cancer treatment grew and his orgone accumulators began to be utilized around the world, so too did the contempt for him grow on the political side of medicine, from organizations like the AMA to government agencies like the Food and Drug Administration (FDA).

Reich was soon branded a quack, a charlatan only out for money. Of course, the declaimers never asked Reich about his methods or theories, nor were they interested in his results. But they *were* interested in the fact that Reich was offering to sell Orgone Accumulators through the mail from his compound in Maine. That was interstate commerce in quackery, and things were getting out of hand. It was time to put a stop to this Dr. Reich, who talked about orgasms all the time. It was time to bring in the Feds. It was 1954. Wilhelm Reich was fifty-seven years old.

Reich was in the crosshairs, and he helped the Feds pull the trigger. He refused to comply with the injunction to cease his activity with the Orgone

Accumulator, taking the stand that monumental scientific discoveries were above the law.

Backed by the courts, the FDA made its move. On February 22, 1954, a decree of injunction was filed. His devices were ordered seized and destroyed, as were all of his writings—including his monumental works in psychotherapy—something entirely independent of orgone. Reich refused to comply, and the case eventually went to a trial by jury in May 1956.

Reich entered a plea of not guilty, believing, as he had so long insisted, that the findings of natural science were above legislation. The jury didn't see it that way. Reich was sentenced to two years in prison, the Wilhelm Reich Foundation was fined $10,000, and one of his fellow Orgonomic physicians was sentenced to one year and a day in prison. Reich didn't last through his punishment, and died on November 3, 1957, at the Federal penitentiary at Lewisburg, Pennsylvania. He was sixty years old. The FDA continued to burn his books, the last event occurring on March 17, 1960.[5]

There's much more to the story of Wilhelm Reich. Throughout his life, Reich wrote extensively on psychotherapy, social psychology, religion, and other topics of importance to mankind. His foundation still exists in Rangeley, Maine, and Orgonomy is still practiced by a handful of physicians worldwide, with a center in New York. His concept of character analysis remains an important element in psychology today, and Reich himself now enjoys a bit of a cult status among freethinkers, New Age people, and the like.

But it is Reich's discovery of orgone that remains his greatest—and most infamous—work. He did much more research than I have reported here. In the early 1950s, he experimented with orgone as a method of counteracting radiation poisoning, something of great interest at the time, during the height of the Cold War.

He obtained some radium and exposed it to orgone radiation, with disastrous results, in the so-called "Oranur" experiment of 1951. Radiation levels went through the roof, and Reich was forced to evacuate his compound.

The combination of radioactivity with orgone produced what Reich called *deadly orgone radiation*, or DOR. It spread into the atmosphere as a chain reaction, causing a panic for Reich and his associates until it dissipated.

Although the conventional scientific community laughed at the idea, the *New York Times* on February 3, 1951, reported an unusually high count of background radiation present in an area of some 300 to 600 miles across, with Rangeley, Maine, as its epicenter.[6] Physicists attempted to explain away the phenomenon as being due to nuclear tests conducted a week earlier in Nevada, but they failed to explain how the radiation traveled 2,300 miles to Maine without leaving traces of radiation in its wake. Some have suggested this episode may have caused the government intervention.

Reich's further studies revealed the extent to which DOR negatively affected plant life and atmospheric conditions. These findings led him to determine that DOR was the causative agent in desert formation, which has progressed at an alarming rate in recent geological time. As a result, Reich experimented with weather control, using his famous "cloud busting" apparatus.

Based on the principles he had discovered with orgone energy, Reich designed a simple device that reportedly could, depending upon the application, cause the formation of rain clouds and heavy rains or, when tuned in the opposite manner, could cause them to dissipate. He called it his *Cloud Buster*. The device employed a series of metal tubes mounted on a rack, with hoses that ran into a stream or river. It was built for him by the Southwest Machine Company of Portland, Maine. According to independent experimentation, the Cloud Buster could apparently affect the weather, specifically with rain produced on application.

In a famous incident in 1953, Reich saved the Maine blueberry crop. After weeks of a severe drought, the local farmers were in a panic. They came to Reich begging for help. Although the weather bureau predicted no rain for days, Reich assembled the Cloud Buster and got to work. After two hours a light rain began to fall. Over the next several days nearly two full inches of rain watered the crop and prevented a catastrophe.

The farmers gave all the credit to Reich and his Cloud Buster in a local newspaper article.[7]

At the very height of his career, before his downfall, Reich met with Albert Einstein at Princeton. Einstein graciously gave Reich one full afternoon out of his busy schedule to listen to his findings concerning orgone energy. Reich set up an Orgone Accumulator for the great scientist and allowed him to view the energy flux through an Orgonoscope. Einstein was at a loss to explain the magnification of the energy pulses and vapors, as well as the increased temperature present in the box, significantly higher than the surrounding air. Einstein admitted he was puzzled by what he saw but was hesitant to attribute it to a new, unknown form of energy.

Reich was very excited, and he told his wife he hoped to work with the great Einstein on the further development of orgone. Einstein later explained away the temperature differences in the accumulator by air current convections, although he had no explanation for the visual phenomena he had witnessed through the Orgonoscope. Einstein later stated, "He's crazy, of course, but very nice."[8] Reich was crushed. The big fall soon followed.

Modern physics and cosmology continue to predict the existence of large quantities of an unknown, undiscovered form of energy. Finding this energy *could* be relatively simple. Let's repeat Reich's experiments with orgone, investigate the bion phenomenon, check out the strange energy he found in the Orgone Accumulator and the Faraday cage, and repeat his experiments with cancer, perhaps on animals to begin with.

First, though, someone has to demonstrate an interest, procure funding, and allow it all to happen. Like other researchers in any area unfashionable to conventional science, Reich had to make do with tiny amounts of money for his research, depending upon his own resources and grants from individuals. Some topics are beyond the interest of the scientific establishment, and none so much as the idea of a "vital energy," an energy common to living things, an energy that makes things *alive*. Reich was not the first to investigate such a phenomenon in Western scientific history, but he was the most thorough.

Although still terribly underfunded, as is all parapsychology today, the search for a vital force continues. The evidence for its existence is mounting all the time. Notice, if you will, a common thread through much of the data about the vital force. We keep coming back to the importance of the vital energy in the growth and development of living things, which is why it's referred to as the *vital* force. This is the Spirit that makes things alive. As such, the flow and balance of this energy is of great importance to proper functioning of an organism.

The ancients knew about vital energy. They were aware of the connection between stress and energy flow. They knew tight muscles inhibit the flow, and they were careful to include techniques to correct this condition. Meditation, yoga, and kung fu all emphasize proper breathing, relaxation, centering, and energy flow. Moreover, the ancients were fully aware of the importance of sex, not just for reproduction, but for its health and energy benefits as well. In fact, they saw vital energy balance as the key to health.

Many forms of healthcare actively work with vital energy, with the goal of achieving a more balanced flow. That's what makes "alternative healthcare" the hottest thing going, and for good reason. It works. In fact, modern, scientific medicine is giving alternative care the ultimate compliment: they are attempting to use it, too. More and more physicians are incorporating natural-medicine concepts into their practices, and many large hospitals throughout the country now have an alternative or integrative care department. This development can only be beneficial, for both our bodies and spirits.

Healing the Rift:
Alternative Medicine Arrives

The doctor of the future will give no medicine, but will instruct his patient in the care of the human frame, in diet, and in the cause and prevention of disease.

—Thomas Edison, inventor

Remember the intrepid medical student David Eisenberg, who raised eyebrows in the seventies by studying Chinese medicine and ch'i kung? He shocked everyone again in the nineties, this time with some jaw-dropping statistics showing just how fast the methods he learned about in China have caught on in the West. The use of complementary and alternative medicine, or CAM, has been on the rise for some time now, but no one guessed just how much. Dr. Eisenberg, who now follows healthcare trends at Harvard Medical School, conducted two studies in 1991 and 1997. The results were astonishing.

The preliminary survey in 1991 showed more and more folks were utilizing CAM, but the follow-up study, published in the November 11, 1998, issue of the *Journal of the American Medical Association* (JAMA), surprised everyone. Incredibly, in 1997, *there were almost twice as many visits to CAM practitioners as there were to primary care physicians!* To be exact, there were 628,825,000 visits to chiropractors, massage therapists, and acupuncturists, to name the top three alternative practices surveyed, compared with 385,919,000 to primary care physicians.[1]

Most CAM treatments are not covered by insurance, yet people are not letting that stop them. In the 1991 study, out-of-pocket expenditures for CAM were $10.3 billion. For conventional hospital treatment, the amount was $12.8 billion. By the 1997 study, the amount paid out of pocket by patients for CAM was an astounding $21.2 billion, and with the resource-based relative value scale (RBRVS), a less conservative set of prices, the figure was as high as $32.7 billion![2]

Of course, patients typically visit a practitioner of CAM several times over the course of a year, whereas they may see their family physician only a time or two, but the statistics are still astounding. Eisenberg commented on the trend: "Alternative medicine use and expenditures increased substantially between 1990 and 1997, attributable primarily to an increase in the proportion of the population seeking alternative therapies, rather than increased visits per patient."[3]

In May 2004, the prestigious National Institutes of Health (NIH) announced the results of a 2002 survey by the National Center for Health Statistics (a branch of the Centers for Disease Control and Prevention) and the National Center for Complementary and Alternative Medicine (a branch of NIH). Of American adults, 74.6 percent had used some form of CAM; 62.1 percent had used CAM within the last twelve months, and 54.9 percent had used CAM in conjunction with conventional medicine. The same survey demonstrated a 75 percent usage of CAM across the life-span.[4] The United States is not alone in this trend. In the United Kingdom, a 2000 report by the House of Lords stated, "Limited data seem to support the idea that CAM use in the United Kingdom is high and is increasing."[5]

Although most forms of alternative medicine are genuinely comforting and often preventative in nature, that's not all there is to it. Alternative methods don't just treat the patient; they activate the Force as well. In fact, it wouldn't be out of line to state that most of such methods were created with just such a goal in mind. And compared with their long history, Western disdain for the vital force has lasted only the blink of an eye. One researcher who could put some cracks in that disdain is Bernard Grad.

Dr. Bernard Grad was a faculty member at Montreal's McGill University. In the 1960s, he grew curious about claims of psychic healing, particularly laying on of hands, a treatment known since ancient times. Grad wanted to investigate the phenomenon, but he was well aware it might just be attributable to a placebo effect. Since this investigation would also be one into the paranormal, the experimental protocols had to be especially tight. Grad decided on something cheap and simple for his experiments— he would test laboratory rats.

After some thought, he decided to see whether a psychic healer could affect the formation of goiters in rats. A goiter is an enlargement of the thyroid gland usually due to a deficiency of iodine, a chemical necessary for the synthesis of thyroid hormones. Grad eliminated iodine from the rats' diets and, for good measure, dosed their water supply with thiouracil, a known blocker of thyroid hormones. The rats were divided into the traditional test and control groups. Next, enter the healer.

Grad decided to use a well-known healer, a former Hungarian military colonel named Oscar Estebany. Estebany had a history of helping heal goiters. The rats in the test group were placed in a special cage with separate compartments, somewhat like an oversized ice-cube tray. By holding this cage, Estebany could treat whole groups of rats at once, which he did for 15-minute sessions.

The study continued for 40 days. At the end of that time, the rats were evaluated. All had developed goiters, but those in the experimental group were significantly smaller, with a slower growth rate.[6] Grad decided to take the experiment a step further. He wanted to see if healing could occur without the healer's touch.

Grad decided to use pieces of cotton and wool cloth that had been held and "charged" by Estebany. The energized fabrics were placed on the floor of the rat's cages for an hour in the morning and again in the evening. The control animals received normal cloth cuttings. The experiment was allowed to run its course. Once again Grad was in for a surprise. The rats housed in the cages with the charged fabrics had less goiter development than the control rats! Psychic energy could be stored in fabrics, just as the ancient teachers, as well as Mesmer and Reich, had maintained.

Particularly striking to Grad was the larger implications of the study. The psychic healing had not cured an existing illness, but it had minimized the development of a well-known physiological phenomenon. Basic biochemistry had been altered. Grad's study had done something that was—for all practical purposes—impossible.

Grad next chose to investigate the phenomenon of wound healing. Once again he used rats. In a careful sequence, the backs of the rats were shaved and a precise amount of tissue was removed from the anesthetized subjects and measured. The resulting wounds were carefully measured, and the animals were divided into three groups of 16 each. One group was used purely as a control, the second group was held by Estebany in its ice-cube-tray cage as before for active healing (although he was not allowed to physically touch them in any way), and the third group had precise amounts of heat applied to the cage to simulate the heat of human hands. This study lasted 30 days.

When the results were in, Grad and company once again were mildly shocked. The wounds of the healer-treated rats were nearly healed; the healing had progressed much further than in the control groups.[7] Psychic healing had significantly enhanced wound healing in a controlled study that used subjects without a belief system, so the placebo effect could not be a factor. Psychic energy appeared to be a genuine phenomenon.

Grad's next experiment would involve plants. Seeking other "belief-free" subjects, he decided to use barley seeds. The seeds were divided into two groups, and both were watered once with a 1-percent saline solution, a known growth retardant to barley plants (thereafter they received tap water). The saline solution received by the two groups differed in one important respect, however. One batch had been psychically treated by Estebany for 15 minutes while enclosed in a sealed flask. The other was just ordinary saline solution. None of the assistants knew which was which as they set about watering the seeds. Also, the seeds didn't have any "beliefs" about which treatment they were receiving. Under these double-blind conditions—which are essential to rule out the famed "experimenter effect" (the possibility of belief by the scientists affecting the outcome of the test)—the seeds were transferred to numbered pots and incubated for 48 hours. They were then arranged randomly in ordered rows for the duration of the experiment and watered with ordinary tap water.

At the end of a 12- to 15-day period, the experiment was terminated, and the small plants were analyzed for percentage of germination, height, and individual chlorophyll content. After all the statistics were in, Grad found that the plants treated with the special saline solution had a higher germination rate, were larger, and had increased levels of chlorophyll.

The fact that water could be psychically charged intrigued Grad. In another test, he tried another angle on testing charged water. He gave sealed samples of water to people with known "green thumbs"—people who had a knack for growing plants—and to depressed and neurotic patients, with instructions to hold the flasks. Later testing showed the water was altered in opposite directions. The green-thumb people had charged the water in some positive manner that would be stimulating to plant life. The opposite was true of the psychologically infirm.[8] In some strange way, they had negatively charged the water, resulting in samples that were harmful to growing plants. The really big question remained: *what was happening to the water?*

Water is such a simple substance, really. Just two hydrogen atoms bonded to one atom of oxygen—two common gases that chemically bind to form the liquid so familiar to us all. It appears that psychic energy affects the chemical bonds *between* water molecules. Molecules of water form what is known as hydrogen bonding, the attraction between the slightly negative aspect of oxygen to the slightly positive charge of the hydrogen atoms of neighboring molecules. This bonding gives water its familiar characteristics, such as capillary action and surface tension. By using infrared absorption spectrometry, Grad discovered that in healer-treated water, the angle of these tenuous molecule-to-molecule bonds, the actual three-dimensional alignments of the atoms, was altered in a small but significant way. This small shift allowed for a slight change in the surface tension of the water. And surface tension is easily measured.

With this discovery, it was now possible to directly quantify the effect on water by a psychic healer.[9] Bernard Grad provided some of the first direct evidence of a physical system being affected by psychic energy. Thanks to his groundbreaking work, others were able to take the ball and run with it. One such man was Dr. Robert Miller, a research chemist from Atlanta.

Robert Miller had long been interested in the biochemical effects of psychic healers. When he heard of Grad's work, he determined to replicate it in his own lab—and succeeded. He also discovered something else. Like water that had been treated psychically, water treated magnetically also had a reduced surface tension. After a lot of experimentation, Miller became convinced that water could indeed become charged with either psychic energy or magnetism, with a measurable reduction in surface tension as a result.[10]

As he investigated further, he found that the energy would be gradually released over a 24-hour period, at which time the surface tension and the hydrogen bond angles would return to normal. However, an exception happened when a metal rod was inserted into a sample or the water was poured into a metallic container. The metal caused an almost instantaneous release of the energy. This effect was precisely what Mesmer had found more than two hundred years ago.

Miller became intrigued by the similar results for psychic energy and magnetism. He began to ask: is there truly any difference between these energies, or are psychics simply using biomagnetism in some strange way? (As we have seen Dr. Tiller's work demonstrate, there is definitely a magnetic quality to psychic phenomena, but the relationship isn't entirely understood.)

To explore the question, Miller decided to try a variation on one of Grad's experiments, using rye seeds to evaluate the growth potential of magnetic and psychically treated water.

He used three groups of rye seeds, with 25 seeds per group, and watered each of the groups with a different type of water. The first group received tap water, the second was watered with special samples of healer-treated water, and the third received water samples that had been exposed to a magnetic field. The results were surprising. The germination rate in the tap-water group was 8 percent; in the healer-treated group, 36 percent; and in the magnetically treated group, 68 percent! This last group produced sprouts that were 28.6 percent taller than the others as well.[11]

Although Miller got the most remarkable results by using magnetism, subsequent studies would show that there is more to the phenomenon than mere growth. One study concerned enzyme activity. Biochemical reactions are totally dependent upon the chemical entities known as *enzymes*. Without these biological catalysts, life as we know it could not exist. Particularly in complex life forms, the vast enzymatic system forms a delicate balance, regulating the myriad chemical reactions that take place in our cells by the thousands every second, allowing them to proceed faster and with less energy. Some scientists were beginning to think that the results of Grad and Miller were due, at least in part, to the effects healers have on enzyme systems, especially since recent research had shown enzyme activity could be affected by magnetic fields.

One researcher who has investigated the role of enzymes in psychic healing was a Catholic nun and biochemist named Dr. Justa Smith, who worked at the Human Dimensions Institute of Rosary Hill College in New York. In 1970, she had just recently completed her dissertation on the effect of magnetism on enzymes. After hearing of Grad's work, she had a hunch the healers were affecting the enzymes themselves, accelerating them in some unknown manner.

Pursuing this hunch was an easy step for Smith. All she needed was a healer. Once again, Colonel Estebany was willing to cooperate. Smith decided to test his ability to activate the common digestive enzyme trypsin. Estebany was instructed to hold test tubes containing laboratory-grade trypsin and simulate a laying-on-of-hands session. Smith took periodic samples of the trypsin solution while Estebany was at work and ran them through a spectrophotometer, a sophisticated instrument that could measure the level of enzyme activity.

What she found was very similar to her studies of enzyme activation in magnetic fields. The longer Estebany held the sample, the higher the level of enzyme activation. That is, there was a direct correlation.[12] A natural conclusion would be that psychic healing must be a magnetic phenomenon after all! However, when Smith attempted to measure the magnetic field around Estebany's hands, she drew a blank. There was little, if any, measurable magnetic field, little more than the body's normal magnetism.

Her curiosity aroused, Smith tested other healers and other enzyme systems. She was soon in for a big surprise. With some enzymes, a healer's intervention actually decreased the activity. In other tests with the same enzyme, the activity increased. This equivocal pattern occurred repeatedly. The results were puzzling until Smith saw a new way to think about the problem. *The enzymes were always altered in a way that was in the best interests of the health of the cell!* Intelligence was at work here. The vital force appeared to be . . . *conscious.*

Here was the important difference between psychic energy and magnetism that Robert Miller had searched for. Magnetism activated *all* enzymes, regardless of their specific function. On the other hand, psychic healers, using a force that contained a consciousness of its own, only activated enzymes in a manner beneficial to the health and well-being of the organism.

Justa Smith was excited. The time had come to see if psychic healers could affect damaged enzyme systems as well. Smith conferred with Grad, and they decided to use ultraviolet (UV) radiation to alter the three-dimensional structure of trypsin. It was one thing to activate an enzyme, but quite another to repair physical damage to the complex 3-D structure of proteins.

Once again, Oscar Estebany was the healer. He received tubes of UV-damaged trypsin with the instruction to "heal them." The baseline enzymatic activity had been recorded; it was low as a result of the UV damage. After the healing sessions, the chemical activity of the sample was restored to normal levels and remained so indefinitely. The conclusion was inescapable. Estebany's psychic energy had repaired the damage to the complex proteins of the enzyme, something generally thought to be impossible. This reversal was unprecedented. *The enzymes were displaying negative entropy!* Here was bio-PK at its best.

As for the magnetic qualities of psychic energy, later studies by Dr. John Zimmerman using an ultra-high-sensitivity magnetometer (officially, a superconducting quantum interference device, or SQUID) confirmed that the energies of psychic healers do contain magnetic fields, some one hundred times higher than the normal fields associated with humans.[13] These biofields were still much weaker than the synthetic ones Justa Smith used to activate enzymes, yet their effects were similar. Although the vital force has a magnetic quality to it, and just as the ancients insisted, there is far more to it. In short, it has consciousness. One woman has explored this consciousness in a spectacularly successful way.

Dolores Krieger has a Ph.D. in nursing and has taught at New York University. She is also an internationally known psychic researcher and practitioner who has sent shock waves around the world in recent years. Krieger has done what many thought impossible: she has made psychic healing a part of modern medicine, through a method she calls *Therapeutic Touch.*

It all started back in the 1960s when Krieger happened upon some of Bernard Grad's work with plants. If you recall, one effect of psychic healing was increased chlorophyll levels in the test plants. This result caught Krieger's attention. She remembered from her basic chemistry that chlorophyll, the green pigment in plants that is so vital to photosynthesis, is very similar to the human blood component hemoglobin. This oxygen-carrying molecule is similar in structure to chlorophyll: both are organic compounds with a metal atom at the core—iron in hemoglobin and magnesium in chlorophyll.

Krieger had a crazy thought. If psychic healers could increase levels of chlorophyll in plants, perhaps they just might be able to do something with hemoglobin levels in humans. After all, the two compounds were so alike structurally, and both served an important role in energy production. Best of all, hemoglobin was vital to human health—and easily measured in standard blood tests.

If psychic healers could alter hemoglobin levels, blood-test results would serve as a reliable, easily obtained quantifier for measuring psychic effects. More importantly, such quantifiable results might help open a new door in healthcare. Already, the workings of the basic experiment were taking shape in her mind.

Krieger looked around and got lucky. Just such a study was already planned, supervised by Otelia Bengssten, M.D., and Dora Kunz, a clairvoyant. Krieger managed to sign on, having convinced Bengssten and Kunz to let her take data on hemoglobin levels as an adjunct to their study on the overall benefits of psychic healing. The study began in 1971, and once again Estebany was the healer. It took place on a farm owned by the Theosophical Society in the foothills of the Berkshire Mountains, in upstate New York. The subjects, who had a variety of illnesses, joined the study through medical referrals. The procedure was similar to what Estebany had done before. Interestingly, just as with the rats in Grad's experiments, the test patients were given rolls of cotton batting that Estebany had charged with energy. Some claimed that they still felt emanations from the rolls as much as a year after the study.

At the end of the experiment, while the others were assimilating their data, Krieger got to work on hers. Just as her hypothesis had predicted, in comparison to the control group the experimental group had significantly increased levels of hemoglobin.[14]

Krieger was excited! None of the subjects knew their hemoglobin values were being studied. All they knew was that Dr. Bengssten was looking at the effects of psychic healing on their various illnesses. Here was the quantifier Krieger was looking for. Hemoglobin levels could serve as the key.

In 1973 Krieger repeated the study, again using Estebany as the healer and with larger test and control groups. The results were the same. Ill people treated by Estebany had increased hemoglobin levels. The control group did not. However, what particularly struck Krieger were the cancer patients.

Anemia is a common problem in cancer patients, resulting both from the treatments they receive and from the disease itself. Even in these difficult cases, hemoglobin levels typically increased after the healing activities of Estebany. In fact, nearly the entire test group treated by Estebany showed marked improvement, not just in hemoglobin levels, but in overall symptomatology as well. Krieger became convinced that a true bioenergetic process was taking place. Whatever Estebany was doing had a positive effect on living beings—people, plants, and animals. It wasn't just a coincidence.

The next question was an important one: could psychic healing be taught to others, or was it an inborn talent, available only to a chosen few? Krieger of course asked Estebany. He was adamant—it was a gift. Only a chosen few could perform such tasks. It could not be taught to others. Krieger was disappointed. But she decided to also ask Dora Kunz, the psychic involved in the original study. Kunz had quite a different opinion. Healing could definitely be taught to others. In fact, she was starting a workshop soon to do just that! Dolores Krieger became one of her first students.

In a short time, under Kunz's tutelage, Krieger had developed the ability to perform psychic healing at a beginner level. It is important to note that Kunz was not teaching Krieger the traditional laying on of hands. Rather, her style of healing involved manipulation of the patient's energy field. The healer used his or her hands first to "sense" the energy field of the patient from a short distance and then to charge and project the flow to the areas in need. The healer did not actually touch the patient.

Krieger was ready to take her skills mainstream, yet she knew the health profession would be appalled by terms like *psychic energy* or *vital force*. She had to come up with something that got the idea across, but without offending the educated, materialistic Western mind. After some thought, she decided on Therapeutic Touch, or TT.

Her first class on Therapeutic Touch was offered as a master's level course at New York University entitled *Frontiers in Nursing: The Actualization of Potential for Therapeutic Field Interaction*.[15] Before long, the students were beginning to practice a bit of healing on their regular patients. Sure enough, the patients started getting better. As they continued the practice and observed the benefits, they got so excited that they had T-shirts printed up with "Krieger's Krazies" emblazoned on the front. The students were convinced. They even experimented with healing on pets and other animals and were amazed at the results. It was time for the real litmus test. Could the newly trained nurse-healers achieve elevated hemoglobin levels like "professionals" such as Estebany had? Krieger decided it was time for another study.

She created an experiment that used two sets of patients, 32 in the experimental group and 32 in the control group, all in hospitals and healthcare facilities in the New York area. As healers, Krieger used 32 nurses, half of whom were her students trained in Therapeutic Touch. All the patients continued with their normal medical care, and the experimental group also received TT. Initial hemoglobin values were documented and the study began.

At the end of the experimental period, hemoglobin levels were measured again. After the data were compiled, the results were clear: the nurses trained in Therapeutic Touch had raised hemoglobin levels in their test patients, just like Estebany had. There was no change in the control group. Krieger became even more committed to her cause.

By 1979, 350 nurses had taken Krieger's course at New York University, and another 4,000 healthcare professionals had been exposed to the technique in continuing education classes throughout North America.

Some of Krieger's former students were now teaching the technique to others. In 1979, Krieger published a book on her experiences, entitled *The Therapeutic Touch: How to Use Your Hands to Help or to Heal.*

Therapeutic Touch continues to thrive in many healthcare settings, the subject of awe in many instances and ridicule in others. Open-minded people who take the time to examine the evidence and clinical successes are supportive. Those who bristle at the idea of an unrecognized form of "energy" that can be transferred from a healer to a patient are, of course, appalled. It remains to be seen how much evidence would be required to convince them otherwise.

While the methods I've described so far deal with a person's energy field as a whole, another practice treats the whole by treating one part: the spine. The ancients attached a special significance to the human spine. They were fully aware of the vital relationship between the spine and the extraordinarily complex and delicate spinal cord, as well as the spinal nerves that course throughout the body. But it went much further than biomechanics.

The ancients felt that the human spine also served as a conduit for the Force, a major channel for the vital energy that connects the brain and the all-important crown chakra with the rest of the body. We can see from their records the importance they gave the spine, with Hippocrates going so far as to say that a physician should look to the spine first for the source of all disease. Late in the nineteenth century, Daniel David Palmer returned to that ancient advice.[16]

The modern art and science of *chiropractic* sprang from Palmer's rediscovery of the importance of spinal manipulation in Davenport, Iowa, in 1895. The late nineteenth century was a time of change in healthcare. Homeopathy was as popular as allopathic (modern) medicine, but Roentgen had just discovered X-rays, so things were in a state of transition. D. D. Palmer would eventually be a major player in healthcare worldwide.

Palmer had been, among other things, a teacher, a farmer, a beekeeper, and, later in his career, an alternative healer. Although he did not have a medical degree, he practiced as a magnetic healer, applying small magnets to problem areas in his patients, something that was perfectly legal and respectable in his day. He eventually maintained a busy practice in the Mississippi River town of Davenport.

Palmer rented office space in a building in downtown Davenport that employed a black janitor named Harvey Lilliard. Harvey was nearly deaf, the result of an incident in which he felt a sudden pop in his upper back, after which he immediately lost most of his hearing in both ears. It was said he was unable to hear the considerable noise produced by the horse-drawn wagons on the cobblestone streets below.

Palmer was a compassionate man, as well as Lilliard's friend. He was well aware of the story behind Lilliard's hearing loss, and after a conversation about it one particular day in September 1895, he convinced Lilliard to let him do something about it. Although it's a safe bet that Lilliard was a bit apprehensive, he consented to allow Palmer to examine his neck and back. Palmer palpated his upper back (the medical way of saying he felt around on Lilliard's body for abnormalities) and found one of the thoracic vertebrae grossly misaligned. He instructed Lilliard to lie down, and using the spinous process of the vertebra (that is, one of the bony projections we see as small bumps on the back), Palmer wrenched the vertebra back into place with a large pop. Lilliard was immediately able to hear the clanging of hoofs on the cobblestone street below the second-story office. His hearing was fine for the remainder of his life. At that moment, modern chiropractic was born.

Palmer did not claim to have invented the art of spinal manipulation. He was fully aware that the ancients practiced and spoke of it a great deal. He did claim to be the first to use the spinous and transverse processes of the vertebrae as levers to realign or "adjust" the bones back into position. As time went on and Palmer refined his art, he began to notice that, in addition to being a wonderful cure for most back and neck pain, adjustments also had a systemic effect on the body. Often, after a series of adjustments, other illnesses seemed to improve as well.

Palmer hit the books, reviewing neuroanatomy, physiology, and ancient philosophy. He had used his intuition to diagnose and treat Harvey Lilliard, and now he continued, as so many other innovators have over the years, to use his gut feelings, the guidance of his higher self, to develop an entirely new system of healthcare. A minister friend suggested he called it *chiropractic*, from the Greek for "done by hand," and Palmer started the first college to teach his techniques in Davenport, Iowa, called, appropriately enough, the Palmer College of Chiropractic.

Central to the development of chiropractic was the condition Palmer termed a *subluxation*. It was well known that a vertebra can become dislocated, a serious medical condition. What Palmer discovered was that the vertebrae of the spine can also become just slightly misaligned, far from a dislocation, yet off enough to affect the nervous system substantially via the spinal nerves that exit between the vertebrae. Such misalignment also produces a painful musculoskeletal condition as well. What really set Palmer and his "subluxations" apart, though, were his ideas concerning vital energy.

As a result of his studies, and perhaps his intuition, Palmer became convinced that a vital energy flows from the brain down throughout the nervous system and back to control and coordinate the functioning of the body. He called this energy *innate intelligence*, the life-giving energy of the Creator.

From its very beginning, chiropractic was a form of healthcare that, much like acupuncture, dealt with the manipulation of vital energy. It was great for sore backs, but it was much more. It was said to restore the flow of vital energy in the body. Eventually chiropractors were using spinal adjustments to treat a wide variety of illnesses, with very considerable success. The system grew rapidly.

It is now the second leading system of healthcare in the United States, second only to allopathic medicine. It is licensed in every state and in many countries. Graduate chiropractors are full-fledged physicians, although they are not trained in pharmacology or surgery. They are experts in spinal anatomy and physiology as well as in the diagnosis and treatment of most musculoskeletal disorders. In many subjects, including nutrition, anatomy, and X-ray diagnosis, they have more training than medical students.

Chiropractic continues to grow, and most good-sized towns now have a practice on just about every corner. It is the only fully licensed, fully recognized, portal-of-entry healthcare system that deals with the flow of the vital force. Although it is touted nowadays as the treatment of choice for conditions such as back pain and headaches, which indeed it is, chiropractic is also a powerful tool for the manipulation of subtle energies.

Perhaps when the government subsidizes chiropractic research to the same degree it does traditional medical research, and chiropractic has sources of income to rival the millions supplied to medicine each year by the big drug companies, its underlying mechanisms will be discovered. For the time being, the clinical and empirical evidence is overwhelming. Chiropractic is great. It is just as important as diet, exercise, and daily nutritional supplementation for optimal health.

Many researchers interested in vital energy have explored the concept that all things possess a characteristic resonant frequency through which they interact with the world. One of the more interesting among that crowd was a man who did most of his original work in the 1920s and 1930s, a gentleman in San Diego, California, named Dr. Royal R. Rife.

He was most interested in finding a successful cure for one of the true scourges of modern industrial societies, the set of some two hundred disorders we call, collectively, *cancer*. Of course, to examine a disorder that seems to occur at the cellular level, as cancer does, a special microscope is required, one that allows us to see the tiny structures involved. Therein lies a fundamental problem.

Modern microbiologists and histologists (specialists in cell anatomy) have advanced the field of microscopy to a remarkable degree, and sophisticated technologies exist, like the scanning electron microscope, that can view matter down nearly to the atomic level. However, the problem with these marvelous microscopes is that they all examine *dead matter*. Biological specimens are cut and pasted, sliced and diced, slip-covered and stained until they bear little resemblance to the pulsating, living organisms they once were.

At some point during his initial search for a cancer cure in the 1920s, Rife developed the Rife universal microscope, a device that used special optics constructed of quartz crystal rather than glass. With it, Rife was able to magnify biological specimens up to thirty thousand times, enough for him actually to see them while they went about their normal functions. He could even see viruses, which are notoriously tiny. In addition, Rife discovered that if he used polarized light to illuminate the samples, each type of sample glowed with a distinctive color.[17] This method led Rife to the discovery that every living thing was associated with a specific energy level that he termed its *mortal oscillatory rate*, or MOR.

After a great deal of study, Rife cataloged the MOR for a number of organisms and developed an instrument he called the *Rife beam ray*, which could deliver a matching electromagnetic frequency. Rife found that if he projected the specific MOR frequency for a species of bacteria, for instance, the bacteria stopped their normal activity and quickly died.

It wasn't long before Rife was having incredible success curing patients with chronic infections, all at a time before the advent of modern antibiotics. By using the principle of vibratory resonance, Rife could tune the ray to the precise MOR and destroy the bacteria within the patient's body. He also found he could destroy cancerous tissue as well.

In 1934, he was involved with a classic study in cancer research at the University of Southern California. Rife and the staff treated 16 terminal cancer patients using his beam-ray device. Three months later, 14 of the 16 were pronounced totally cancer free by the five medical physicians involved with the study. Once the results were released, the AMA wanted in. When the parties couldn't resolve the details of a deal for rights to the method and equipment, the AMA immediately branded Rife a quack, and one night his laboratory mysteriously burned to the ground. Rife was taken to court, and all doctors using his methods were warned to cease immediately or face being blacklisted. Without any official support, Rife continued his amazing work on his own for decades but suffered from depression and alcoholism. He died without seeing his work go any further in official circles, although it is still carried out today by alternative researchers.

In another byway of research we can find several obscure practices that echo the discoveries of Wilhelm Reich, whose work we saw in chapter 8. Reich believed that under conditions of physical or emotional stress, the energy vesicles he discovered could degenerate into other microorganisms, including bacteria and a type of pathogen he called T-bacilli. He reportedly had direct, photographic evidence of this transformation, but conventional science scorned him. Others, including Royal Rife, found evidence of transformation as well. Rife had discovered something he called the *BX organism*, which he felt was directly responsible for cancer. He observed the BX organism to be *pleomorphic*, to shape-change into other forms.

Modern French biological researcher Gaston Naessens, once again using a specialized microscope that allowed him to observe living microorganisms under high magnification, discovered something very similar.[18] While conducting a careful study of human blood, Naessens discovered what he thought was the very essence of life—minute, subcellular energy particles, living condensers of energy he called *somatids*, something that sounds an awful lot like Reich's bions.

Naessens continued the investigation and found the somatids to be vital components of both human and animal blood, essential to the health of the organism. He also found that they underwent a pleomorphic, three-stage cycle in the bloodstream. During times of normal functioning, the somatids remained in their usual appearance and organization. When a patient was immunosuppressed, they changed into *one of sixteen different forms*, ranging from bacteria to spores and fungi.[19]

Something similar was also found by German bacteriologist Günter Enderlein, who, using microscopy to view living blood samples, found minute, flourishing microorganisms that he called *protits*. Enderlein found that during times of normal health the protits appeared to remain in their normal state, but with exposure to stress, radiation, carcinogens, or improper diet they would morph into pathological forms that were destructive to tissues.[20] His research showed that the new, sinister forms were quite dangerous, causing various cancers, including leukemia, and acquired immune deficiency syndrome (AIDS). Eventually, Enderlein used fungal cultures to develop both homeopathic and isopathic remedies. The homeopathic remedies stop pathological development and shift the protits back into their beneficial state; the isopathic remedies employ a product of the disease itself to combat it. Sanum Kehlbeck, the company Enderlein started, continues to thrive worldwide. And the research he started continues as well, but the concept is so far from the beliefs of conventional microbiologists and medical researchers that it is ignored.

In the meantime, Naessens continued to develop effective treatments based on his somatid theory of disease. After a great deal of study, he determined that the sixteen microbial end products of somatid degeneration contribute to a wide range of pathological agents responsible for such diseases as cancer, multiple sclerosis, AIDS, and rheumatoid arthritis. He found that a by-product of cells affected by the pathogenic somatids, a compound he called *co-cancerogenic K factor* (CKF), caused immunosuppression. Since cancer is thought to be a disease of improper immune function at its most basic level, the involvement of somatids in cancer appeared reasonable. Naessens eventually developed a camphor compound called *714-X* that inhibited the action of CKF when injected into the lymphatic system.[21] His findings are just too far beyond conventional thinking to be accepted at this time by orthodox science and medicine.

We've covered a lot of ground in this chapter. We've found that vital energy can be restored to a balanced state by manual manipulation, laying on of hands, and the use of strange energy devices like the Rife beam ray. We've found that a loving, healing intent can go a long way. Sometimes, however, we have to call on a higher power for help. Yes, I'm talking about that most basic, and probably most ancient, of human mental and emotional practices . . . *prayer*!

Studies have demonstrated that plants and animals—everything from rye grass to red blood cells, from algae to moth larvae—can indeed be positively affected by prayer. Prayer has been shown to affect the activity of enzymes, mutation rates of bacteria, the healing rate of wounds, the firing rate of cardiac "pacemaker" cells, and the growth rate of leukemic white blood cells. In humans, just being "religious" has been shown to have a powerful effect on health and recovery from illness, something orthodox medicine is beginning to notice.[22]

In a 28-year study, religious persons had a 25 percent lower mortality rate than others, and when only the females were considered, it rose to 35 percent. Studies have shown that those who consider themselves religious and attend church regularly have improved immune function.[23] In the United States, the Mormons have been shown to be the healthiest members of society as a group.[24] Naturally, it is assumed that these people pray a good deal, both for themselves as well as for each other. But what happens when a group of people prays for an ill person without the patient knowing about it, in so-called "intercessory" prayer?

The idea is simple. Get a group of religious people together; have them pray for seriously ill patients, such as cardiac cases; use a control group of patients to compare to the experimental group; and then see what happens. This is exactly the study done by William S. Harris, Ph.D., of Saint Luke's Hospital in Kansas City, Missouri, who gathered a team of experts to investigate the phenomenon further.[25] Harris's study of prayer's effect on cardiac patients eventually proved to be a groundbreaking event, hitting the big time on October 25, 1999, when it was published in the *Archives of Internal Medicine*, a respected journal published by the AMA.

A key reason for the study's success was its careful design. For starters, Harris decided to make his study truly double-blind. So first of all, none of the patients knew they were the subjects of a study on prayer, although it took a bit of sidestepping to get around the problem of informed consent. It was ultimately decided prayer could do little if any harm, and the requirement of consent was waived. The next step was to get the doctors and staff out of the loop, too. This "blinding" was done in a novel way. During the period of the study, the chaplain's secretary, who had access to lists of new admissions but didn't even know where the coronary care unit (CCU) was, randomly assigned the new coronary care patients to either the control or test group. With this technique, no one else associated with the hospital even knew the study was being conducted.

During the 12 months of the study, 990 patients fit the criteria for the test and were admitted to the program, 466 in the prayer group and 524 in the "usual care group," the control portion of the test. Lists giving only the patients' first names were supplied to teams of "intercessors," the people who would pray for them each day for 28 days. No other personal or medical information was given. At no time did the intercessors actually meet the patients. They only offered a simple prayer each day for a "speedy recovery with no complications," as well as anything else the intercessors deemed important. The 28-day study length was chosen to ensure that patients with typical CCU stays would receive steady prayer throughout their hospitalization.

The intercessors were chosen through contacts in the local community. No particular religious beliefs were necessary; the only requirement was that the participant be willing to state, "I believe in God. I believe that He is personal and is concerned with individual lives. I further believe that He is responsive to prayers for healing made on behalf of the sick."

Eventually 75 intercessors were used, organized into 15 teams of five members each. Members were randomly assigned to the teams, and all members of a team received the same patient names. They were kept blinded to the identity of their fellow team members, and all prayer was offered privately. With all the pieces in place, Harris and his team were ready to set things in motion.

Previously, Harris and his team of experts had consulted with a team of cardiologists and an internist about how to record the patient's condition. No standard set of criteria was quite right for their needs, so the doctors had to invent a new system of scoring, one that took into account a number of variables, such as the need for cardiac resuscitation, bypass surgery, and cardiac catheterization.

With all the pieces in place, the study began. Each of the 990 patients who would eventually be involved in the study was observed and carefully scored using Harris's new method. When the final data were analyzed and the results tallied, the team found that the earlier studies had been correct. There was a statistically significant difference between the improvements of the prayer group when compared to the "usual care" group. Although the lengths of hospital stay were the same, the patients in the prayer group displayed—you guessed it—generally speedier recoveries with fewer complications, which is pretty much what the intercessors had asked of God!

As for the underlying mechanism, two possibilities were suggested: one, that some unknown force or energy was generated by prayer and transmitted to the intended individuals, or two, that God really does exist and really does answer prayers, something the authors say would be "beyond the ken of science." Harris admitted that the odds of all this just happening by chance were one in twenty-five, not an immensely huge amount. He also commented on some other important items:

> Although we cannot know why we obtained the results we did, we can comment on what our data do not show. For example, we have not proven that God answers prayer or that God even exists. It was intercessory prayer, not the existence of God, that was tested here. All we have observed is that when individuals outside of the hospital speak (or think) the first names of hospitalized patients with an attitude of prayer, the latter appeared to have a "better" CCU experience.[26]

At the very least, the Harris study shows us that earlier experiments were not flukes and that prayer is not just the stuff of ancient superstition but something of significant medical value, possibly as important as the medical procedures themselves.

Fortunately, even though the medical profession may be deaf, the American public is listening. The Harvard study on the use of complementary and alternative medicine surprised a lot of people. Alternative healthcare is on the move for the most fundamental of reasons: it works remarkably well for a wide variety of common medical conditions. Of course, for some things, modern medicine works wonders. Although I am frequently critical of organized medicine, I have respect for the physicians working in the field. Most I've met are hard-working, compassionate men and women, professionals who face difficult situations nearly every working day.

Of course, it has always been difficult to change the official scientific version of things. Often the changes don't occur until the members of the old guard die off and younger people rise to take their place. The question of why the scientific orthodoxy is so resistant to the examination of certain topics is an interesting area of study all its own, one that has not gone unnoticed by the psychologists and epistemologists who examine such things. In the next chapter we'll look at several famous scientific discoveries that sparked outrage of a type usually reserved for studies of the paranormal, and we'll see how that mindset has taken root in some organizations that specifically set out to discredit paranormal research.

CHAPTER NINE

Schlock Science:
Who Makes the Call?

I maintain that the cosmic religious feeling is the strongest and noblest motive for scientific research.

—Albert Einstein

So far we've seen several cases of researchers who study the paranormal being brutally rejected, but it's worth remembering that scientists can also be brutal to respected "big names" if it looks like they've strayed from the straight and narrow. In 1879, Thomas Edison was unquestionably a "big name." More than 150 patents were already on the books for his inventions, which included the stock market ticker tape and the phonograph. The latter had been introduced the year before and was now a sensation, its popularity helped by the fact that Edison demonstrated it at the White House and in the editorial offices of *Scientific American*.

However, for his next great invention, Edison would feel the sting of sharp criticism. When Edison announced (after a great deal of trial and error) that he had succeeded in creating the incandescent lamp, the scientific world attacked him.

The world was ready for a new form of illumination. Some experimental models and carbon arc lamps had already been around for a few years, but they proved unsatisfactory for wide-scale commercial use. There was also the problem of the primitive electrical circuitry of the day. Items had to be rigged in a series, and a malfunction in one would cut power to everything else, just as in a string of cheap Christmas-tree lights. Edison knew the future of home electrical power required both the discovery of a functional electric light and the development of a practical parallel circuit system.

In Menlo Park, New Jersey, Edison had already designed and built the world's first research and development facility, and he soon employed all of his energies in developing a practical electric lamp and parallel circuit. He spent most of 1879 working on the problem, as he and his research team tried everything imaginable. Nothing would burn for more than a few hours, whether in the open air or in a vacuum. Then Edison stumbled upon the combination of a carbonized thread contained in a sealed vacuum. This model burned for 40 continuous hours. Edison was overjoyed, especially when he discovered that the use of high-resistance filaments allowed him to achieve parallel circuits.

In spite of a surprising amount of professional criticism, Edison continued his work and eventually staged a public demonstration of his newest invention, rigging a series of outdoor lights around his laboratories. People traveled for miles to witness his wondrous invention, which lit the night skies for the first time in history.

Unfortunately, the scientific community would have nothing to do with it, not even Edison's neighbor Professor Henry Morton. Refusing to go around the block and see for himself, Morton wrote that he felt the need "to protest in behalf of true science," and that Edison's work on the light bulb was "a conspicuous failure, trumpeted as a wonderful success. A fraud upon the public."[1]

Fortunately for Edison and the world at large, big-money people like J. P. Morgan and William Vanderbilt respected Edison enough to invest in his new invention in spite of the outcry from orthodox science. Unlike Edison's respected colleagues, the business tycoons knew a good thing when they saw it.

It is only natural that people are hesitant to accept new ideas. This is nothing new. Western science is full of such examples. People of status and power who have spent their lives and careers representing certain ideas and scientific models are naturally unwilling to accept new theories that change the way we think about the world. There's a lot of ego and status at stake. Sadly, there can also be a lot of money at stake as well, and money can dictate the behavior and ideals of the best of us, especially when billions of dollars are on the line.

Imagine for a moment that you have discovered an innovative way to generate energy, something so simple and so inexpensive that it could solve the energy woes of mankind for centuries to come. By rights, you should be championed as an international hero, maybe even get on *The Tonight Show*! But wait! Energy is big, big business. How do you think the oil companies, electric and nuclear power people, coal and natural gas producers, and others involved in the business of modern energy production would react? Surely you're not so naive as to think they would welcome you with open arms? We're talking about something that could wipe them out, crash their stocks, make them obsolete, shake the world's economy to the very core. No, the powers-that-be would never permit that, not if they could stop it. You see, this scenario has already occurred. Big business can't allow such a thing to happen, so what they do is simple. They do to you what they did to Martin Fleischmann and Stanley Pons, the scientists who discovered cold fusion.

Energy production has been a royal pain for mankind, one could imagine, ever since there was an early Neolithic hunter who stumbled into a pile of mastodon dung while gathering firewood. Today, with the skyrocketing worldwide demand for energy, it isn't getting any easier, either. We sure have some grand ideas, though. Humans have dreamed for centuries of harnessing the power of the sun, but photoelectric cells are currently too expensive for wide-scale application and are often not powerful enough in cooler climates with less sunshine.

Nuclear fission, once touted to be the energy savior of society, has proven to be a disappointment. In spite of President Eisenhower's promise to produce electricity that would be "too cheap to meter," nuclear fission has proven to be just the opposite—an expensive, dangerous game with minimal, disappointing results. However, if we could just harness the real secret of nuclear power, *nuclear fusion*, the process that fuels the stars, our energy woes would be solved.

Nuclear fission, the process used in nuclear power plants around the world, requires the expensive, heavy elements uranium and plutonium and produces dangerous wastes as by-products, materials that remain charged with deadly radioactivity for thousands of years. One advantage to it, though, is that it can be carried out in a reasonably simple chamber.

Nuclear *fusion*, on the other hand, is an entirely new ballgame. In this process of the stars, hydrogen atoms, in the form of plasma, fuse together to form the stable atom helium, something we all know from party balloons.

For decades now, some of the top physicists in the world have been exhaustively studying the process of hot fusion with no real solution in sight for how to harness it. No material on earth can act as a vessel to withstand the heightened temperatures and pressures required for nuclear fusion to occur. Although heroic efforts have been tried using magnetic fields as containment vessels, nothing has worked so far.

With this background in mind, imagine the shock when, in March 1989, two scientists announced during a press conference at the University of Utah that they had achieved something unimaginable—*cold fusion*, the production of usable amounts of energy from water in a jar at ordinary, room temperatures! The headlines circled the globe and sent the scientific world, both amateur and professional, into a frenzy.[2]

The usual protocol would have been to submit a paper to a journal like *Nature*, where it would be reviewed by peers in the same scientific discipline. But Professor Martin Fleischmann of Southampton University and Professor Stanley Pons of the University of Utah, a former student of Fleischmann's, had taken the unusual step, perhaps with some suggestion from superiors, of making their paradigm-smashing discovery known to the world through a press conference. There was method to their madness, however.

For starters, Fleischmann and Pons were electrochemists, not physicists. Unfortunately, their discovery of cold fusion was outside the box of chemists, deep into the territory of fusion physics. The two scientists were rightfully concerned that their work might not be the flavor of the month with fusion experts, who might skewer their chances at publishing in a top physics journal just out of spite (and anti-chemist prejudice).

And then, there was the little matter of money. Consider that this was potentially Nobel Prize–winning, billionaire-producing stuff. The patents and developmental head start resulting from the first workable fusion, hot or cold, would likely be the most lucrative discovery in the history of mankind, because the technology would supply the world's energy needs for generations to come. With billions of dollars on the line, Fleischmann and Pons were taking no chances that they and the University of Utah would not be the benefactors of such a magnificent—if puzzling—discovery. Something this big required a change in protocol.

What Fleischmann and Pons had discovered was, if proven to be repeatable, extraordinarily profound. With equipment that was later valued at less than two hundred dollars, the good professors made a startling find. They filled a glass jar with "heavy water" (the deuterium-rich water of World War II nuclear development fame), inserted electrodes made of platinum and palladium, and dropped in a few lithium salts for good measure. When they switched on the juice, approximately 50 percent more energy was produced in the form of excess heat than was supplied as electricity. All in an ordinary beaker at room temperature.

No chemical process could account for such a high yield of energy, so the scientists considered the next amazing possibility. It must be a *nuclear* process, they concluded. On later evidence, they proclaimed it nuclear fusion. Since it occurred at room temperatures they called it "cold fusion," the first reported case in history! The energy yield approached that of a conventional nuclear reactor without the gigantic cost and dangerous waste materials. Could this be the magic answer so long awaited for the world's energy woes?

It appeared that it could, and for a month or so Fleischmann and Pons were the darlings of the media. The headlines flashed around the world, but because of the secrecy inherent in patent-worthy discoveries, the details were slow in coming. The two professors were even on TV, with an ordinary Mason jar filled with nearly boiling water, heated by the mysterious nuclear fusion occurring under such simple circumstances.

Almost overnight, Texas A&M and Brigham Young Universities reported similar findings. Steve Jones at Brigham Young even revealed his team had been achieving similar results for years, but the energy outputs had been too small for practical application. A month after the original announcement, Robert Huggins of Stanford University reported he had duplicated Fleischmann and Pons's results and added a control jar of ordinary tap water.[3] The experimental device produced a whopping 50 percent more energy than the control jar. Huggins had placed the devices in a red plastic picnic cooler during the test. The press had a field day!

Things were on the move and by April 1989, when the American Chemical Association had its annual meeting in Dallas, Fleischmann and Pons surely were feeling heady with success. The energy production was approaching that of conventional nuclear fission, and Pons had detected some crucial data that confirmed the fusion process: the existence of tritium, another isotope of hydrogen, and the presence of gamma rays and helium. When the power to the jar was cut, the gamma radiation stopped, too! Things were looking up.

By the end of April, Fleischmann and Pons found themselves standing before the U.S. House Science, Space, and Technology Committee, requesting a nice, round sum of $25 million with which to start a center for cold fusion research. They must have felt like rock stars, but their ratings were just about to go way down.

I'm going to let you draw your own conclusions about the next chain of events. Suddenly, in spite of reports of replication around the world, the scientific community was skeptical. In spite of finding gamma rays, tritium, and helium in samples where there were none to start with—a direct indication nuclear fusion was taking place—the powers-that-be decided that no . . . it was not. Seemingly overnight, many of the labs that initially reported success with Fleischmann and Pons's simple apparatus were now changing their stories.

The press picked up on it and, by the early summer of 1989, cold fusion was being discussed as a "flawed idea." Things were starting to look bad, and then the coup de grace was delivered by that bastion of engineering and technological science, the Massachusetts Institute of Technology (MIT).

By the early summer of 1989, MIT had investigated the cold fusion phenomenon, and Dr. Richard Petrasso of MIT's Plasma Fusion Center reported the findings of Fleischmann and Pons were most likely a "glitch" and suggested there may have been no gamma radiation at all. He stated, "We can offer no plausible explanation for the feature other than it is possibly an instrumental artifact with no relation to gamma ray interaction." After that, the director of the Plasma Fusion Center, Dr. Ronald Parker, also commented, "We're asserting that their neutron emission was below what they thought it was, including the possibility that it could have been none at all."[4]

There was an ironic twist to it all. If Parker had stopped there, the subject of cold fusion probably would have slipped away to be rediscovered another day. Instead, he went for the jugular, attempting to discredit Fleischmann and Pons personally by planting a story in the *Boston Herald* that accused them of fraud and "scientific schlock."

The story caused quite a bit of excitement in Boston, and Parker later tried to change it and accuse the writer, Nick Tate, of embellishing the negative comments. Tate simply produced his original transcripts of the interview, where Parker had indeed used the word "fraud" numerous times. Parker was about to feel the sting of his own bad karma.

It started with the chief science writer in MIT's press office, Dr. Eugene Mallove. The good doctor was hip to Parker's manipulation of the *Boston Herald*, and he didn't like it. As he and other insiders at MIT began to examine the in-house evidence, they found some startling facts.

The first graph from the MIT study of the experimental cold fusion apparatus did indeed show more heat produced than electricity put in, just as Fleischmann and Pons had stated. But when Mallove's team examined the graph of the control jar, they were surprised. *The two graphs were virtually identical!* Yet the control jar had contained just plain water, in which case no significant heat production would have been possible from fusion or anything else.

Although it was hard to accept, the evidence was staring them in the face. *MIT had cheated*, fudging the experimental data to discredit cold fusion! Even after so-called "data reduction" and statistical manipulation, there was no way the two graphs could appear identical, unless, of course, they were *made* to look that way. Unfortunately, it was this very data that was eventually used by the U.S. Department of Energy and the U.S. Patent Office to deny cold fusion.

Eugene Mallove became so disgusted that he resigned from MIT at a public meeting and openly accused the institution of submitting fudged experimental data with the precise intention of discrediting cold fusion. After all the smoke had cleared and the news of MIT's fiasco had spread around the world, the MIT representatives attempted to save face with the usual song and dance about data reduction, finally changing their official stance of being "unable to reproduce [the experiment of] Fleischmann-Pons" to the more innocuous statement that the results were "too insensitive to confirm."[5]

Normally, that would be the end of that. However, it's hard to suppress something that has genuine value and, by all accounts, the process of cold fusion does. In spite of the U.S. House Committee recommendation, in spite of the MIT debacle, and in spite of the rejection by the Department of Energy and the U.S. Patent Office, the research and development of cold fusion is growing by leaps and bounds. Let's examine some facts.

Within four years after the original announcement by Fleischmann and Pons, cold fusion had been reproduced and documented by ninety-two different groups in ten countries throughout the world. A team at Stanford Research Institute (yes, the SRI of remote viewing fame), led by Dr. Michael

McKubre, reported that they had successfully replicated the cold fusion process and could produce excess energy at will. But there's more.

Cold fusion has been confirmed at the following institutions: Los Alamos National Laboratory, Oak Ridge National Laboratory, the U.S. Naval Research Laboratory, the Naval Air Warfare Center Weapons Division at China Lake, the Naval Ocean Systems Center, Texas A&M University, and California Polytechnic Institute, where Dr. Robert Bush and associates have achieved levels of energy production thirty times greater than the power density of nuclear fuel rods in a typical fission plant.[6]

The Electric Power Research Institute was deeply involved in cold fusion research and had allocated millions of dollars by the mid-1990s. Additionally, a consortium of five major utility companies has budgeted $25 million for further research. Commercial companies are well into development of 10-kilowatt cold fusion heating devices for home use. They are expected to be available on the open market soon.[7]

It certainly appears that a lot of attention has been paid to something that officially doesn't work. *Nature* still continued the criticism of cold fusion, running an editorial in the March 1990 issue replete with phrases such as "farewell (not fond) to cold fusion," "discreditable to the scientific community," "a shabby example for the young," and "a serious perversion of the process of science."[8] There is a change in the air, however. A July 17, 2007, broadcast on the History Channel was of particular interest. During the program *Doomsday Tech I*, both cold and hot fusion were mentioned. It was refreshing to see cold fusion discussed in a positive light. The narrator stated, "Although largely discredited in the past, it is now being examined again . . . and studies at SRI International have shown cold fusion to create *30 times the energy yield of the same amount of gasoline!*"[9] (The italics are mine.) Dr. Eugene Mallove knew there was something to it all, and for fifteen years he continued the fight, traveling the world to promote cold fusion as something he believed could save mankind, allowing energy for all of us. And then something terrible happened.

After single-handedly convincing the U.S. Department of Energy to reexamine the process of cold fusion, Mallove, who was beloved by all who knew him, was found bludgeoned to death on May 14, 2004. Officials have no leads and no clues in the murder. The only explanation had been a highly suspicious "landlord-tenant" dispute, something all who knew him say is absurd. Perhaps cold fusion works *too* well.

During the summer of 1976, Americans were well into their year-long celebration of the United States bicentennial. There were picnics, parties, and pie-eating contests across the land, but the folks at NASA were in a jovial mood for a different reason. Viking Orbiter I had made a successful rendezvous with the planet Mars and was busy photographing the surface of the Red Planet, searching for suitable landing sites for Viking Orbiter II, a robot craft that would be launched from Viking Orbiter I to make the first soft landing on Mars.

After launching its precious cargo, Viking Orbiter I continued to sweep across the Martian landscape at an altitude of 1,000 miles, taking thousands of unprecedented photographs. The planetary scientists were in a fever of excitement. These would be the first extensive images from the surface of Mars, the planet of myth and fable from time immemorial, the only heavenly body in our solar system besides our own likely to support life.

On the thirty-fifth orbit, while the spacecraft was photographing an area known as *Cydonia* about 41 degrees above the current equator of Mars, something occurred that no one was prepared for. There were thousands of images to analyze, in a process that would take years of scientific study by many, many experts, but when imaging technician Toby Owen first spotted a certain frame, something about it caught his eye. He was crawling on his hands and knees over images that carpeted the floor, examining them with a magnifying glass, when his gaze stuck on that frame, numbered 35A72. In that moment, he felt a chill run down his spine and the hair stood up on the back of his neck. "Oh my God, look at this!" There, on an isolated, windblown mesa in the Cydonia region of

Mars, was . . . *a face* . . . an enormous humanoid face gazing solemnly out into space. It had to be huge to be visible from orbit, maybe a mile or more across, and much of it was in shadow, but it sure looked for all the world like a . . . *face*!

Naturally, no one at NASA really thought it was a face. After all, it was a lot more likely to be the creation of natural forces than of little green men. In a press conference shortly afterward, Viking project scientist Gerry Soffen flashed a slide of the face, which was about to explode in press releases around the world, and remarked, "Isn't it peculiar what tricks of lighting and shadow can do? When we took a picture a few hours later it [the appearance of a face] all went away; it was just the way the light fell on it."[10]

There was a huge media presence for the conference, and among the reporters was a science writer of some note, Richard Hoagland—a brilliant man, passionate about science and technology, particularly space science. A friend of writer and inventor Arthur C. Clarke, Hoagland was the man personally responsible for the inclusion of a gold-plated message plaque on Pioneer 10, the first man-made device to leave our solar system. (Hoagland took the last-minute idea to the famed astronomer Carl Sagan, who had enough clout to get it included on the probe. The plaque included diagrams of humans and the solar system, as well as recordings of common earth sounds and music. NASA was even hip enough to include Chuck Berry's classic "Johnny B. Goode"!) Richard Hoagland didn't know it at the time, but his life was just about to take off in a new direction.

For two and a half years after the Mars mission, nothing happened with the mysterious image. Then two imaging experts named Vincent Di Pietro and Gregory Molenaar invented a new and improved technique to clean up electronic data, such as the Viking photos of Mars. Di Pietro had seen the picture of "the Face" and accepted the official ruling that it was all the result of erosion—that is, until he ran the data through his new process. The Face looked more like a face than ever, even showing evidence of pupils in the eyes and teeth in the dispassionate mouth. Puzzled and suspicious,

Di Pietro and Molenaar began to search for NASA's "other photo taken a few hours later."

It turned out that those few hours later, the Cydonia region of Mars was experiencing nighttime, when no decent images were possible. It was only after months of searching through the official images from NASA, which were available to the public, that they found another shot of Cydonia— misfiled, incidentally—that had been taken 35 days later, at an entirely different sun angle. Lo and behold, they still saw what looked like a face, carved out of a dry Martian mesa.

Di Pietro and Molenaar continued an exhaustive search for anything similar throughout the maze of Viking photographs and found nothing. Only the Face seemed to stand out, along with some nearby hills that seemed oddly symmetrical. They looked an awful lot like pyramids. It was time to hold a press conference. Unfortunately, the two men became involved in scientific turf wars between geologists and biologists until things bogged down. The issue would likely have slipped from view had not Richard Hoagland happened to examine the images carefully with a magnifying glass. It was July 1983.

As Hoagland carefully explored the photos with magnification, he found himself becoming more and more convinced that the face, the pyramids, and a nearby area of parallel lines, redundant angles, and strange honeycomb-like cells—something he thought of as "the City"— were indeed structures of artificial origin. He comments, "I realized that I was looking at something that was either a complete waste of time, or the most important discovery of the 20th Century, if not of our entire existence on Earth."[11] Hoagland was hooked.

When it comes to analyzing something as puzzling and controversial as the Cydonia region, which could contain either very intriguing natural formations or ancient artificial structures of unknown origin, one must search for clues. Natural formations do not form straight lines. They do not form redundant angles. The new images had lots of both; in fact, the Cydonia region was literally teeming with formations that screamed artificial origin. The structures recalled Carl Sagan's comment about extraterrestrial life: "Intelligent life on Earth first reveals itself through the geometric regularity of its constructions"; Sagan, however, didn't seem to think the definition applied when the Cydonia region was considered.[12] That situation he compared to "those who see Jesus Christ in a tortilla chip."

In addition to the Face, there were dozens of other "mounds," "pyramids," and city-like formations. Any one of these objects, with the exception of the Face, if found at random in the Martian deserts, would have scarcely caused a moment's hesitation. It was the fact they were all within a single "complex" and, furthermore, precisely aligned to one another that made the idea of random erosional formation so remote.

Imaging specialist Dr. Mark Carlotto spent years examining the data from the Cydonia region and became convinced that the features were of intelligent design. His resulting paper, featured on the cover of the May 1988 issue of *Applied Optics*, concluded with the following statement: "The results of the 3-D analysis show that the impression of facial features is not a transient phenomenon. Facial features are evident in the underlying topography and are shown to induce the visual impression of a face over a wide range of illumination conditions and perspectives."[13]

Later, reporters questioned Bill Rhodes—the editor of *Applied Optics* and an engineering professor at Georgia Institute of Technology—about the level of "science" contained in Carlotto's work. Rhodes replied, "Carlotto has been impartial and objective in the methods he chose to use; they were classical [imaging] techniques."[14] Like it or not, the Face appeared to be real. Now, if Hoagland could only get NASA to agree. The problem continues to this day, and it is the reason why I've included this story in this particular chapter.

The chain of events following the time Hoagland first brought the Cydonia region to the attention of the world reads almost like a pulp mystery novel. For whatever reason, NASA went to a lot of trouble to avoid budging on their position that Cydonia was just an odd geological formation. For starters, they simply . . . *lied*.

For years NASA officials insisted they had other images of Cydonia that demonstrated the "tricks of light and shadow" they kept talking about. For some strange reason, however, those images never seemed to be available. Finally, years after the initial discovery, the truth came out. There *were* no other images, at least none that showed the features to be a pile of rubble. There were plenty of images with something that looked like a face, though. Future missions to Mars were already on the planning books. Many voices asked, "Just please, please take some more images so we can clear this matter up once and for all." It would seem to be a reasonable request.

Another mission had indeed been scheduled for Mars already, the Mars Observer spacecraft that would launch in 1993. Initially no photographic cameras were included in the mission plan, but after public interest in the "face and pyramids of Cydonia" had grown to such mammoth proportions that they could no longer be ignored, a high-tech Malin camera was included in the mission profile, a device that could acquire images fifty times sharper than the original equipment.

While lecturing about the wondrous merits of the camera and the upcoming mission at a technical college in Michigan, Dr. James Zimbelman, a formal member of the Mars Observer team, remarked on the fine studies of Martian geology that would result. Finally, the inevitable happened. An audience member asked the Big One: "Given, as you say, the superb nature of the new camera on the [Mars Observer] spacecraft—are you planning to take new pictures of 'the Face and Pyramids'?" Astoundingly, Zimbelman replied, "We'd like to . . . but we can't *focus* the camera."[15]

Finally, after numerous setbacks, official arguments, and a congressional investigation, as well as many unusual events concerning the launch itself, the vehicle approached Mars. In what was perhaps the strangest event in the brief history of space exploration, the Mars Observer, just six days short of entering an orbit around Mars, suddenly, without any warning at all . . . simply . . . *disappeared*!

Based upon a startling series of events, Hoagland became convinced that insiders at NASA had deliberately staged the "disappearance" of the

Observer so that they could convert its flight into a stealth mission. Big Brother wanted to check out Cydonia without any public knowledge or interference. If this is true, the big question remains—*why*?

It is important to realize that by the time of the Mars Observer mission, the existence and controversy surrounding the Face had grown to the point where it had become an item of pop culture. Even the average Joe on the street knew about it, and most thought it was a genuine artificial structure. This being the case, the measures NASA took to avoid the subject of the Monuments of Mars (a name popularized by Hoagland's book of that title) bordered on neurosis. It wasn't long before somebody noticed. The somebody was Dr. Stanley V. McDaniel, professor of epistemology and chair of the Department of Philosophy at Sonoma State University in northern California.

Epistemology is a major branch of philosophy that studies how we know what we know, how science itself works. Dr. McDaniel took an interest in Hoagland's 17-year study of the Cydonia area, and, more importantly, in NASA's reaction to the subject, particularly their insistent stonewalling on the matter of a future, in-depth reexamination. McDaniel, who like any reasonable person felt as though this topic should be of the utmost importance to NASA, thought the space agency's behavior itself warranted a bit of further examination.

He did exactly that, publishing the results of his exhaustive, year-long study under the impressive title *The McDaniel Report: On the Failure of Executive, Congressional, and Scientific Responsibility in Investigating Possible Evidence of Artificial Structures on the Surface of Mars and in Setting Mission Priorities for NASA's Mars Exploration Program*.[16] It was McDaniel who finally got NASA to admit that there was no "other photograph" that proved their claim of the Face being just a "trick of light and shadow."

In the report, McDaniel made this exceptionally strong statement: "Because of the position NASA has taken, a massive failure of NASA's public responsibility is imminent. NASA may, in fact, be *about to commit one of the most egregious crimes against the ethics of science in all of history*."[17]

The report was hand delivered to NASA spokesperson Dr. Bevan French on Thursday, August 19, 1993. French refused to comment on it during a *Good Morning America* debate with Hoagland on August 22. However, worth noting is that it was less than forty-eight hours after NASA received copies of *The McDaniel Report* that radio contact was lost with the Mars Observer and it disappeared.

Of course, we have yet to comment on the really big question: *why*? Why would NASA and the U.S. government be so hesitant to sanction such an investigation? What was there about Cydonia and the Monuments of Mars that they went to such exhausting and unusual lengths to hide? Many feel the reason might be the supposed "shock" to society that would be caused by the revelation that we are not alone, with the rash of suicides and cultural unrest all the "experts" predict would result.

In fact, back in its infancy NASA itself had been involved in just such a study; the results appeared in a document known as the Brookings Report. When NASA was created by Congress in the 1958 Space Act, panels of experts throughout the country considered the potentially important implications of space travel. A 1959 study was commissioned by the Brookings Institution to deal with such issues, a year-long review that resulted in a 264-page document entitled "Proposed Studies on the Implications of Peaceful Space Activities for Human Affairs."

Near the end of the work was a section entitled "Implications of a Discovery of Extraterrestrial Life." After having mentioned that many experts considered it very likely that life exists elsewhere in the cosmos, Brookings scientists suggested that "artifacts left at some point in time by these life forms might possibly be discovered through our [future] space activities on the Moon, Mars, or Venus."[18] They suggested keeping such discoveries all tightly under wraps.

It appeared to most that the day had indeed come, and the folks at NASA were following the recommended advice to the letter. However, Hoagland thinks there's even more to the story. He believes that the true reason behind all the secrecy may be the potential discovery of something of monumental importance: an unlimited supply of energy, the intrinsic energy of the cosmos itself.

I have included the story of the Monuments of Mars for two reasons. The first is to establish the fact that science is often a bedfellow of politics. Of greater importance is the second reason, the possible verification of something the ancients have long spoken of, the existence of the subtle energy that permeates the cosmos. Richard Hoagland believes that he and his crew have found it.[19]

In a sense, it all goes back to sacred geometry. For eons, sages have stated that certain shapes contain or harness a cosmic energy. Some think this geometry is the underlying reason for why our system of measurement is based on units of 60, such as the 360 degrees contained in a circle, or our measures of time, with 60 seconds in a minute, 60 minutes in an hour, and so on.

For centuries scholars have wondered why the ancients chose this particular series, seemingly plucking it out of the air at random. After years of study, Hoagland and his associates discovered that Cydonia displays much of the same geometry seen in ancient structures in Egypt, China, Mexico, and Greece. In particular, they noted the importance of an *inscribed tetrahedron*

The most basic of the ancient Platonic solids is a tetrahedron, a perfect example of which is the Great Pyramid at Giza. Encase the pyramid in a huge sphere and you have a "circumscribed tetrahedron." If a corner of the pyramid is located on the north or south polar axis of a rotating sphere, then the other corners align at 19.5 degrees either north or south of the equator of the sphere. Hoagland found these particular values evident again and again at Cydonia, including the physical location of the Cydonia complex itself.

Other researchers have found that energy centers exist on Jupiter and Neptune at this precise location—19.5 degrees. In the case of Jupiter, it's the Great Red Spot; on Neptune, the Great Dark Spot. *And both of these giant planets radiate into space more energy than they receive from the Sun.*[20] In fact, the Sun itself seems to follow this rule. The peak location of the eleven-year sunspot activity occurs at . . . you guessed it . . . 19.5 degrees north or south of the solar equator. Even here on earth, natural formations seem to follow this finding. The largest volcanic "upwelling" on our planet, the Hawaiian Shield Volcano, lies at exactly 19.5 degrees, as do the two largest known active volcanoes on Venus—Alpha and Beta Regio.

Although these are just some of the parallels Hoagland's group has found, they collectively lead to something that, to Hoagland's mind, is of vast importance: the belief that Cydonia holds the key to the legendary energy so common and so emphasized in sacred ancient writings. And it all may just have been done on purpose.

Hoagland and crew have come to the conclusion that the Cydonia complex was built, among other reasons, as a marker to others, perhaps the citizens of earth, as an eventual tool to educate us about this most basic characteristic of ourselves and our world. The gigantic humanoid face, gazing out onto the heavens, would indeed serve as a marker, something to get our attention when the time came.

If this is indeed the case, then the Face has already served its intended purpose. It was found in 1976. Since then, NASA and the government have been acting strangely, leaving us with a question: are they just following the original guidelines of *The Brookings Report*, or are they afraid for us to know what they've found? After all, the truth might just set us free.

Up to now we've discussed matters concerned with conventional science, and more specifically the reluctance of the scientific establishment to accept new concepts if they stray too far from the current version of the Truth. If you think recognized scientists and institutions receive brutal treatment, just imagine the witch hunt that results when the psychic world is considered. Some establishment members have become so offended they created an organization to investigate and discredit psychical research.

Such is the case with the Committee for the Scientific Investigation of Claims of the Paranormal, the fabulous CSICOP (pronounced "psi cop"— get it?). Established in 1976, the organization changed its name in 2006 to the Committee for Skeptical Inquiry (CSI), but I prefer the snappier acronym; besides, it's truer to the organization's attitude.

To understand the mentality behind CSICOP, we have to backtrack a hundred years or so. By the late nineteenth century, paranormal and psychical research had become firmly entrenched in both America and Great Britain. Although shunned by orthodox science, there was a growing movement interested in the unexplained events that seemed such a part of human existence. As with so many other topics with religious or spiritual overtones, feelings ran deep both for and against psychic phenomena and the paranormal.

Those who believed in the possibility of psychic events wanted further research conducted. But among those who disbelieved in it, the responses ranged from mild disgust to absolute hatred. In their view, and for several decades into the twentieth century, things weren't too bad. Then the New Age movement came along in the 1960s and really mucked things up. Before that time, the paranormal had been just an obsession of a few crackpots, but now . . . now it was mainstream! The popular media were having a field day with all this hogwash! Expanded consciousness, love-ins, rock music, robes, beads, Shirley MacLaine . . . what nonsense! Something had to be done to smooth the ruffled feathers of the humanists, atheists, and science junkies who were so aggravated by this sort of thing.

A small group was already waiting in the wings. At first they called themselves Resources for the Scientific Evaluation of the Paranormal, or RSEP, and were rather low key, although their views on the paranormal were said to range "from moderate skepticism to militant hostility."[21] The original members were writer Martin Gardner, psychologist Ray Hyman, magician James "The Amazing" Randi, and sociologist Marcello Truzzi, who also published their newsletter *The Zetetic*, which dealt with academic research into occultism and the paranormal.

By 1975, when RSEP was first getting together, philosopher Paul Kurtz, a professor at the State University of New York at Buffalo and editor of *The Humanist* magazine, was upset by the growing popularity of astrology. Kurtz collected one hundred eighty-six signatures from scientists opposed to astrology and put together a brief paper entitled "Objections to Astrology." It got a lot of attention, including an item on the front page of the *New York Times*.

Thus the stage was set for the formation of CSICOP, although not before a bit of initial criticism was offered by, of all people, famed astronomer Carl Sagan, who would later be a member of CSICOP himself. Sagan wrote a letter to *The Humanist* in response to the article "Objections to Astrology." In it he stated:

> I find myself unable to endorse the "Objections to Astrology" statement . . . not because I feel that astrology has any validity whatever, but because I felt and still feel that the tone of the statement is *authoritarian*. The fundamental point is not that the origins of astrology are shrouded in superstition. *This is true as well for chemistry, medicine, and astronomy, to mention only three.* To discuss the psychological motivations of those who believe in astrology seems to be quite peripheral to the issue of validity. . . . Statements contradicting borderline, folk, or pseudoscience that appear to have an authoritarian tone can do more damage than good. They never convince those who are flirting with pseudoscience but *merely seem to confirm their impression that scientists are rigid and closed-minded*" [italics added].[22]

This argument is important because, in the near future, this very same conflict would cause significant internal strife within the fledgling organization. Later, one writer would say, "Although they were operating in the name of science, theirs was not in any traditional sense a 'scientific' enterprise but an ideological, political, or even—to the extent that the humanist agenda was being served—theological one."[23]

The problem was that the leadership saw only black and white. They collectively lumped the occult, bona fide religious beliefs, and popular paranormal topics into the same category as serious parapsychological research and disliked them all equally. I would like to think that a reasonable person might see a slight difference between someone chasing the Loch Ness monster and the excellent work done at Princeton by Robert Jahn and his associates on psychokinesis.

On the other hand, we have a man like Marcello Truzzi, skeptical of the paranormal to be sure, but open to the serious investigation of psychic and paranormal topics. In an article in *Fate* magazine, a leading paranormal publication, Truzzi admitted that some paranormal subjects were "amenable to investigation and justification just like any scientific statement."[24] So the stage was set, and when Paul Kurtz learned of Truzzi and RSEP, he contacted him immediately with a deal to join forces in what would become CSICOP.

Truzzi was initially concerned by the fact that he himself was not a humanist and did not share in humanistic beliefs. He was also worried about Kurtz's zealous attacks on paranormal subjects. Truzzi agreed to help if such topics were investigated fairly, but he was not interested in being part of a rabid debunking campaign. Kurtz assured Truzzi that he and his colleagues would indeed be fair and impartial. Truzzi was enlisted, and he even allowed *The Zetetic* to become CSICOP's official publication, though the name was quickly changed to the *Skeptical Enquirer*, the popular magazine we see today.

It wasn't long before Truzzi realized that he had been misled and that the true goal of CSICOP was to debunk anything smacking of the paranormal. He resigned his position as cochairman in August 1977. Shortly afterward, Kurtz and crew went after NBC television and *Reader's Digest* for giving favorable coverage to psychic topics. One CSICOP official, a magician named Milbourne Christopher, made the statement that more than two hundred people around the world had killed themselves over disappointing horoscopes or unfavorable palm readings. The media struck back, however, and when this claim could not be documented, CSICOP never used this bit of verbal ammunition again.

CSICOP gained considerable power, though, because they were able to recruit some serious scientists to their cause, although the only ones recognizable to the public were celebrity scientist Carl Sagan and behavioral psychologist B. F. Skinner. It is important to note that, with the partial exception of Sagan, who had investigated UFO phenomena and had written a paper critical of Immanuel Velikovsky of *Worlds in Collision* fame, *none of these people had any experience whatsoever in paranormal or psychic phenomena!* Additionally, several members had no scientific background at all, including magician James Randi; aviation journalist Philip Klass, a critic of UFO study; and one of the founders, Martin Gardner, an author on science and related topics who had long been a critic of anything outside solidly orthodox beliefs.

The irony of it all is that any parapsychological researcher would absolutely *love* for his or her work to be the subject of serious, orthodox scientific investigation. Robert Jahn used to comment how disappointing it was to achieve such monumental data, as he did during the Princeton PEAR program, and then be unable to convince his colleagues simply to walk across the lawn of the Princeton campus and examine his results.

Only once did CSICOP attempt any scientific research. It concerned Paul Kurtz's favorite pet peeve, astrology. Needless to say, astrology has been a stone in the craw of orthodox science since the beginning of . . . orthodox science. From a strictly mechanistic view, it makes no sense at all. Heavenly bodies, basically huge chunks of dead rock, perhaps with a sliver of gaseous atmosphere, millions of miles away, having a direct bearing on the living? Heck, even the minute gravitational effects would be too tiny to measure. Utter nonsense. However, I hope it is evident by now that not everything in this world can be explained by the current paradigm, and astrology is no exception.

One key to the importance of astrology is longevity. A belief in astrology, in different forms, has been part of human society for as far back as we care to look. It predates written history and is found across time and across cultures worldwide. It is my opinion that the ancients knew more about some aspects of reality than we do today, and that when a discipline has been kept around for that long, it is because it has genuine value.

If we accept the modern theories that everything is energy, which is exactly what ancient religions have maintained for eons, then the enormous energy fields from stars and planets interact with the fields of everything else. Isn't this what astrology is saying? If future studies show that astrology has validity, then it should be seriously considered as a genuine phenomenon, even if some consider it distasteful. That's what French researchers Michel and Françoise Gauquelin thought about their revolutionary study on the "Mars effect."[25]

The familiar astrological signs are "sun signs" that relate to the sun's placement in the constellations of the zodiac known since ancient times, such as Aquarius, Taurus, Libra, and Pisces. However, astrology also takes into account many other factors, such as the effects of the moon and the planets. In current interpretations, those born during the time Mars is rising or transiting are said to have naturally superior physical abilities— the Mars effect.

Of course, if one were skeptical, it would be a relatively simple matter to survey a large group of top jocks and compile the data to see whether a disproportionate number were in fact born under the Mars sign. That is precisely what the Gauquelins did, back in the late 1970s. The French psychologists, a married couple who have since parted ways, indeed found that a statistically significant number of world-class athletic champions were born with Mars in this special position.

But when the results eventually got to CSICOP, they did not agree. Kurtz, statistician Marvin Zelen, and astronomer George Abell compiled a study of American champion athletes. They were quick to claim no apparent "Mars effect" in their study and were just as quick to report their findings in the *Skeptical Enquirer*. Although the Gauquelins were outraged and claimed the study was flawed, it made little difference. CSICOP's star was rising (I'm sorry—I couldn't resist!) and their fans in the scientific world were apparently happy.

For a while all was good, in CSICOP terms. Then an exiled CSICOP insider, Dennis Rawlins, a planetary-motion specialist and an original member of CSICOP's executive council who was canned in December 1979, published an article in *Fate* magazine entitled "sTARBABY." The following account tells it best:

> Rawlins reported that the CSICOP test of the Mars effect on a sample of American athletes had been botched from the beginning and that Kurtz, Abell, and Zelen had repeatedly ignored his warnings. *When the results came in, confirming the Mars effect, the three CSICOP officials covered them up and eventually so distorted them that it appeared the results had disproved the Mars effect.* As this was going on, Rawlins repeatedly but futilely warned CSICOP officials that the test was being poorly and even dishonestly handled. According to his account, CSICOP notables including Kurtz, Abell, Gardner, Randi, Klass, and Frazier seemed concerned only that he keep quiet. When Rawlins refused to drop the issue, he was removed from the organization [italics added].[26]

What may immediately come to mind is that Rawlins was simply a disgruntled employee with a personal axe to grind. However, an independent investigation conducted by Patrick Curry, notably well before Rawlins's article appeared in print, concurred that CSICOP *cheated*—mishandling the entire study. He stated that CSICOP's "work could now best function as a model and a warning of how not to conduct such investigations."[27] A former CSICOP member named Richard Kammann, a New Zealand psychologist, reached a similar conclusion, and it was reported by Marcello Truzzi in his *Zetetic Scholar*. And then, finally, the guilty parties themselves came out of the closet, admitting that "errors" had been made and that CSICOP would retire from the scientific investigation business, after this episode of bungling had been made public through a controversy reported by the popular media and scientific journals.

The bottom line, of course, is that CSICOP is an advocacy group for a particular point of view. Paul Kurtz's humanist zeal against religion and all things of a spiritual nature has grown to include aspects of legitimate science as well. With the support of many respected scientists, and the success of the *Skeptical Enquirer,* CSICOP continues to thrive.

The really intriguing question about the common response by members of the scientific orthodoxy to areas they disagree with is ... *why*? Why do they go to such lengths to disprove, to eradicate, to destroy the topics they don't like? Psychologists have taken note of this and similar examples of human behavior over the years and have discovered that it lies rooted in an important area—*belief.* In many ways our belief system functions as a filter, a qualifier through which we "judge" the phenomena of our world, including our sensory information.

Belief systems can actually make us see a physical object in an incorrect way. A novel study was reported in the *Journal of Personality.* The authors, psychologists J. S. Bruner and Leo Postman, designed a clever experiment to test this idea.[28] They took decks of ordinary playing cards and changed their color or configuration. For example, a normally black card such as a spade was changed to red, keeping, however, the same numeric suit, or vice versa for a normally red card, such as a diamond or heart. The altered cards were shuffled back in with the rest, and the altered deck was given to the test subjects, who briefly examined it. If the subjects were only allowed brief glances, they invariably reported the deck to be normal. It really got interesting, however, when the subjects were allowed longer and longer periods of examination.

What the psychologists found was that, eventually, if enough time were allowed, most subjects would recognize that some of the cards were incorrect. What the psychologists weren't prepared for were the *emotional responses* they observed. Some subjects actually became angry, others upset. Some could never figure out why they were annoyed by the incorrect cards, and some 10 percent of the subjects never saw the cards for what they really were, even after being exposed for forty times the normal amount of time required. Even the experimenters themselves reported being upset. Leo Postman complained to a colleague that "though [he knew] all about the apparatus and display in advance, he nevertheless found looking at the incongruous cards acutely uncomfortable."[29]

About this time, another group of psychologists at Stanford University were also examining the importance of belief and its effects on behavior. Leon Festinger and associates formulated the theory of *cognitive dissonance*. They proposed it as the mechanism by which we cope with any discrepancies we may stumble upon between how we think and feel, and between what we believe and other information that may contradict that belief.

In other words, we hold—for numerous reasons—certain beliefs concerning our little corner of reality. If we are presented with data that are in opposition to our beliefs, we experience a "dissonance," a sense of distress. Since this dissonance is uncomfortable, we seek to reduce it in various ways, and such attempts are perhaps the key to much of the behavior displayed by orthodox science that we have discussed up to now.

When it came to examples of social disagreement, Festinger advanced three mechanisms he felt many people use to reduce areas of dissonance. One is to change our own opinion to more closely match that of the group, a strategy he felt explains the behavior of much of the general population. People often show a tendency to work toward a consensus viewpoint. We are social animals, and we want others to agree with us. The second mechanism is to attempt to change the opinions of others in an effort to get them to agree with our own. But the third mechanism is the most interesting: Festinger found that, if one's perception of dissonance were sufficiently high, then the subject would often *find fault with the individual causing the dissonance*. We have already seen numerous examples of this mechanism at work. When paranormal or psychic phenomena are involved, such a reaction is almost the default for orthodox science.

By the very nature of what scientists are attempting to do, they should be open-minded, skeptical of some things to be sure, but open nonetheless to whatever evidence presents itself. Many are, but much of the leadership is not.[30] Certain personality types seem to desire positions of authority. Often these people are not necessarily the most knowledgeable about their field or the best suited to getting things done. Rather, they are people skilled at playing The Game. To me, leadership in science seems much like leadership in the military, where the real hard-chargers, the professional warriors who can lead men on the battlefield, often aren't politically astute enough to make the higher ranks. Instead, many of the top generals are politicians first and warriors second, if at all. What often happens as a result—although certainly not in all cases—is that staff officers who are highly skilled at ticket punching, socializing, and the like are the ones who end up in top leadership positions.

I strongly suspect science operates in much the same way, with those who can really perform limited to the lab or work bench, either by choice or by lack of the proper political skills. So, we end up with authoritarians in positions of authority, people who enjoy, perhaps a bit *too* much, the power and prestige that accompanies these positions. And guess what, folks? According to studies, these are exactly the types most resistant to change, to innovation!

Ordinary taxpayers such as you and me have no say in such things, the belief being that we're too ignorant of the lofty field of scientific endeavor to know why and how the money should be spent. With all this in mind, is it any wonder that there's a stigma attached to anything to do with energy medicine, psychic research, or the vital force? They're nonmaterialistic and nonreductionistic. Current science simply cannot handle the dissonance.

When all is said and done, the catch phrase of the early twenty-first century could be "*There is no scientific evidence to support. . . .*" In our times, that's all it takes to squelch investigation and hide the truth—as long as the declaration comes from the proper source, of course. How many times in recent years have we seen the same, tired old nonsense on scientific studies? Ideas fall in and out of fashion as quickly as the changing seasons. So much of scientific inquiry is politically based. Often, small, insufficient studies are promoted by the media to sway public opinion, while major works of an unpopular nature languish. "There's no scientific evidence to support" . . . lots of things, but they're still here, still part of our world. It may be the most currently misused phrase in the English language.

The bottom line in science is the same as in all human endeavors—*money and power*. Funds control science. Funding can be quickly cut from a young scientist who ventures into forbidden territory. Dollars are doled out to projects that are politically correct and withheld or denied for ideas that are deemed unsavory.

And the top journals, along with their editors, hold the keys to what is accepted science and what is not. The top scientific journals are some of the most powerful entities on earth. Although it may come as a shock, a surprisingly small number of people around the globe control what is— and isn't—science. And all too often, *science* is what those in charge want it to be.

CHAPTER TEN

A Path with Heart:
The Way Back Home

For me there is only the traveling on paths that have heart, on any
path that may have heart. There I travel, and the only worthwhile
challenge is to traverse its full length. And there I travel, looking,
looking, breathlessly.

— Don Juan, in Carlos Castaneda, *The Teachings of Don Juan*

The ancient Egyptians were obsessed with life after death. Of course, it could be said that all of us are to a point, but none quite like the Egyptians. They really went extra lengths to assure the proper passage from the world of the living to the plane of the afterlife. Their hieroglyphs are filled with detailed instructions about the proper preparations for the journey. They even prepared a book about it, a kind of owner's manual and travelogue rolled into one called the Egyptian Book of the Dead. How's that for a gripping title? But what really demonstrates their commitment is the thing Egypt is best known for, the one romantic notion that is known around the world, the stuff of Hollywood feature films and ancient legends . . . *mummies*!

Even today, with all the technology we're so proud of—with advanced knowledge of chemistry, magnetic resonance imaging, gas chromatography and the like—we still aren't sure exactly how the Egyptians achieved mummification. Their climate helped; hot, dry conditions by themselves go a long way toward making mummies. However, there's more to it than that; the process involved, by all accounts, a complicated, well-crafted procedure. After the body was ritually washed and perfumed, the internal organs were carefully removed for special processing. These precious tissues were placed in their own containers—solid gold jars in the case of the elite—and were arranged within the burial chamber with extra care.

The human heart was given exceptional attention, as a mark of the respect due to the organ the Egyptians believed was not only the center of emotion, but, more importantly, *the center of reason and thought as well!* On the other hand, about the brain, that unimaginably complex mass of neurons and supporting tissues, the ancient Egyptians were rather blasé. For this critical human organ, the Egyptians had no special plan, no golden chalice. Instead, the squashy mass was unceremoniously yanked through the nostrils and—without pomp, circumstance, or ceremony—dumped into the trash! The brain wasn't given a second thought. It was the heart that was held in high regard; and, just maybe in that respect, the Egyptians were onto something big, something we are just now beginning to rediscover.

Neurochemicals have now been found throughout the tissues of the human body. This fact brings to mind an interesting question: *why*? The short answer is that "thinking" occurs in many places in the body besides the brain. And if cells can "think," then are they also aware? Preposterous, you say? Maybe not. Memory also appears to be a function found throughout the tissues of the body, all the way down to the cellular level. Interestingly, the heart seems to be of special importance.

For eons, people have placed special significance on the heart as the seat of emotions. Science tells us, to the contrary, that emotion all takes place in the brain, that the heart is just simply a dual-action, four-chambered pump, nothing more. Yet all of us, at one time or another, have felt our own heartstrings plucked (there really are strings in the heart—the chordae tendineae, connective tissues that keep the mitral and tricuspid valves from prolapsing, at least most of the time). We have all experienced feelings of profound joy or sorrow and felt them exactly, precisely . . . *in the heart.*

Spiritually inclined people attribute this sensation to the heart chakra, which connects us from the physical plane to our higher energy bodies. Now we have some scientific evidence to corroborate this experience. We need briefly to examine the work of Paul Pearsall, Ph.D., a pioneer explorer of the world of "energy cardiology."[1]

For starters, the human heart is unique in several ways. It is composed of its own special type of muscle tissue, found only in the heart, which is called, appropriately enough, *cardiac muscle*. Besides having its own unique anatomical structure, the heart also has something other tissues don't have—an innate, inherent ability to beat, a capacity entirely independent of the brain or of any other portion of the nervous system.

A heart completely disconnected from the body and placed in a nutrient solution will continue to beat for a long time. Even more interesting is that if two hearts are placed in separate containers close together, in short order their beats will become synchronized, regulated by some unseen energy present in the tissues. If we find this phenomenon unusual, what are we to make of the recent reports from heart transplant patients who suddenly find themselves experiencing memories of their donors? Is this all just fantasy?

After working as a psychologist for hundreds of such cases, Paul Pearsall doesn't think so. Taking the lessons gained from years of working with heart transplant patients, he searched out others who were working with subtle energy and energy cardiology. He soon came upon the work of Gary Schwartz and Linda Russek. Schwartz is a professor of neurology, psychology, and psychiatry at the University of Arizona and director of the Laboratory for Advances in Consciousness and Health there. At the time Russek, who formerly taught at Harvard, was his assistant. The two scientists feel that, given the great complexity of living things, informational systems of some kind must be at work in biology, systems that modern science has failed to recognize. As a result, they have advanced their view of "info-energetics," the belief that biological energy is itself a form of information. Personally, I don't see how it could be any other way.

After combining modern biological concepts with the new findings of subtle energy and quantum mechanics, Schwartz and Russek concluded that the heart is an important center of energy in the body, and that this energy is a vital source of bioinformation. They developed their concept of energy cardiology into what they termed the "dynamic systems memory theory," which Pearsall describes as "the idea that all systems are constantly exchanging mutually influential energy, which contains information that alters the systems taking part in the exchange."[2] The theory is based upon four central hypotheses:

1. Energy and information are the same thing. Everything that exists has energy; energy is full of information; and stored info-energy is what makes up cellular memories.
2. What we call mind, consciousness, or our intentions are really manifestations of information-containing energy.
3. The heart is the primary generator of info-energy.
4. Because we are manifestations of the info-energy coming to, flowing within, and constantly being sent out from our total cellular systems, who and how we are is a physical representation of a recovered set of cellular memories.[3]

Whether or not the heart is the major center of informational energy is subject to debate, but one thing that *has* been demonstrated is the concept of cellular memory. Dr. Candace Pert is a former researcher at the National Institute of Mental Health, the author of *Molecules of Emotion*, and the star of the great film, *What the Bleep Do We Know?* She is also a world-renowned authority on neuropeptides, short protein strands that are active in the central nervous system and are at the very neurological core of memory. Her work is some of the first to demonstrate that these chemicals are active in the brain during emotional experiences. However, further study showed something that came as a shock.

Rather than just existing within the barriers of the brain, these special chemicals were found throughout the blood circulation system, floating to all areas of the body. But without the specialized receptor cells in the brain that the neuropeptides activate, it looked as though the neuropeptides were of no functional use to the organism as a whole. At least that was the thinking, until receptors were found to exist in many places throughout the body, including the heart (of course), the immune system, and even the gastrointestinal tract. As for her revolutionary findings, Dr. Pert commented:

> In the beginning of my work, I matter-of-factly presumed that emotions were in the head or brain. Now I would say they are really in the body as well. They are expressed in the body and are part of the body. I can no longer make a strong distinction between the brain and the body . . . the more we know about neuropeptides, the harder it is to think in the traditional terms of a mind and a body. It makes more and more sense to speak of a single integrated entity, a "body-mind."[4]

At a later date, when Pearsall discussed some of his ideas of memory transfer with heart transplantation, Pert was not at all surprised or inclined to disagree. Pearsall recalls, "She pointed out that, since the cells in the heart are loaded with molecules that necessarily contain at least some form of memory, these memories could well come along with the heart to join with the new body and brain."[5]

Almost from the very start of heart transplantation, strange things began to be reported. Granted, heart transplant patients have been through an extremely stressful, challenging ordeal; but even allowing for that reality, something profound seemed to be happening. One of the most unusual cases was related to Pearsall by a female psychiatrist who was attending an event where Pearsall was the keynote speaker. After the presentation, the psychiatrist approached Pearsall and began relating the event to him. In short order she began to cry gently and had difficulty discussing her experience, and within a few moments Pearsall understood why. As the psychiatrist described the event:

> I have a patient, an eight-year-old little girl who received the heart of a murdered ten-year-old girl. Her mother brought her to me when she started screaming at night about her dreams of the man who had murdered her donor. She said her daughter knew who it was. After several sessions, I just could not deny the reality of what this child was telling me. Her mother and I finally decided to call the police and, using the descriptions from the little girl, they found the murderer. He was easily convicted with evidence my patient provided. The time, the weapon, the place, the clothes he wore, what the little girl had said to him . . . everything the little heart transplant recipient reported was completely accurate.[6]

In another instance, a family physician named Glenda had been involved in a tragic automobile crash resulting in the death of her husband. Some years later, perhaps to bring things to a close, she sought to meet the young man who had been the recipient of her husband's heart. Pearsall made the arrangements and waited in the hospital chapel with Glenda for the appointment. After a half hour had elapsed, Pearsall suggested they leave, but Glenda was hesitant. Saying she "knew" her late husband's heart was nearby, she exclaimed, "Oh no, we have to wait. He's here in the hospital. I felt him come about thirty minutes ago. I felt my husband's presence. Please wait with me."

Glenda was correct. Almost immediately a young Hispanic man and his mother hurried into the chapel, explaining that they had had difficulty finding the room and had searched for half an hour. After introductions Glenda asked to feel her husband's former heart, and, as she did so, she softly said a prayer to her late husband with the words, "I love you David. Everything is copacetic." The mother and son were shocked. That word, *copacetic*, was the very first one the young man had uttered after awaking from anesthesia with his new heart!

Within the next few moments, they related how the young man's tastes had changed in other ways, as well. It seems, for instance, that while he had once been a practicing vegetarian, he now craved junk food. While he was formerly a heavy-metal rocker, he now only listened to vintage rock and roll. Moreover, he was frequently plagued with dreams of an automobile collision, with bright headlights getting closer and closer until a horrendous crash occurred. By the time Glenda verified that these characteristics were all specific to her late husband, everyone was in tears.

Glenda frequently experienced the very same dream. Although she was a highly trained physician, with all the science background that entails, she now became a believer in the phenomenon of cellular memory transference. She knew in her heart that it wasn't all just a matter of coincidence.

In another instance, a woman received a heart transplant and almost immediately began to complain of sharp, shooting pains in her lower back. The doctors explained the pain away as a response to surgery. However, years later she still suffered, awakening suddenly at night with shooting pains in her lumbar area. What's more, her husband noticed a significant change in her personal tastes; she now chose very feminine attire over the casual, unisex styles she had preferred before her surgery. And once they were able to resume sex, the wife seemed preoccupied with gay fantasies, asking her husband if he ever experienced them, too, which came as a shock. This went on for three years, at which time the woman met with the parents of the donor. He had been a young, gay artist who had died during a robbery. He was killed by a gunshot wound to the lower back.

Pearsall mentions that other organs, as well as the heart, seem to demonstrate the same odd behavior of having the capacity to transmit memory. Although the stories of heart transplant patients are often more dramatic than others, he states: "I have never spoken to a transplant recipient who did not have a story to tell"[7]

Besides the exciting stories of cellular memories and changing personalities associated with the heart, that organ seems to be of supreme importance in other ways as well, not the least of which is as a source of vitally important energy and information. We may tend to forget that the heart is an organ of considerable power. A wonderfully designed hydraulic pump, it sends the fresh, nutrient-laden blood from the lungs throughout the miles of tubes that comprise the vascular tree, contracting about once per second for every moment of our lives—sometimes a bit slower, sometimes a bit faster, but continuing with its job until it finally stutters to a stop and life itself stops with it.

There's a lot of kinetic energy associated with all this pumping, but what we're concerned with at the moment are the *other* forms of energy generated by the heart. For one thing, the heart is also an organ of *profound electromagnetic energies.* We all know of the legendary electrical activity of the brain, the wave patterns that are measured and evaluated via EEGs, but compared to the heart, the brain is an electro-magnetic pipsqueak.

Only in recent times have the electromagnetic fields of living things been generally recognized. Now we know that electromagnetism is an essential part of living things, as important as genetics, cellular respiration, or any of the dozens of processes that make up life.[8] And the heart is an organ of powerful electromagnetic activity, operating at a level five thousand times higher than that of the human brain.[9] We have spent significant portions of this book discussing the importance of electromagnetic fields as the organizing force within living things, so it shouldn't come as a shock to see such high values in the heart, the organ the ancients traditionally named as the real seat of the human experience.

Like so many before him, Pearsall became intrigued with the question of what coordinates the massive amounts of energy present in the human body. We know the brain does some of it, and the instructions from DNA are a major player, but part of the puzzle appears to be missing. Pearsall commented on the known energies at work, starting with the source of all cellular energy for living things, the molecule adenosine triphosphate (ATP), which fuels everything from elephants to E. coli:

> A very powerful, sensitive, centrally located instrument is required to coordinate the immense energy and information generated by the billions of cellular vibrations taking place every second of our life. Multiply two million vibrations of ATP molecules by 75 trillion cells, multiply that number by the 51 to 78 billion cycles per second at which human DNA resonates and conveys its information within each cell, and multiply yet again by the energetic vibrations of the sixty or so neuropeptides that are the biochemical means by which our emotional state is manifested throughout our body. The total number would be a very rough low estimate of the energy surging within you as you read these words.[10]

Based on his years of experience and on the work of Gary Schwartz and Linda Russek, Pearsall believes that the heart, in ways that are just now being understood, is the primary organizer of the body. He comments:

> Every cell is literally a mini-heart humming with the energy. The ultimate biomedical illusion has been the view that the body is made of solid matter with fluid pumped through it by an unconscious heart and a powerful conscious brain that is the primary controller of the entire system. Energy cardiology suggests, however, that the heart and not just the brain is what holds this system together by *a form of spiritual info-energy*, in a temporary and ever-changing set of cellular memories we refer to as "the self." This "self" is the dynamic gestalt of information that might be considered the code that constitutes our soul [italics added].[11]

Yes, Paul Pearsall also strongly believes in the Force. He chooses to call it *L* energy, as in *life energy*, but the meaning is the same. At other times he refers to it as the *fifth force*, the other four being the primary forces of the universe recognized by modern physics: electromagnetism, gravity, and the strong and weak forces of atomic attraction and decay.

The heart is also important within the context of these primary forces, particularly in terms of Pearsall's preference for following one's heart rather than one's brain. As he states, "The heart has its own form of wisdom, different from that of the rational brain but every bit as important to our living, loving, working and healing."[12] It is my personal belief that there are indeed two centers of focus in the body—the brain *and* the heart—but even if we take the idea of the heart as the center of consciousness simply as a metaphor, it still provides us with another perspective on life.

It is particularly interesting that Pearsall discusses heart problems, because cardiovascular disease has become the number-one killer in industrialized nations in just a few generations. At the beginning of the twentieth century, infectious diseases were still the primary cause of death. Halfway through the century they were replaced by cardiovascular problems—strokes and heart attacks. The traditional explanation for this change is the lack of exercise and activity resulting from the use of modern conveniences and the increased rate of atherosclerosis resulting from modern, high-fat junk diets. But there might be a little more to the picture.

In modern medicine the list of risk factors for heart disease includes high blood pressure, smoking, high cholesterol, and obesity. *Yet, half of the people who experience their first heart attack exhibit none of these factors.* And 80 percent of those with at least three of these factors never experience a heart attack. How do we explain these discrepancies? It would appear that some other dynamic is at work.

Pearsall discovered something interesting in the years he has worked with cardiovascular disease patients. He began to inquire about . . . *sex.* In many cases the victims of heart disease had often been celibate for long periods of time. Again and again he found that the patients had gone for a year or more without being intimate, even though most were married.

Pearsall had also worked for years as a sex counselor. He had been a director at the Kinsey Institute, had trained at the Masters and Johnson Institute, and had founded and directed a sexual dysfunction clinic in Michigan for several years. He knew a lot about human sexuality, and he was struck by the fact that so many victims of heart disease showed few of the traditional risk factors, yet had little if any sexual contact.

Pearsall immediately thought of the importance of sex to the flow of "L" energy, something we have already discussed regarding Wilhelm Reich. He became convinced of the relationship, and he felt even more confident when he discovered current research that backed up his hunch. More than 50 percent of heart attack patients had had no sexual contact of any kind for the entire year preceding their attack! This finding was published in 1996 in *JAMA*, yet the medical establishment ignored it.[13]

Another thread in the weave comes from Dr. Dean Ornish, a leading authority on heart disease. He appears frequently on television as a guest discussing the near epidemic of cardiovascular problems in the industrialized world. Among other factors, Ornish has found that anger is a major factor. Ornish is a cardiologist and a proponent of a change in lifestyle for heart patients, including diet and exercise; but he also advocates anger management and a more gentle style of interacting with others.

His research has shown that reducing stress and anger, along with other lifestyle modifications, can reduce arterial clogging without the need for invasive surgery. He is convinced that, in many cases, this is the road to take. Of course, many people are unwilling or unable to comply with significant lifestyle changes, and consequently the medical profession can continue to emphasize bypass surgery and other invasive techniques as their standard treatment.

Sexual abstinence in adults impedes the vital energy flow, as do anger and stress. All these states have a common result: they cause our muscles to tense. The result is a condition recognized both in ancient times and today; Reich called it *muscular armoring*. What we need is a change of heart and, perhaps most of all, to decide to follow our hearts. A path with heart is one of meaning; it is a choice to pursue worthwhile things in life rather than to lust after money, power, and material objects.

Our wondrous human brain has devised heaps of modern technology to make life "easier"— things like microwaves, cable TV, computers, push-button windows, heated car seats, cell phones, pagers, palm-sized computers, cordless phones, Internet banking and shopping and socializing and what have you—yet people report that they are busier and more stressed out than ever. They are working more hours than people did just a generation ago. Families hardly see one another during the course of the day. Fast food has become the dietary staple; the resulting obesity and other health problems have become, sadly, a worldwide phenomenon. In a typical American marriage both partners work, yet they're in hock up to their necks as they go crazy accumulating more and more "things," while the children are allowed to raise themselves.

As Castaneda's Don Juan recognized, and now more than ever, "We need a path with heart."

Afterword

When I started this project in 1995, I set out to gather as much information as I could concerning the idea of a vital force, the intrinsic energy of ancient lore that fills and creates the cosmos, giving movement and life to everything. Based on decades of experience in the martial arts and alternative healthcare, I strongly suspected that there was something to those old stories. You can *feel* the energy in certain situations and with specific exercises. The search led to many things.

It has long been my belief that there is another aspect to our world beyond the everyday humdrum perceptions of our five senses, levels of higher-frequency vibrations that are entire worlds unto themselves. I believe that at least some people can leave their physical bodies with their spiritual essence and visit these other planes, and I believe that all of us do so at the time of our death.

I believe that each human possesses an immortal soul, as do animals and plants and all living things, and that life here on the physical plane is largely a learning experience, one we likely repeat several times throughout the course of our development. I believe that there is a purpose to it all, something that was planned ahead of time. And it appears as though, based on thousands of personal testimonies, we ourselves do much of the planning, with some sort of spiritual guidance from those more evolved than we are.

I've used the word *believe* a great deal here, because, until further data are collected, psychic phenomena are very much just a matter of belief, as are all theories. The wondrous field of philosophy defines *knowledge* as "verified true belief." Belief in the phenomena discussed in this book has been widely held throughout most of human history, across time, space, and cultures, until modern, materialistic science appeared in the last four centuries. Only science asks us to believe that the universe is a dead place with a few bits of living tissue scattered—by pure accident—among the stars. But the magnificent writings and legends of the ancients tell us exactly the opposite—*the universe is nothing if not alive!*

Since I was a young man, I have operated with a simple premise concerning things of a spiritual nature. The advanced cultures of antiquity were extremely sophisticated. They were extraordinarily advanced on our physical plane, and they were just as advanced on a spiritual level. What's more, they were fully aware that human *intention* is a true force in the universe.[1]

Of course, materialism is . . . well . . . *materialistic!* Pyramids and relics of unexplained ancient technology are fascinating, but what really amazes me is the enormous effect on modern society of the religious and spiritual beliefs of ancient cultures. What is it about these ancient beliefs that have such a hold on us today? Civilization itself virtually revolves around, in one way or another, a handful of religious beliefs that all started within a few centuries of one another thousands of years ago.

Think of the impact! Enter a courtroom today and before you can issue a statement, you must "swear in" in the name of a deity while—in some instances—your right hand rests on a modern copy of an ancient Hebrew text. If we examine this custom from a purely objective point of view, doesn't it seem strange? This is the twenty-first century, for Christ's . . . er . . . for heaven's . . . er . . . for Pete's sake! (See what I mean?) And what really brings it all home is when something very bad, or very good, happens to us. Oh, brothers and sisters, when our backs are against the wall, it's amazing how quickly people get religion.

The first explanation that comes to mind for religious belief is the simplest—that we fat, soft, wimpy, pampered, overindulgent, excessive people are . . . *afraid*! I wouldn't doubt that for a moment, but why turn to religion? Atheists and science enthusiasts devoid of spiritual beliefs would have us think that religion is all a silly superstition, something the unwashed, foolish masses cling to when times get tough, and that could indeed be the case. Our modern beliefs may be no different, when we get down to the bottom line, from those of a caveman clinging to his carved wooden idol while the wooly mammoth is about to squash him to pulp. It could be that simple. But it's not.

The reason it's not is also simple—*we have direct evidence to the contrary that there is a spiritual side to the world, and much of this evidence suggests that religion is on the right track.* The reason we come back to such knowledge during hard times is because we intuitively know that life has meaning and we and the world matter. There *is* a purpose to everything. Our hearts tell us so, if we will shut up long enough to listen. Spiritual marvels are a matter of verified true belief.

One pressing question remains. If the phenomena we've spoken of are true, why aren't they officially recognized? Or, perhaps more importantly, why was the ancient knowledge about them lost? I can't be sure, but I enjoy speculating. Here's what I think:

Things happen for a reason. The great power that created the universe had a purpose in mind, even though we may not be able to understand it for a while yet. We're masters of our destiny and slaves to it at the same time. And, if the subjects we've examined are any indication, there is a spiritual dimension that makes the physical world, the little corner of materialistic reality we cling to during life, appear as only the opening act of a grand play. The physical world is an important scene—vital even—but it's only the *prelude* to eternity.

The thought I keep coming back to is that humankind is not yet ready to realize its full spiritual potential. Our collective consciousness is still in the minor leagues. As long as we are prone to violence, greed, selfishness, and all the other human emotions, grand and petty, that are celebrated so eternally in the great arts of our world, maybe we're just not trustworthy enough to have the keys to heaven yet.

Then there is another consideration. If the physical plane is one of fundamental spiritual development, then perhaps it *has* to remain as it is, with all our human achievements and all our shortcomings. Who knows? Perhaps there's a new class waiting in the wings, excited about its chance at experiencing a little of the "real" world. If that's the case, then things need to stay much as they are to provide the proper backdrop for what may be the greatest adventure of all . . . life as we currently know it.

Some say life is just an extraordinarily vivid dream. Maybe it is. Perhaps the physical world is ultimately just a matter of perception—the result of the mystery of consciousness. And sometimes, when I wake at night thinking about these things, it occurs to me that some of us see the world as a wave and some of us see it as a particle, and the rest of us are floating out there in the vastness, somewhere in between.

Notes

Foreword

1. Marcello Truzzi, "On Some Unfair Practices towards Claims of the Paranormal," in *The Parapsychology Revolution: A Concise Anthology of Paranormal and Psychical Research*, eds. Robert M. Schoch and Logan Yonavjak (New York: Tarcher Penguin, 2008), 261–62.

Introduction

Epigraph: Albert Einstein, in Gary E. Schwartz, *The Truth about Medium: Extraordinary Experiments with the Real Allison DuBois,* with William L. Simon (Charlottesville, VA: Hampton Roads, 2005), 73.

1. Lee Smolin, *The Trouble with Physics: The Rise of String Theory, The Fall of Science, and What Comes Next* (New York: Houghton Mifflin, 2006), 20.

2. Peter Woit, *Not Even Wrong: The Failure of String Theory and the Search for Unity in Physical Law* (New York: Basic Books, 2006), 211.

3. Ervin Laszlo, *Science and the Akashic Field: An Integral Theory of Everything* (Rochester, VT: Inner Traditions, 2007), 103.

4. Fritjof Capra, *The Tao of Physics: An Exploration of the Parallels between Modern Physics and Eastern Mysticism* (Boston: Shambhala, 1991), 11.

5. Ibid., 17–18.

6. Werner Heisenberg, *Physics and Philosophy: The Revolution in Modern Science* (Harmondsworth, UK: Penguin, 2000), 157–202.

Chapter 1

Epigraph: Albert Einstein, in Gary E. Schwartz, *The G.O.D. Experiments: How Science is Discovering God in Everything, Including Us,* with William L. Simon (New York: Atria, 2006), 197.

1. Capra, *The Tao of Physics,* 214 (see introduction, n. 4).

2. Ibid., 213.

3. David M. Eisenberg, *Encounters with Qi: Exploring Chinese Medicine*, with Thomas Lee Wright (New York: W. W. Norton and Co., 1995), 202–3.

4. Sidney Rose-Neil, "The Work of Professor Kim Bong Han," *The Acupuncturist* 1 (1967): 15.

5. Ibid.

6. Eisenberg, *Encounters*, 48.

7. Ibid., 202.

8. Ibid., 202–3.

9. Ibid., 213–14.

10. Ibid., 228.

11. Lynn McTaggart, *The Field: The Quest for the Secret Force of the Universe* (New York: Quill, 2003), 194.

12. Elmer E. Green, Peter A. Parks, Paul M. Guyer, Steven L. Fahrion, and Lolafaye Coyne, "Anomalous Electrostatic Phenomena in Exceptional Subjects," *Subtle Energies* 2, no. 3 (1991): 69–97.

13. Craig J. Hogan, Robert P. Kirshner, and Nicholas B. Suntzeff, "Surveying Space-Time with Supernovae," *Scientific American*, January 1999, 51.

14. Ibid.

15. Lawrence M. Krauss, "Cosmological Antigravity," *Scientific American*, January 1999, 53.

16. Ibid., 55.

17. Charles Muses, "Working with the Hypernumber Idea," in *Consciousness and Reality*, eds. Charles Muses and Arthur M. Young (New York: Avon Books, 1972), 448–69.

Chapter 2

Epigraph: J. B. S. Haldane, in Richard Milton, *Alternative Science: Challenging the Myths of the Scientific Establishment* (Rochester, VT: Park Street Press, 1996), 207.

1. Charles T. Tart, ed., *Body Mind Spirit: Exploring the Parapsychology of Spirituality* (Charlottesville, VA: Hampton Roads, 1997), 193–94.

2. Ibid., 194.

3. Ibid., 178–79.

4. Michael Talbot, *The Holographic Universe* (New York: HarperCollins, 1991), 14–17.

5. Capra, *The Tao of Physics*, 180 (see introduction, n. 4).

6. Alson J. Smith, "From Miracle to Experiment," in *Religion and the New Psychology* (New York: Doubleday, 1951), 13–22.

7. Ibid., 18.

8. Hans J. Eysenck and Carl Sargent, *Explaining the Unexplained: Mysteries of the Paranormal* (London: Prion, 1997), 17.

9. Joseph Banks Rhine, *New World of the Mind* (New York: William Sloane, 1953), 227.

10. Gary Schwartz, *The Afterlife Experiments*: *Breakthrough Scientific Evidence of Life after Death*, with William L. Simon (New York: Atria, 2002), 14.

11. Quoted in Tart, *Body Mind Spirit*, 75.

12. Harold E. Puthoff and Russell Targ, "Psychic Research and Modern Physics," in Edgar J. Mitchell, *Psychic Exploration: A Challenge for Science*, ed. John White (New York: G. P. Putnam's Sons, 1974), 523–36.

13. Sheila Ostrander and Lynn Schroeder, *Psychic Discoveries Behind the Iron Curtain* (New York: Prentice Hall, 1970, 1984), 6–7.

14. Jim Schnabel, *Remote Viewers: The Secret History of Amercia's Psychic Spies* (New York: Dell, 1997), 88–89.

15. Ibid., 97.

16. Ibid., 90–91.

17. Ibid., 101.

18. Harold E.Puthoff and Russell Targ, "Information Transmission under Conditions of Sensory Shielding," *Nature*, 251, no. 5476 (1974): 602–7.

19. _____, "A Perceptual Channel for Information Transfer over Kilometer Distances: Historical Perspective and Recent Research," *Proceedings of the IEEE* 64, no. 3 (1976): 329–54.

20. Schnabel, *Remote Viewers*, 142.

21. Leon Jaroff, "Boom Times on the Psychic Frontier," *Time*, March 4, 1974.

22. Bernard Haisch, *The God Theory: Universes, Zero-Point Fields, and What's Behind It All* (York Beach, ME: Red Wheel/Weiser, 2006), 86–96.

23. See for example Bernard Haisch, Alfonso Rueda, and Harold E. Puthoff, "Physics of the Zero-Point Field: Implications for Inertia, Gravity And Mass," *Speculations in Science and Technology* 20 (1997): 99–114; Harold E. Puthoff, "Polarizable Vacuum [PV] Approach to General Relativity," *Foundations of Physics* 32 (2002): 927–43; Harold E. Puthoff, "Searching for the Universal Matrix in Metaphysics," *Research and Opportunities in Science and Theology* 2, no. 8 (2002): 22.

24. McTaggart, *The Field*, 152 (see chap 1, n. 11).

Chapter 3

Epigraph: Michael Faraday, in Milton, *Alternative Science*, 3 (see chap. 2, epigraph).

1. Harold S. Burr and F. S. C. Northrop, "Evidence for the Existence of an Electrodynamic Field in Living Organisms," *Proceedings of the National Academy of Sciences of the United States of America* 24 (1939): 284–88.

2. Peter Tompkins and Christopher Bird, *The Secret Life of Plants: A Fascinating Account of the Physical, Emotional, and Spiritual Relations between Plants and Man* (New York: Avon Books, 1973), 197.

3. Ostrander and Schroeder, *Psychic Discoveries*, 165 (see chap. 2, n. 13).

4. Thelma Moss, "Puzzles and Promises," *Osteopathic Physician*, February 1976, 30–37.

5. Ion Dumitrescu, *Electrographic Imaging in Medicine and Biology,* ed. Julian Kenyon (Suffolk, UK: Neville Spearman, Ltd., 1983), 158.

6. See for example Laszlo, *Science and the Akashic Field* (see introduction n. 3); Dean I. Radin, *Entangled Minds: Extrasensory Experiences in a Quantum Reality* (New York: Paraview Pocket Books, 2006); Rupert Sheldrake, *A New Science of Life: The Hypothesis of Morphic Resonance* (Rochester, VT: Park Street Press, 1995); Talbot, *The Holographic Universe* (see chap. 2, n. 4).

7. Ostrander and Schroeder, *Psychic Discoveries*, 325.

8. Fred Alan Wolf, "The Physics of Dream Consciousness: Is the Lucid Dream a Parallel Universe?" *Second Lucid Dreaming Symposium Proceedings/ Lucidity Letter* 6, no. 2 (December 1987), 133.

9. Robert Miller, "Bridging the Gap: An Interview with Valerie Hunt, Ed.D.," *Science of Mind*, October 1983, 12.

10. Talbot, *The Holographic Universe*, 175.

11. Richard M. Restak, "Is Free Will a Fraud?" *Science Digest*, October 1983, 52.

12. Talbot, *The Holographic Universe*, 192.

13. William Tiller, "Theoretical Modeling on the Functioning Man," in *Healers and the Healing Process*, ed. G. Meek (Wheaton, IL: Theosophical Publishing House, 1977), 192.

14. See for example Annie Besant, *Theosophical Manual No. VII: Man and His Bodies* (London: Theosophical Publishing House, 1914); Barbara Ann Brennan, *Hands of Light: A Guide to Healing through the Human Energy Field* (New York: Bantam, 1987); Richard Gerber, *Vibrational Medicine for the 21st Century: A Complete Guide to Energy Healing and Spiritual Transformation* (New York: HarperCollins, 2000); C. W. Leadbeater, *Man, Visible and Invisible* (London: Theosophical Publishing House, 1902).

Chapter 4

Epigraph: Edmund Spenser, *The Faerie Queene*, bk. 1, canto 9, st. 40.

1. Pirn van Lommel, Ruud van Wees, Vincent Meyers, and Ingrid Elfferich, "Near-death Experience in Survivors of Cardiac Arrest: A Prospective Study in the Netherlands," *Lancet* 358, no. 9298 (December 15, 2001), 2039–45.

2. Raymond Moody, *The Light Beyond: New Explorations,* with Paul Perry (New York: Bantam, 1988), 14–15.

3. James Christopher and Ellen Burgess, "Brain Death: Resolving Inconsistencies in the Ethical Declaration of Death," *Canadian Journal of Anesthesia* 50 (2003), 725–31.

4. Kenneth Ring, *Life at Death* (New York: Quill, 1980), 247.

5. Moody, *Light*, 8.

6. Joel L. Whitton and Joe Whitton Fisher, *Life Between Life* (New York: Doubleday, 1986), 39.

7. Allan L. Botkin, *Induced After-Death Communication: A New Therapy for Healing Grief and Trauma*, with R. Craig Hogan (Charlottesville, VA: Hampton Roads, 2005), 144–59.

8. Raymond Moody, *Life After Life*, 2nd ed. (St. Simons Island, GA: Mockingbird Books, 1975), 75.

9. Moody, *Light*, 13.

10. Kenneth Ring, *Heading Toward Omega : In Search of the Meaning of the Near-Death Experience* (New York: HarperPerennial, 1985), 186–87.

11. Moody, *Life*, 22.

12. Schwartz, *The G.O.D. Experiments*, 213–14 (see chap. 1, epigraph).

13. McTaggart, *The Field*, 138 (see chap. 1, n. 11).

14. Talbot, *The Holographic Universe*, 213 (see chap. 2, n. 4).

15. Ibid., 214.

16. Whitton and Fisher, *Life*, 43.

17. Ibid., 156.

18. See for example Ian Stevenson, *Twenty Cases Suggestive of Reincarnation* (Charlottesville, VA: University Press of Virginia, 1974); *Cases of the Reincarnation Type*, vols. 1–4 (Charlottesville, VA: University Press of Virginia, 1974); and *Children Who Remember Previous Lives: A Question of Reincarnation* (Charlottesville, VA: University Press of Virginia, 1987).

19. _____, *Twenty Cases*, 240–43.

20. Lester S. King, "Reincarnation," *Journal of the American Medical Association* (*JAMA*) 234, no. 9 (1975): 978. King was reviewing Ian Stevenson's *Cases of the Reincarnation Type, Volume I: Ten Cases in India* (Charlottesville, VA: University Press of Virginia, 1975). See also Ian Stevenson and Bruce Greyson, "Near-death Experiences: Relevance to the Question of Survival after Death, *JAMA* 242. no.3 (1979): 265–67.

21. Schwartz, *The Afterlife Experiments*, 222 (see chap. 2, n. 10).

22. Ibid., 254–55.

23. Joel Martin and Patricia Romanowski, *We Don't Die : George Anderson's Conversations with the Other Side* (New York: G. P. Putnam's Sons, 1988), 268.

24. Ibid., 266.

25. Ibid., 275.

26. Don Piper, *90 Minutes in Heaven: A True Story of Death and Life*, with Cecil Murphey (Grand Rapids, MI: Revell, 2004), 201.

Chapter 5

Epigraph: Saint Augustine, see http://en.proverbia.net/citasautor. asp?autor=10339& page=5 (accessed March 2009).

1. Eysenck and Sargent, *Explaining the Unexplained*, 25 (see chap. 2, n. 8).

2. Schnabel, *Remote Viewers*, 168 (see chap. 2, n. 14).

3. Puthoff and Targ, "Information Transmission," 602–7 (see chap. 2, n. 18).

4. John M. Taylor, *Superminds: A Scientist Looks at the Paranormal* (London: Pan, 1976), 47–54.

5. Schnabel, *Remote Viewers*, 168–69.

6. Ibid., 168.

7. Ibid., 33.

8. Ibid., 107.

9. Robert G. Jahn and Brenda J. Dunne, "On the Quantum Mechanics of Consciousness with Application to Anomalous Phenomena," *Foundations of Physics* 16, no. 8 (1986): 721–72.

10. Radin, *Entangled Minds*, 102–4 (see chap. 3, n. 6).

11. McTaggart, *The Field*, 116 (see chap. 1, n. 11).

Chapter 6

Epigraph: Roger Bacon, in Christopher Bird, *The Persecution and Trial of Naston Naessens: The True Story of the Efforts to Suppress an Alternative Treatment for Cancer, AIDS, and Other Immunologically Based Diseases* (Tiburon, CA: H. J. Kramer Inc, 1991), xiii.

1. Tompkins and Bird, *Secret Life,* 170 (see chap. 3, n. 2).

2. Ibid., 171.

3. Ibid.

4. Milton, *Alternative Science*, 63 (see chap. 2, epigraph).

5. Tompkins and Bird, *Secret Life*, 171.

6. Karl Baron von Reichenbach, *Researches on Magnetism, Electricity, Heat, Light, Crystallization, and Chemical Attraction in Their Relations to the Vital Force,* trans. William Gregory (London: Taylor, Walton & Maberly, 1850), 487.

7. Ibid., 488.

8. Ibid., 495.

9. Brennan, *Hands of Light*, 30 (see chap. 3, n. 14).

10. Ibid.

11. Ibid., 31.

12. Walter J. Kilner, *The Human Atmosphere* (London, 1911); revised as *The Human Aura* (New Hyde Park, NY: University Books, 1965), 3–4.

13. Ibid.

14. Milton, *Alternative Science*, 67.

15. William Tiller, *Science and Human Transformation: Subtle Energies, Intentionality, and Consciousness* (Walnut Creek, CA: Pavior, 1997), 5–12.

16. Gerber, *Vibrational Medicine*, 298–99 (see chap. 3, n. 14).

17. Ibid.

18. Ibid., 137–38.

19. Fritz-Albert Popp and Jiin-Ju Chang, "Mechanism of Interaction between Electromagnetic Fields and Living Systems," *Science in China* (*Series C*) 43 (2000): 507–18.

Chapter 7

Epigraph: Wilhelm Reich, in Milton, *Alternative Science*, 1 (see chap. 2, epigraph).

1. Wilhelm Reich, *Selected Writings* (New York: Farrar, Straus, and Cudahy, 1960), 3–5.
2. Gerber, *Vibrational Medicine*, 297–98 (see chap. 3, n. 14).
3. Reich, *Selected Writings*, 189.
4. Ibid., 190.
5. Ibid., 548.
6. George A. Katchmer, *The Tao of Bioenergetics: East and West* (Jamaica Plain, MA: YMAA Publication Center, 1993), 186.
7. The Wilhelm Reich Museum—Orgonon (Rangely, ME), "Biography," http://www.wilhelmreichmuseum.org/biography.html (accessed April 2009).
8. Denis Brian, *Einstein: A Life* (New York: John Wiley and Sons, 1996), 382.

Chapter 8

Epigraph: Thomas Edison, in *The Fort Wayne Sentinel*, December 31, 1902; see also http://snopes.com/quotes/edison.asp (accessed March 2009).

1. David M. Eisenberg, Roger B. Davis, Susan L. Ettner, Scott Appel, Sonja Wilkey, Maria van Pompay, and Ronald C. Kessler, "Trends in Alternative Medicine Use in the United States, 1990–1997: Results of a Follow-up National Survey," *Journal of the American Medical Association* 280, no. 18 (1998): 1569–75; David M. Eisenberg, Ronald C. Kessler, Cindy Foster, Frances E. Norlock, David R. Calkins, and Thomas L. Delbanco, "Unconventional Medicine in the United States: Prevalence, Costs, and Patterns of Use," *New England Journal of Medicine* 328, no. 4 (1993): 246–52.
2. Eisenberg et al., "Trends in Alternative Medicine Use," figure 2.
3. Ibid., 1569.
4. Patricia A. Barnes, Eve Powell-Griner, Kim McFann, and Richard L. Nahin, "Complementary and Alternative Medicine Use among Adults: United States, 2002," *CDC Advance Data from Vital and Health Statistics*, no. 343 (May 27, 2004), 1–20.
5. Michael McIntyre, "The House of Lords Select Committee's report on CAM," *Journal of Alternative and Complementary Medicine* 7, no. 1 (2001): 9–11.
6. Bernard Grad, "Some Biological Effects of 'Laying-on of Hands': A Review of Experiments with Animals and Plants," *Journal of the American Society for Psychical Research* 59 (1965): 95–127.

7. _____, Remi Cadoret, and G. I. Paul, "An Unorthodox Method of Treatment on Wound Healing in Mice," *International Journal of Parapsychology* 3 (Spring 1961): 5–24.

8. McTaggart, *The Field*, 185 (see chap. 1, n. 11).

9. Bernard Grad, "A Telekinetic Effect on Plant Growth, Part 2: Experiments Involving Treatment of Saline in Stoppered Bottles," *International Journal of Parapsychology* 6 (1964): 473–98.

10. Robert Miller, "Methods of Detecting and Measuring Healing Energies," in *Future Science: Life Energies and the Physics of Paranormal Phenomena*, eds. John White and Stanley Krippner (Garden City, NJ: Anchor/Doubleday, 1977), 431–44.

11. Ibid.

12. Ibid.

13. Dolores Krieger, "Therapeutic Touch: The Imprimatur of Nursing," *American Journal of Nursing* 75 (1975): 784–87.

14. _____, "The Response of In-Vivo Human Hemoglobin to an Active Healing Therapy by Direct Laying-on of Hands," *Human Dimensions* 1 (Autumn 1972): 12–15.

15. Gerber, *Vibrational Medicine*, 376–77 (see chap. 3, n. 14).

16. Bruce Lipton, *The Biology of Belief: Unleashing the Power of Consciousness, Matter, and Miracles* (Santa Rosa, CA: Mountain of Love/Elite Books, 2005), 119.

17. Thomas Valone, *Bioelectromagnetic Healing: A Rationale for Its Use* (Beltsville, MD: Integrity Research Institute, 2000), 58.

18. Gerber, *Vibrational Medicine*, 576–77.

19. Bird, *Persecution and Trial*, 4–17 (see chap. 6, epigraph).

20. Erik Enby, Peter Gosch, and Michael Sheehan, *The Revolutionary Medical Discoveries of Günther Enderlein* (Saratoga, CA: S & G Communications, 1990), 5–9.

21. Ibid., 578.

22. Jeffery S. Levin, "How Religion Influences Morbidity and Health: Reflections on Natural History, Salutogenesis, and Host Resistance," *Social Science and Medicine* 43, no. 5 (1996): 849–64.

23. Herbert Benson, et al., "Study of the Therapeutic Effects of Intercessory Prayer (STEP) in Cardiac Bypass Patients: A Multicenter Randomized Trial of Uncertainty and Certainty of Receiving Intercessory Prayer," *American Heart Journal* 151, no. 3 (April 2006): 934–42.

24. Associated Press, "Mormon Fasting Heart-Healthy, Study Says," posted by CBC News, Canada, December 10, 2007, http://www.cbc.ca/health/story/2007/12/10/mormon-meals.html (accessed March 2009).

25. McTaggart, *The Field*, 192.

26. William S. Harris, Manohar Gowda, Jerry W. Kolb, Christopher P. Strychacz, James L. Vacek, Philip G. Jones, Alan Forker, James H. O'Keefe, and Ben D. McCallister, "A Randomized, Controlled Trial of the Effects of Remote, Intercessory Prayer on Outcomes in Patients Admitted to the Coronary Care Unit," *Archives of Internal Medicine* 159 (October 25, 1999): 2273–78.

Chapter 9

Epigraph: Albert Einstein, *The World As I See It* (New York, Philosophical Library, 1949), 24–28.

1. Milton, *Alternative Science*, 18 (see chap. 2, epigraph).

2. Ibid., 25.

3. David Lindley, "Commentary: The Embarrassment of Cold Fusion," *Nature*, 344 (March 29, 1990): 375.

4. *Daily Telegraph*, May 2, 1989, 1; cited in Milton, *Alternative Science*, 29.

5. D. Albagli, R. Ballinger, V. Cammarata, X. Chen, R. M. Crooks, C. Fiore, M. P. J. Gaudreau, et al., "Measurement and Analysis of Neutron and Gamma-ray Emission Rates, Other Fusion Products, and Power in Electrochemical Cells Having Pd Cathodes," *Journal of Fusion Energy* 9 (1990): 33.

6. Edmund Storms, "Review of Experimental Observations about the Cold Fusion Effect," *Fusion Technology* 20 (December 1991): 433–77.

7. Milton, *Alternative Science*, 33.

8. "Farewell (Not Fond) to Cold Fusion," *Nature* 344 (March 29, 1990): 365.

9. *Doomsday Tech 1*, *Modern Marvels* series, History Channel, July 17, 2007.

10. Richard Hoagland, *The Monuments of Mars: A City on the Edge of Forever*, 4th ed. (Berkeley, CA: Frog, Ltd., 1996), 5.

11. Ibid., 16.

12. Carl Sagan, "The Man in the Moon," *Parade Magazine*, June 2, 1985, 7.

13. Mark Carlotto, "Digital Imagery Analysis of Unusual Martian Surface Features," *Applied Optics* 27 (1988): 1926–1933; see also *The Martian Enigmas: A Closer Look* (Berkeley, CA: North Atlantic Books, 1991), 62.

14. _____, "Digital Imagery Analysis," 62.

15. Hoagland, *Monuments*, 332.

16. Stanley McDaniel, *The McDaniel Report: On the Failure of Executive, Congressional, and Scientific Responsibility in Investigating Possible Evidence of Artificial Structures on the Surface of Mars and in Setting Mission Priorities for NASA's Mars Exploration Program* (Berkeley, CA: North Atlantic Books, 1993), 174.

17. Ibid.

18. Report of the Committee on Science and Astronautics, U.S. House of Representatives, 87th Congress, First Session, No. 242, "Proposed Studies on the Implications of Peaceful Space Activities for Human Affairs," 215. Prepared for NASA by the Brookings Institution and delivered to the Committee of the Whole House of the State of the Union, April 18, 1961.

19. Hoagland, *Monuments*, 350–60.

20. B. Conrath, F. M. Flasar, R. Hanel, V. Kunde, W. Maguire, J. Pearl, J. Pirraglia, et al., "Infrared Observations of the Neptunian System," *Science* 246, no. 4936 (1989): 1454–59; see also Hoagland, *Monuments*, 397.

21. J. Gordon Melton, Jerome Clark, and Aidan A. Kelly, *New Age Almanac* (Detroit: Visible Ink Press, 1991), 105.

22. Ibid., 106.

23. Ibid.

24. Jerome Clark and J. Gordon Melton, "Marcello Truzzi Talks about . . . the Crusade Against the Paranormal," Part 1, *Fate* 83, no. 9 (1979): 70–76; Part 2, *Fate* 83, no. 10 (1979): 87–94.

25. Michel Gauquelin, *The Cosmic Clocks* (London: Peter Owen, 1969), 10–14.

26. Dennis Rawlins, "sTARBABY," *Fate Magazine* 34, October 1981, 67–98.

27. Melton, Clark, and Kelly, *New Age Almanac,* 109–10.

28. Thomas Kuhn, *The Structure of Scientific Revolutions* (Chicago: University of Chicago Press, 1970), 64.

29. Ibid.

30. Schwartz, *The Afterlife Experiments*, 216 (see chap. 2, n. 10).

Chapter 10

Epigraph: Carlos Castaneda, *The Teachings of Don Juan: A Yaqui Way of Knowledge* (Berkeley, University of California, 1968), 11.

1. Paul Pearsall, *The Heart's Code: Tapping the Wisdom and Power of Our Heart Energy* (New York: Broadway Books, 1998), 13–14.

2. Ibid.

3. Gary E. Schwartz and Linda G. S. Russek, "Energy Cardiology: A Dynamic Energy Systems Approach for Integrating Conventional and Alternative Medicine," *Advances: The Journal of Mind-Body Health*, 12 (1996): 4–24.

4. Candace Pert, "The Wisdom of the Receptors: Neuropeptides, the Emotions, and BodyMind," *Advances* 3 (1986): 9.

5. Ibid., 12

6. Pearsall, *Heart's Code*, 7.

7. Ibid., 83.

8. Laszlo, *Science and the Akashic Field*, 157 (see introduction, n. 3).

9. John Clarke, "SQUIDS," *Scientific American*, August 1994, 46–53.

10. Pearsall, *Heart's Code*, 103.

11. Ibid., 101.

12. Ibid., 73.

13. Robert F. DeBusk, "Sexual Activity Triggering a Myocardial Infarction: One Less Thing to Worry About," *Journal of the American Medical Association* 275 (1996): 1447–48.

Afterword

1. Lynn McTaggart, *The Intention Experiment: Using Your Thoughts to Change Your Life and the World* (New York: Free Press, 2007), 178.

Bibliography

Arntz, William, Betsy Chasse, and Mark Vicente. *What the Bleep do We Know!?: Discovering the Endless Possibilities for Altering your Everyday Reality*. Deerfield Beach, FL: Health Communications, Inc., 2005.

Backster, Cleve. "Evidence of a Primary Perception in Plant Life." *International Journal of Parapsychology* 10 (1967): 141.

Barnes, Patricia A., Eve Powell-Griner, Kim McFann, and Richard L. Nahin. "Complimentary and Alternative Medicine Use among Adults: United States, 2002." Centers for Disease Control Advance Data from Vital and Health Statistics, no. 343 (May 27, 2004).

Barrow, John, and Frank Tripler. *The Anthropic Cosmological Principle*. London: Oxford University Press, 1986.

Becker, Robert, *Cross Currents: The Perils of Electropollution, the Promise of Electromedicine*. New York: Tarcher/Putnam, 1990.

———, and Gary Selden. *The Body Electric: Electromagnetism and the Foundation of Life*. London: Quill/William Morrow, 1985.

Blavatsky, Helena, P. *The Secret Doctrine*. Wheaton, IL: Theosophical Publishing House, Quest Books, 1993.

Bohm, David. *Wholeness and the Implicate Order*. London: Routledge, 1980.

Botkin, Allan L. *Induced After-Death Communication: A New Therapy for Healing Grief and Trauma*. With R. Craig Hogan. Charlottesville, VA: Hampton Roads, 2005.

Brennan, Barbara Ann. *Hands of Light: A Guide to Healing through the Human Energy Field*. New York: Bantam, 1987.

Brian, Denis. *Einstein: A Life*. New York: John Wiley and Sons, 1996.

Broderick, Damien. *Outside the Gates of Science: Why It's Time for the Paranormal to Come in from the Cold*. New York: Thunder's Mouth Press, 2007.

Broughton, Richard. *Parapsychology: the Controversial Science*. London: Random Century, 1992.

Bibliography

Bruyere, Rosalyn. *Wheels of Light*. Glendale, CA: Healing Light Center, 1983.

Burr, Harold Saxton, Ph.D. *The Fields of Life*. New York: Ballantine, 1972.

Byrd, Robert. "Positive Therapeutic Effects of Intercessory Prayer in a Coronary Care Unit Population." *Southern Medical Journal* 81, no. 7 (1988): 826–29.

Capra, Fritjof. *The Tao of Physics: An Exploration of the Parallels between Modern Physics and Eastern Mysticism*. Boston: Shambhala, 1991.

Castaneda, Carlos. *The Art of Dreaming*. New York: HarperPerennial, 1993.

———. *The Teachings of Don Juan: A Yaqui Way of Knowledge*. Berkeley: University of California Press, 1998.

Davies, Paul. *The Mind of God: The Scientific Basis for a Rational World*. New York: Touchstone, 1992.

DeBusk, Robert F. "Sexual Activity Triggering a Myocardial Infarction: One Less Thing to Worry About." *Journal of the American Medical Association* 275 (1996): 1447–48.

Dossey, Larry. *Space, Time, and Medicine*. Boulder, CO: Shambhala, 1982.

Drake, Frank. *Intelligent Life in Space*. New York: Macmillan, 1964.

Dumitrescu, Ion. *Electrographic Imaging in Medicine and Biology*. Edited by Julian Kenyon. Translated by C. A. Galia. Sudbury, Suffolk: Neville Spearman, Ltd., 1983.

Dunne, Brenda. "Gender Differences in Human/Machine Anomalies." *Journal of Scientific Exploration* 12, no. 1 (1998): 3–55.

———, et al. "Operator-Related Anomalies in a Random Mechanical Cascade." *Journal of Scientific Exploration* 2, no. 2 (1988): 155–79.

Ehrman, Bart D. *Misquoting Jesus: The Story Behind Who Changed the Bible and Why*. San Francisco: HarperSanFrancisco, 2005.

Einstein, Albert, Boris Podolski, and Nathan Rosen. "Can Quantum Mechanical Description of Physical Reality Be Considered Complete?" *Physical Review* 47 (1935).

Eisenberg, David M. *Encounters with Qi: Exploring Chinese Medicine*. With Thomas Lee Wright. New York: W. W. Norton and Co., 1995.

Eisenberg, David M., Roger Davis, Susan Ettner, Scott Appel, Sonja Wilkey, Maria van Pompay, and Ronald Kessler. "Trends in Alternative Medicine Use in the United States, 1990–1997: Results of a Follow-up National Survey." *Journal of the American Medical Association* 280, no.18 (1998): 1569–75.

Eisenberg, David M., Ronald Kessler, Cindy Foster, Frances Norlock, David Calkins, and Thomas Delbanco. "Unconventional Medicine in the United States: Prevalence, Costs, and Patterns of Use." *New England Journal of Medicine* 328, no. 4 (1993): 246–52.

Eysenck, Hans J., and Carl Sargent. *Explaining the Unexplained: Mysteries of the Paranormal.* London: Prion, 1997.

Festinger, Leon. *A Theory of Cognitive Dissonance.* Palo Alto, CA: Stanford University Press, 1962.

Fleischmann, Martin, and Stanley Pons. "Electrochemically Induced Nuclear Fusion of Deuterium." *Journal of Electroanalytical Chemistry* 261, no. 2, pt. 1 (April 10, 1989): 301–8 and 263: 187–88.

Gauquelin, Michel. *The Cosmic Clocks.* London: Peter Owen, 1969.

Gerber, Richard. *Vibrational Medicine for the 21st Century: A Complete Guide to Energy Healing and Spiritual Transformation.* New York: HarperCollins, 2000.

———. *Vibrational Medicine: New Choices for Healing Ourselves.* Sante Fe: Bear, 1988.

Grad, Bernard. "Some Biological Effects of 'Laying-on of Hands': A Review of Experiments with Animals and Plants." *Journal of the American Society for Psychical Research* 59 (1965): 95–127.

———. "A Telekinetic Effect on Plant Growth, Part 2; Experiments Involving Treatment of Saline in Stoppered Bottles." *International Journal of Parapsychology* 6 (1964): 473–98.

———, et al. "The Influence of an Unorthodox Method of Treatment on Wound Healing in Mice." *International Journal of Parapsychology* 35 (1963): 24.

Green, Brian. *The Elegant Universe: Superstrings, Hidden Dimensions, and the Quest for the Ultimate Theory.* London: Vintage, 2000.

Green, Elmer E., Peter A. Parks, Paul M. Guyer, Steven L. Fahrion, and Lolafaye Coyne. "Anomalous Electrostatic Phenomena in Exceptional Subjects." *Subtle Energies* 2, no. 3 (1991): 69–97.

Guth, Alan. *The Inflationary Universe: The Quest for a New Theory of Cosmic Origins.* New York: Perseus, 1997.

Haisch, Bernard. *The God Theory: Universes, Zero-Point Fields, and What's Behind It All.* York Beach, ME: Red Wheel/Weiser, 2006.

Haisch, Bernard, Alfonso Rueda, and Harold Puthoff. "Beyond E=MC2: A First Glimpse of a Universe without Mass." *Sciences* (November/December 1994): 26–31.

Bibliography

———. "Inertia as a Zero-Point-Field Lorentz Force." *Physical Review A* 49, no. 2 (1994): 678–94.

Hameroff, Stuart. "'Funda-Mentality': Is the Conscious Mind Subtly Linked to a Basic Level of the Universe?" *Trends in Cognitive Sciences* 2, no.4 (1998): 119–27.

Harris, William S., Manohar Gowda, Jerry W. Kolb, Christopher P. Strychacz, James L. Vacek, Philip G. Jones, Alan Forker, James H. O'Keefe, and Ben D. McCallister. "A Randomized, Controlled Trial of the Effects of Remote, Intercessory Prayer on Outcomes in Patients Admitted to the Coronary Care Unit." *Archives of Internal Medicine* 159, no. 19 (October 25, 1999): 2273–78.

Heisenberg, Werner. *Physics and Philosophy: The Revolution in Modern Science.* Harmondsworth, UK: Penguin, 2000.

Hoagland, Richard. *The Monuments of Mars: A City on the Edge of Forever.* 4th ed. Berkeley, CA: Frog, Ltd., 1996.

Hogan, Craig J., Robert P. Kirshner, and Nicholas B. Suntzeff. "Surveying Space-Time with Supernovae." *Scientific American* (January 1999): 51.

Hoyle, Fred. *The Intelligent Universe.* London: Michael Joseph, 1983.

Jahn, Robert G.. "The Persistent Paradox of Psychic Phenomena: An Engineering Perspective." *IEEE Proceedings of the IEEE* 702 (1982): 136–70.

Jahn, Robert G., and Brenda J. Dunne. *Margins of Reality: The Role of Consciousness in the Physical World.* New York: Harcourt Brace Jovanovich, 1987.

———. "On the Quantum Mechanics of Consciousness with Application to Anomalous Phenomena." *Foundations of Physics* 16, no. 8 (1986): 721–72.

———. "Science of the Subjective." *Journal of Scientific Exploration* 11, no. 2 (1997): 201–24.

Kilner, Walter J. *The Human Atmosphere.* London, 1911. Revised as *The Human Aura.* New Hyde Park, NY: University Books, 1965.

Kirlian, Semyon D., and Valentina H. Kirlian, *Investigation of Biological Objects in High Frequency Electrical Fields, etc.* Alma Ata: USSR, 1968.

———. "Photography and Visual Observations by Means of High Frequency Currents." *Journal of Scientific and Applied Photography* 6 (1961): 145–48.

Krauss, Lawrence M. "Cosmological Antigravity." *Scientific American* (January 1999): 53.

Krieger, Dolores. "The Response on In-Vitro Human Hemoglobin to an Active Healing Therapy by Direct Laying-on of Hands." *Human Dimensions* 1 (Autumn 1972): 12–15.

———. *The Therapeutic Touch: How to Use Your Hands to Help or to Heal*. Englewood Cliff, NJ: Prentice-Hall, 1979.

———. "Therapeutic Touch: The Imprimatur of Nursing." *American Journal of Nursing* 75 (1975): 784–87.

Kuhn, Thomas. *The Structure of Scientific Revolutions*. Chicago: University of Chicago Press, 1970.

Laszlo, Ervin. *The Interconnected Universe: Conceptual Foundations of Transdisciplinary Unified Theory*. Singapore: World Scientific, 1995.

———. *Science and the Akashic Field: An Integral Theory of Everything*. Rochester, VT: Inner Traditions, 2007.

Leadbeater, C. W. *The Chakras*. Wheaton, IL: Theosophical Publishing House, 1927. Ninth printing, 2001.

LeShan, Lawrence. *The Medium, the Mystic, and the Physicist*. New York: Ballantine, 1966.

Levin, Jeffery S. "How Religion Influences Morbidity and Health: Reflections on Natural History, Salutogenesis, and Host Resistance." *Social Science and Medicine* 43, no. 5 (1996): 849–64.

Lipton, Bruce. *The Biology of Belief: Unleashing the Power of Consciousness, Matter, and Miracles*. Santa Rosa, CA: Mountain of Love/Elite Books, 2005.

Lommel, Pirn van, Ruud van Wees, Vicent Meyers, and Ingrid Elfferich. "Near-death Experience in Survivors of Cardiac Arrest: A Prospective Study in the Netherlands." *Lancet* 358, no. 9298 (December 15, 2001): 2039–45.

Martin, Joel, and Patricia Romanowski. *We Don't Die*. New York: G. P. Putnam's Sons, 1988.

McDaniel, Stanley. *The McDaniel Report: On the Failure of Executive, Congressional, and Scientific Responsibility in Investigating Possible Evidence of Artificial Structures on the Surface of Mars and in Setting Mission Priorities for NASA's Mars Exploration Program*. Berkeley, CA: North Atlantic Books, 1993.

McIntyre, Michael. "The House of Lords Select Committee's Report on CAM." *Journal of Complimentary and Alternative Medicine 7*, no. 1 (2001): 9–11.

McMoneagle, Joseph. *Mind Trek: Exploring Consciousness, Time, and Space through Remote Viewing*. Charlottesville, VA: Hampton Roads, 1997.

McTaggart, Lynn. *The Field: The Quest for the Secret Force of the Universe*. New York: Quill, 2003.

———. *The Intention Experiment: Using Your Thoughts to Change Your Life and the World*. New York: Free Press, 2007.

Melton, J. Gordon, Jerome Clark, and Aidan A. Kelly. *New Age Almanac*. Detroit: Visible Ink Press, 1991.

Miller, Robert. "Methods of Detecting and Measuring Healing Energies." In *Future Science: Life Energies and the Physics of Paranormal Phenomena*, edited by John White and Stanley Krippner, 431–44. Garden City, NJ: Anchor/Doubleday, 1977.

Milton, Richard. *Alternative Science: Challenging the Myths of the Scientific Establishment*. Rochester, VT: Park Street Press, 1996.

Mitchell, Edgar D. "Nature's Mind: The Quantum Hologram." *International Journal of Computing Anticipatory Systems* 7. Partial Proceedings of the Third International Conference CASYS'99 on Computing Anticipatory Systems, August 9–14, 1999, edited by D. M. Dubois, 295–312. Liège, Belgium: Centre for Hyperincursion and Anticipation in Ordered Systems (CHAOS), 2000.

———. *The Way of the Explorer: An Apollo Astronaut's Journey through the Material and Mystical Worlds*. London: G. P. Putnam, 1996.

Monroe, Robert. *Far Journeys*. Garden City, NY: Doubleday, 1985.

———. *Journeys Out of the Body*. Garden City, NY: Doubleday, 1977.

Moody, Raymond. *Life After Life*. 2nd ed. New York: Bantam, 1975.

———. *The Light Beyond*: *New Explorations*. With Paul Perry. New York: Bantam, 1988.

Moss, Thelma. *Body Electric*: *A Personal Journey into the Mysteries of Parapsychological Research, Bioenergy and Kirlian Photography*. New York: Tarcher, 1979.

Motoyama, Hiroshi. *Theories of the Chakras: Bridge to Higher Consciousness*. Wheaton, IL: Theosophical Publishing House, Quest Books, 1981.

Muses, Charles. "Working with the Hypernumber Idea." In *Consciousness and Reality*, edited by Charles Muses and Arthur M. Young. New York: Avon Books, 1972.

Nelson, Roger D. and Dean I. Radin. "When Immovable Objections Meet Irresistible Evidence." *Behavioral and Brain Sciences* 10 (1987): 600–601.

Ostrander, Sheila, and Lynn Schroeder. *Psychic Discoveries Behind the Iron Curtain*. New York: Prentice Hall, 1984.

Pearsall, Paul. *The Heart's Code: Tapping the Wisdom and Power of Our Heart Energy*. New York: Broadway Books, 1998.

Penrose, Roger. *Shadows of the Mind: A Search for the Missing Science of Consciousness*. London: Vintage, 1994.

Pert, Candace. *Molecules of Emotion: Why You Feel the Way You Feel*. New York: Simon and Schuster, 1999.

Piper, Don. *90 Minutes in Heaven: A True Story of Death and Life*. With Cecil Murphey. Grand Rapids, MI: Revell, 2004.

Playfair, Guy, and Scott Hill. *The Cycles of Heaven: Cosmic Forces and What They Are Doing to You*. New York: Avon Books, 1978.

Popp, Fritz-Albert, and Jinn-Ju Chang. "Mechanism of Interaction between Electromagnetic Fields and Living Systems." *Science in China (Series C)* 43 (2000): 507–18.

Popp, Fritz Albert, Qian Gu, and Ke-Hsueh Li. "Biophoton Emission: Experimental Background and Theoretical Approaches." *Modern Physics Letter B* 8 (1994): 1269–96.

Popper, Karl. *The Logic of Scientific Discovery*. London: Unwin Hyman, 1959.

Powell, A. E. *The Causal Body and the Ego*. Wheaton, IL: Theosophical Publishing House, 1928. Reprint Adyar, India: Theosophical Publishing House, 2000.

———. *The Etheric Double: The Health Aura of Man*. Wheaton, IL: Theosophical Publishing House, Quest Books, 1969.

———. *The Mental Body*. Wheaton, IL: Theosophical Publishing House, 1967.

Puthoff, Harold E. "CIA-Initiated Remote Viewing Program at Stanford Research Institute." *Journal of Scientific Exploration* 10, no. 1 (1996): 63–76.

———. "Gravity as a Zero-Point-Fluctuation Force," *Physical Review A* 39, no. 5 (1989): 2333–42.

Puthoff, Harold E., and Russell Targ. "Information Transmission under Conditions of Sensory Shielding." *Nature* 251, no. 5476 (October 18, 1974): 602–7.

———. "A Perceptual Channel for Information Transfer over Kilometer Distances: Historical Perspective and Recent Research." *Proceedings of the IEEE* 64, no. 3 (March 1976): 329–54.

———. "Psychic Research and Modern Physics." In Edgar D. Mitchell, *Psychic Exploration: A Challenge for Science,* edited by John White, 523-36. New York: G. P. Putnam's Sons, 1974.

Radin, Dean I. *The Conscious Universe: The Scientific Truth of Psychic Phenomena*. New York: HarperEdge, 1997.

———. *Entangled Minds: Extrasensory Experiments in a Quantum Reality*. New York: Paraview Pocket Books, 2006.

Radin, Dean I., and Roger D. Nelson. "Evidence for Consciousness-Related Anomalies in Random Physical Systems." *Foundations of Physics* 19, no. 12 (December 1989): 1499–1514.

Reich, Wilhelm. *The Cancer Biopathy*. New York: Farrar, Straus, and Giroux, 1973.

———. *Character Analysis*. London: Vision Press, 1950.

———. *The Discovery of the Orgone*. Vol. 1, *The Function of the Orgasm*. Translated by Theodore P. Wolfe. New York: Orgone Institute Press, 1942.

———. *The Discovery of the Orgone*. Vol. 2, *The Cancer Biopathy*. Translated by Theodore P. Wolfe. New York: Orgone Institute Press, 1943.

———. *Selected Writings*. New York: Farrar, Straus and Cudahy, 1960.

Reichenbach, Karl Baron von. *Researches on Magnetism, Electricity, Heat, Light, Crystallization, and Chemical Attraction in Their Relations to the Vital Force*. Translated by William Gregory. London: Taylor, Walton and Maberly, 1850. Reprint Secaucus, NJ: University Books, 1974.

Restak, Richard M. "Is Free Will a Fraud?" *Science Digest* (October 1983): 52.

Rhine, Joseph Banks. *New World of the Mind*. New York: William Sloane, 1953.

Ring, Kenneth. *Heading Toward Omega: In Search of the Meaning of the Near-Death Experience*. New York: HarperPerennial, 1985.

———. *Life at Death*. New York: Quill, 1980.

———, and Sharon Cooper. "Near-Death and Out-of-Body Experiences in the Blind: A Study of Apparent Eyeless Vision." *Journal of Near-Death Studies* 16 (Winter 1997): 101–47.

Rose-Neil, Sidney. "The Work of Professor Kim Bong Han." *The Acupuncturist* 1 (1967): 15.

Schnabel, Jim. *Remote Viewers: The Secret History of America's Psychic Spies*. New York: Dell, 1997.

Schwartz, Gary E. *The Afterlife Experiments: Breakthrough Scientific Evidence of Life after Death*. With William L. Simon. New York: Atria, 2002.

———. *The G.O.D. Experiments: How Science is Discovering God in Everything, Including Us*. With William L. Simon. New York: Atria, 2006.

———. *The Truth about* Medium: *Extraordinary Experiments with the Real Allison DuBois*. With William L. Simon. Charlotteville, VA: Hampton Roads, 2005.

———, and Linda G. S. Russek. *The Living Energy Universe: A Fundamental Discovery that Transforms Science and Medicine*. Charlottesville, VA: Hampton Roads, 1999.

Schwartz, Gary E., Linda G. S. Russek, Lonnie A. Nelson, and Christopher Barentsen. "Accuracy and Replicability of Anomalous After-Death Communication across Highly Skilled Mediums." *Journal of the Society for Psychical Research* 65 (2001): 1–25.

Sheldrake, Rupert. *Dogs that Know When Their Owners Are Coming Home and Other Unexplained Powers of Animals*. London: Hutchinson, 1999.

———. *A New Science of Life: The Hypothesis of Morphic Resonance*. Rochester, VT: Park Street Press, 1995.

———. *The Presence of the Past: Morphic Resonance and the Habits of Nature*. London: HarperCollins, 1994.

Smith, Alson J. "From Miracle to Experiment." In *Religion and the New Psychology*. New York: Doubleday, 1951.

Smolin, Lee. *The Trouble with Physics: The Rise of String Theory, the Fall of Science, and What Comes Next*. New York: Houghton Mifflin, 2006.

Stevenson, Ian. *Cases of the Reincarnation Type*. 4 vols. Charlottesville, VA: University Press of Virginia, 1975–83.

———. *Children Who Remember Previous Lives: A Question of Reincarnation*. Charlottesville, VA: University Press of Virginia, 1987.

———. *Twenty Cases Suggestive of Reincarnation*. Charlottesville, VA: University Press of Virginia, 1974.

Sturrock, Peter. "Brave New Heresies." *New Scientist* 24 (December 31, 1988): 49–51.

Swann, Ingo. *To Kiss Earth Good-bye*. New York: Dell, 1975.

Swedenborg, Emanuel. *Heaven and Hell: Drawn from Things Heard and Seen*. Translated by George F. Dole. West Chester, PA: The Swedenborg Foundation, 2000.

Talbot, Michael. *The Holographic Universe*. New York: HarperCollins, 1991.

Targ, Russell, and Keith Harary. *The Mind Race: Understanding and Using Psychic Abilities*. New York: Ballantine, 1984.

———, and Harold E. Puthoff. *Mind-Reach: Scientists Look at Psychic Ability*. New York: Dell, 1977. Reprint Charlottesville, VA: Hampton Roads, 2005.

Tart, Charles T., ed. *Body Mind Spirit: Exploring the Parapsychology of Spirituality*. Charlottesville, VA: Hampton Roads, 1997.

Taylor, John M. *Superminds: A Scientist Looks at the Paranormal*. London: Pan, 1976.

Thompkins, Peter, and Christopher Bird. *The Secret Life of Plants*. New York: Avon Books, 1973.

Tiller, William A. "Energy Fields and the Human Body." In *Frontiers of Consciousness*, edited by John White. New York: Avon Books, 1974.

———. *Science and Human Transformation: Subtle Energies, Intentionality, and Consciousness*. Walnut Creek, CA: Pavior, 1997.

———. "Subtle Energies in Energy Medicine." *Frontier Perspectives* 4, no. 2 (1995).

Velikovsky, Immanuel. *Worlds in Collision*. New York: Dell, 1950.

Whitton, Joel L., and Joe Whitton Fisher. *Life Between Life*. New York: Doubleday, 1986.

Wilber, Ken. *The Spectrum of Consciousness*. Wheaton, IL: Theosophical Publishing House, Quest Books, 1977.

———. *A Theory of Everything: An Integral Vision for Business, Politics, Science, and Spirituality*. Boston: Shambhala, 2000.

Woit, Peter. *Not Even Wrong: The Failure of String Theory and the Search for Unity in Physical Law*. New York: Basic Books, 2006.

Wolf, Fred Alan. *The Dreaming Universe: A Mind-Expanding Journey into the Realm Where Psyche and Physics Meet*. New York: Touchstone, 1995.

———. *Star Wave: Mind, Consciousness, and Quantum Physics*. New York: Macmillan, 1986.

Zukav, Gary. *The Dancing Wu Li Masters: An Overview of the New Physics*. New York: William Morrow, 1979.

———. *The Seat of the Soul*. New York: Fireside, 1989.

Index

Index

Quest Books

encourages open-minded inquiry into
world religions, philosophy, science, and the arts
in order to understand the wisdom of the ages,
respect the unity of all life, and help people explore
individual spiritual self-transformation.

Its publications are generously supported by
The Kern Foundation,
a trust committed to Theosophical education.

Quest Books is the imprint of
the Theosophical Publishing House,
a division of the Theosophical Society in America.
For information about programs, literature,
on-line study, membership benefits, and international centers,
see www.theosophical.org
or call 800-669-1571 or (outside the U.S.) 630-668-1571.

Related Titles

The Chakras and the Human Energy Fields, by Dora van Gelder Kunz
The Etheric Double, by A. E. Powell
Man, Visible and Invisible, by C. W. Leadbeater
A New Science of the Paranormal, by Lawrence LeShan
Our Psychic Sense, by Phoebe Bendit, with Laurence Bendit
The Personal Aura, by Dora van Gelder Kunz
Thought Forms, by Annie Besant, with C. W. Leadbeater

To order books or a complete Quest catalog,
Call 800-669-9425 or (outside the U.S.) 630-665-0130.